Alaska Gold Trails
The Pioneers

**With
Jim Madonna**

Volume I

**Life in Alaska's Frontier
as Told by the Pioneers Who Blazed the Trails**

Cover Photo: River Boat Discovery III on the Chena River near Fairbanks, Alaska. Photo courtesy of Jim and Mary Binkley.

ISBN: 1-891733-08-7
All Rights Reserved
© 1999 by James A. Madonna

Published by A.P. Publishing
Fairbanks, Alaska

Table Of Contents

Figure I: Alaska Communities

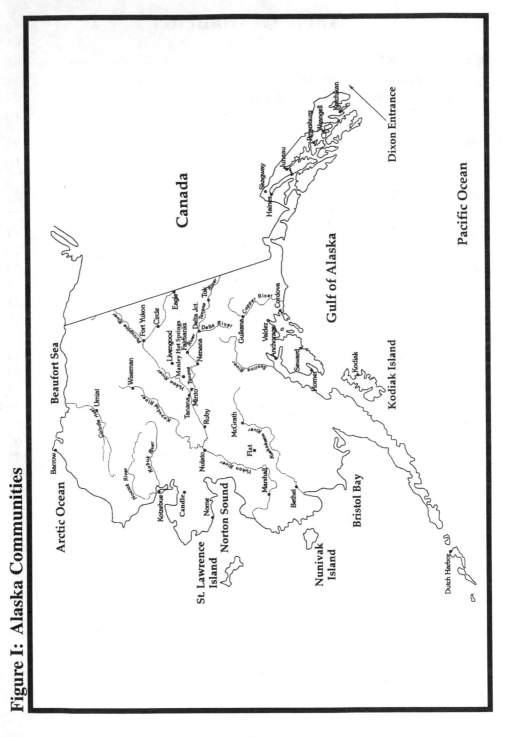

Figure II: Route Of The Alaska Highway

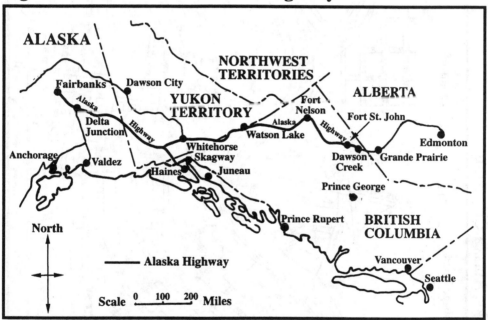

Figure III: 1949 Fairbanks, Alaska City Map

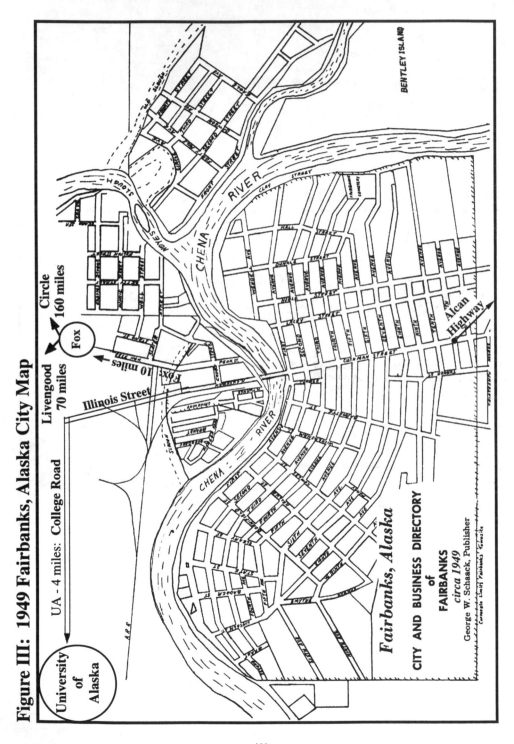

Part I

Destiny

Destiny

There were always challenges we dreamed of facing in our lives but for some reason, only known to us personally, we never quite got around to them. Time alone dictates that we can not be or do all things in this short time we have on earth. Fortunately, those of us interested in the rugged outdoor adventure associated with Alaska's vast wilderness can live some of our dreams through the lives and experiences of the early frontiersmen and settling pioneers. As we read these accounts of their colorful frontier lives and the tasks they faced during the time they blazed the trail into the country, one of their experiences may strike us as exceptionally appealing and guide our destiny by moving us towards taking that one last adventure.

Little did I know when I arrived in Fairbanks in 1948 at ten years old what my destiny was.

Fairbanks, Alaska, was fascinating and a wonderful place for a young boy to grow up. There were so many things to see and do. There was trapping, hunting and gold panning just walking distance from town. I remember on many occasions several of us riding our bicycles ten miles south of town to the Badger Road area which was pretty much wilderness at that time, to go fishing and camping during the spring, summer and fall of the year. Often we would camp in the snow just for the adventure of sleeping out in below freezing temperatures. In the winter there was the Ice Carnival, which hosted dog races, car races and other activities on the solidly frozen Chena River adjacent to first Avenue.

The Avenues run east-west, as shown in Figure 3. First Avenue is adjacent to and parallel to the Chena River. The main business district was on 1st and 2nd between Cushman and Lacey, with some businesses also on 3rd and the Red Light District on 4th. From there the Avenues became residential. The streets which ran north-south were for the most part named after founding pioneers such as Barnette, Noyes, Cowles, Wickersham and Noble. Cushman Street, which was considered the end of the Alcan Highway by many, ended at the bridge that crossed the Chena River. On the north side of the Chena, Illinois Street extended to College Road, which linked the town to the University, approximately four miles away. As I remember it a great many businesses lined Cushman Street as far out as 16th Avenue.

My father first came to Alaska as a welder for the construction companies but in 1949, because it was so difficult to obtain automotive batteries, opened a battery repair shop and service station on South Cushman, at 16th Avenue. Our living quarters, were attached to the business, as were so many in those days.

A young energetic boy could always earn money in Fairbanks. For three years I was a street-hawker for the Fairbanks Daily News Miner, Jessen's

Weekly and the Seattle Sunday Times. Selling papers, I could earn about $15 per week which, even in Fairbanks, Alaska was a lot of money for an eleven-year-old-boy. Then in the summer I would shine shoes on the street for 25 cents. Every morning the bartender at the Silver Dollar Bar would set two pairs of shoes outside the bar. When I arrived I would shine them up perfectly, then set them inside the door. Soon he would come out and give me a silver dollar. The customers would almost always give fifty cents for the shine especially if I worked hard at it and didn't get polish on their socks. I could earn three to four dollars every morning shining shoes. The summer routine was to shine shoes in the morning, go swimming at the swimming pool in the afternoon then sell papers in the late afternoon to early evening. While shoe shining came to an end in the winter when temperatures dipped below freezing, the snowfall provided another means of income. After every major snowfall walks had to be shoveled. I focused on one area of town and that was Fourth Avenue. There was never a need to set a price, I just shoveled snow from the walks and made certain it was perfectly neat, tidy and user friendly. When the girls would come out and inspect the job they would always give me a silver dollar, or sometimes two.

I attended Main School, which was located on Cushman Street. At that time it was the only public school in town and housed all twelve grades. The student population had grown to the point that the building could not accommodate all of us so we were required to attend school in shifts. I chose the morning shift so I could help my father at the battery shop, shovel walks, and sell papers in the afternoon.

Alaskans are always discussing the weather. I learned early that it was hot in the summer and cold in the winter. Summer temperatures in Fairbanks commonly reached the high 90s and the winter lows often reached 60 below zero. The beauty of summer is that it never gets dark. In contrast the winter blues occur for several months when the sun barely breaks the horizon and days are, at best, gloomy-gray.

During the three youthful years I spent in Fairbanks the only pavement was on Second Avenue from Cushman to Lacey and on Cushman Street from the bridge to Fifth Avenue. As I remember it the sidewalks were wooden planks. All the roads and streets were frozen and covered with ice in the winter. During the spring thaw the roads were often knee deep in mud and ruts (at least my knee deep; I wasn't very tall). In the summer the mud changed to thick layers of dust.

The time was just after the war had ended. I remember the military would set up anti-aircraft machine guns at the corner of Second Avenue and Lacy Street as a defense demonstration.

The Alcan was not open to tourism until 1949. It was interesting that a pile of snow was pushed up at the end of the Cushman Street business district when the snow and temperatures reached a point that prevented passage on the highway. A sign was stuck in the snow that said, "Road Closed Until

Spring." As I understand it the only travel to Delta, 90 miles down the road, was by dog team.

While Fairbanks was a true frontier town, it was not a gun packin', rough-tough-town typical of those we read about in the Old West. Perhaps because of the unforgiving environment and the cyclic nature of the work season people had to depend upon one another for survival. As a result there was a sense of comradeship and goodwill in the town.

There were certainly hardships and disasters, both at a personal and community level. Most of these were in the form of floods and fires. I remember that Jessen's Weekly burned as did one of the major drug stores on Second Avenue.

Perhaps the greatest disaster that befell my family happened in the summer of 1950. Several of us kids rode our bicycles out to the Badger area to go fishing and camp overnight. The next afternoon as we rode back into town we could see a great cloud of black smoke hovering over the town. As we approached, horror struck me as I recognized that my dad's battery shop and our home had burned to the ground.

I left Alaska in the summer of 1951. Little did I know that twenty years later I would return to spend the rest of my life.

In 1966, after spending several years working in the limestone mines in the Mojave Desert of California I began taking night courses in geoscience at Victor Valley College in Victorville, California. In 1968 I was elected student body president. Along with the position came an interview with the local paper. I remember clearly the question "What are you going to do after you graduate?" The answer to that question was founded, in large part, on a previously read newspaper article on aspects of geologic hazards in Alaska by an internationally recognized authority on Alaskan geology and professor at the University of Alaska, by the name of Dr. Robert Forbes. That article reinforced the idea that Alaska was the last frontier. The answer given the reporter and that appeared in the Victorville paper stated that the frontier of Alaska had an attraction and that following achievement of a Bachelors degree in geology at a California State University I intended to go to Alaska and study with Dr. Robert Forbes then become an Alaskan "Bush" teacher. All that turned out to be true. It just didn't turn out the way I imagined it at that time. After graduating from Victor Valley College in 1969 I attended Humboldt State College where I earned a Bachelors Degree in geology in 1971. In early May of that year my dream of returning to Alaska came true when I was accepted as a graduate student and traveled to Alaska to attend the University of Alaska Geology Department's six-week field camp. The plane landed in the early evening. During a short tour around town, I recognized that while Fairbanks was still a frontier community it had grown considerably and there were a lot more paved streets. I looked for a landmark where I could stay until contact was made with the Geology Department. The Nordale Hotel on Second Avenue brought back old memories of when I sold papers in the 1950s. The charming Eva McGown, who was known as "The Hostess of the Territory" was there as I checked in. Eva McGown's cheerful personality, Irish Brogue and fragrant perfume added to the wonderful feeling of returning to Fairbanks.

The University is situated on a hill approximately six miles from town. It is a beautiful campus with a picture perfect view of the Alaska Range to the south. In the fall following the summer field camp I entered the geology graduate program and was also given the position as teaching assistant. At that time one of my dreams came true. I met and took courses from Dr. Robert Forbes as well as other well recognized geoscientists including Dr. Daniel Hawkins who later became my graduate thesis advisor. These people were to play important roles in my life, first as my professors then as my colleagues, and finally as my long-time friends.

As in the days of my youth, once again disaster struck Fairbanks in the winter of 1972. We could see flames in the middle of town from our dormitory rooms on the hill at the university. I took pictures from my room. We later learned that the Nordale Hotel had burned and that Eva McGown had been trapped in her little room and had died in the fire. The entire community was saddened over this tragedy.

In the spring of 1973 I graduated with a masters degree in Geology. At about that time Willow Burrand was retiring from his position as Mining Extension instructor, a position that required that the instructor travel to the various towns and villages of Alaska and teach public service prospecting and mining short courses. My geology professors suggested that the position was ready made for me and the frontier life I was seeking and urged me to apply. I was awarded the position, I suspect largely on the basis of the many letters of support provided by the professors. Those first years I worked for many wonderful people, Charles Lafferty, Mildred Mathews, Earl Beistline and of course Dr. Wood who was president of the University at that time and who signed every certificate of course completion for my students. Others who gave guidance along the way included Dr. Ernest Wolff, Doug Colp and Dr. Donald Cook.

The courses were of short duration meeting three hours each evening, five nights a week for four weeks. My first assignment was in McGrath. A couple of months following completion of the course the first of many treasures arrived at my home. A trophy from the McGrath students with the inscription on the plate that reads "Jim Madonna, Traveling Bush Teacher, McGrath Class, 1973" sits on display in my home. My dreams from the Victor Valley College days had come true. I had studied with Dr. Robert Forbes and I had become an Alaskan Bush teacher. It was somewhat different than I had imagined, but there I was. All I had to do was prove myself. To this day I don't know if I have convincingly demonstrated to everyone the skills required to teach the Mining Extension program at the highest level of efficiency but I do know that I have taught thousands of men, women and children the art of mineral identification, prospecting and mining over the past twenty-five years.

Apparently the majority of students benefited and enjoyed the courses. Perhaps the most rewarding element of teaching was knowing that of all the worldly wealth, an education was perhaps the one treasure that cannot be taken away from a person and that I was playing a significant role in enriching the lives of my students by providing the guidance that would lead to expanded enjoyment of outdoor recreational activities, successful development of small businesses, and guidance into professional degree programs. Throughout the years I have been fortunate to have had a life where I could watch my students as they discovered valuable mineral deposits in Alaska and developed them into workable mines. Perhaps others would have to live my experience to understand it but these are the types of rewards that drive a person to work hard to develop and protect a program that provides a valuable education to Alaskan students and ultimately contributes so significantly to the economic development of the State.

Throughout these years I had the good fortune to teach with some of the most recognized geoscience professionals and mining professors in Alaska. The courses in which such people as Ernie Wolff, Doug Colp, Milt Wiltse and Don Cook made contributions were some of the more memorable of my career.

Other colorful events have occurred in Alaska during the past twenty-five years that have influenced our lives. The Trans-Alaska pipeline construction in the 1970s, and what might be called a mini-gold rush that occurred in response to the removal of restrictions on gold ownership by President Gerald Ford in 1974 leading to a significant increase in the price of gold in the late 70s and early 80s. Both of these events led to very colorful periods in Alaskan history. It was interesting and exciting to live in Alaska and witness the rush for riches as they blossomed, peaked and diminished.

The gold rush of the 70s and 80s had an effect on our Mining Extension program development, and by 1985 we took steps to modernize the program in ways that would better serve the general public, teachers and mineral industry. By 1990 the unique reputation of the program began to grow and it became recognized for its high quality on an international scale.

During this same period of time two activities that were for the most part outside my professional career as a professor at the University of Alaska materialized. The first was in 1987 when I began hosting the weekly one-hour Alaska Gold Trails show on KFAR. The second was in 1990 when I was accepted as a Ph.D. candidate at the University of Tasmania in Hobart, Tasmania, Australia.

The five-year experience surrounding the achievement of a doctorate was exceptionally rewarding, as studies in three countries revealed exciting new approaches to creating a stable vocational, technical and continuing two-year geoscience education program. These concepts were applied to the Mining Extension Program for the benefit of the residents of the State of Alaska until 1994.

I have always had an adventurous spirit and a consuming interest in pioneer history. I remember, as a young boy, sitting near the wood stove as the "Old Timers," who by the way weren't so old at that time, sat around drinking coffee in the dimly lighted kitchen telling stories about traveling into the country over the Alcan, fishing, hunting and gold mining. They spoke of hardships associated with breakdowns and flat tires on the Alcan. They told fascinating stories about hiking into their favorite areas and the bountiful fishing in the Alaskan streams. They told of exciting experiences during caribou and moose hunts and close calls with bears. And they shared methods of gold prospecting and mining and spoke of gold pokes and fruit jars full of nuggets. While many of these stories have faded, at the time they were intriguing, captivated my attention and added fuel to my imagination. These were the things that made a young boy dream of becoming a frontiersman.

Perhaps it was this background and interest that made the years of teaching the Mining Extension courses and simultaneously hosting the Alaska Gold Trails Show on KFAR among the most enjoyable of my life.

As the interviews demonstrate, the guests on the show were magical and wove the same spell as the sourdough storytellers of my youth. Clearly, these were the pioneers who formed the link of development between the first Alaskan frontiersmen and the modern conveniences enjoyed by Alaskans today. They tell us where in Alaska they were born or, if not born in Alaska, where they came from and why they came. They often share with us their original vision of freedom their hopes and their dreams of a fresh start with a new and better life when they arrived. They were hard working men and women from all parts of the world and all walks of life, who were gifted with the determination and skills to carve a living out of a country that was often dangerously inhospitable, depressingly remote and simultaneously held breathtaking beauty and peaceful tranquillity that is unequaled in any other part of the world. The one comment that was consistent from all those who entered the country was: "I couldn't believe how friendly the people were." It is clear from the interviews that the people of Alaska lived by a code of good will that went beyond open friendliness but also included helping a neighbor out in a time of need. To a large extent, in many ways this attitude still exists among the people of the State.

As pointed out earlier, whether it could be called destiny, if you believe in a predetermincd course of events, or the course that evolves because of our actions, I feel honored to have had the opportunity to pass along the events of these pioneers lives as they made their valuable contribution to the development of the last frontier.

Part II

The Alaska Gold Trails Radio Show

The Radio Show

The Alaska Gold Trails series had its beginning in the summer of 1987, when Michael Dresser, then program coordinator for KFAR Radio (660 on the a.m. Dial) in Fairbanks, Alaska, approached me regarding hosting a mining related talk show. It was quite a compliment, but only a flattering dream that scarcely had a possibility of coming to fruition. Then in September of 1987 Michael approached me once again and explained that he had submitted the proposal to Bill Walley and Frank DeLong, the station owners, and they were interested in introducing the show. Finally I agreed to a trial period of four weeks. Much caution was exercised because of my total lack of experience. In my view, the first two shows were less than exciting. I dealt primarily with early gold rush history, did not have a guest and got few if any phone calls. Things looked bleak. Michael reassured me that I was doing fine and that it would take a little time to get comfortable. Then a remarkable thing happened. I had Ernie Wolff on as a guest. It was wonderful. I had known Ernie for decades. He had not only been my teacher, he was, and is, a close personal friend. We simply sat there and chatted as if we were in our living room. Over the next week people approaching me in public saying "Great show, Jim. Who you having on next week?" and "You should write a book."

Local business people began supporting the show through sponsorship as it began to take on a delightful character of its own. Some of the businesses sponsored the show in one way or another from the very beginning. Collectively, the sponsors spanned a wide spectrum of services and supplies which were often reflected in their name, as shown in the accompanying list.

Alaskan Prospectors and Geologists Supply - Prospecting and mining equipment.

Arctic Springs - Manufacturers of vehicle leaf springs and U-bolts.

B&L Pawn - Pawn shop.

Fairbanks Boot and Shoe Repair - Leather, boot and shoe repair.

Gabes Truck and Auto - Truck and auto repair.

Golden Nugget Taxi - Transportation.

Hectors Welding - Metal fabrication and manufacture of sluice boxes.

Import Auto Body - Auto body and fender repair.

Larson's Jewelry-Jewelry and gift shop.

Lora's Gold Strike Cafe - Restaurant.

McCaulleys Reprographics - Office supplies and reprographic service.

McKinley Mutual Savings Bank - Banking services.

North Pole Equipment - Equipment rental and small engine repair.

Oxford Assaying and Refining - Gold buyers.

Tip Top Chevrolet - Automobile dealership.

Two Rivers Lodge- Dining.

Within the first two months we began involving the listening audience at the beginning of each show. We would give a sponsor's address, then a caller could win a prize for telling us which sponsor resided at that particular location and what they offered in materials and/or services. In short, the caller was giving the ad. The audience loved it and sponsors were so satisfied with the success of their ads that they soon began volunteering prizes; for example, Laura's Gold Rush Cafe gave a prize of dinner for two, Alaskan Prospectors gave beautiful crystal lined geodes, and Oxford assaying gave away one ounce silver ingots. It was a lively community program focused on the pioneer history and mining in Alaska. But unlike many of the current radio talk shows which are held together by controversy, Alaska Gold Trails was bound together by community respect. It was a program people could call to share some of their favorite frontier experiences or just reminisce about old times for a few minutes.

For almost two and a half years I had the pleasure of hosting 96 shows and interviewing more than 60 interesting Alaskan pioneers with very special backgrounds, regarding their contributions in developing Alaskan history. The show would start at 1:00 PM on Friday. An hour before the scheduled time, our guest and I would have lunch together and just talk about their lives and get acquainted. Within a short period of time the shows were running smoothly. Unfortunately, in 1989 a research project surfaced that required my full attention for several years and the Alaska Gold Trails radio show came to an end. However many people remember the guests and from the very beginning urged me to publish the interviews in book form. The convincing argument was that these contributions to our heritage should not be lost. I fully agreed with this philosophy. As a result beginning in 1987 I took the steps to preserve the interviews on tape until the time became available to begin preparing the Alaska Gold Trails series as a tribute to the Alaskan Pioneers.

Volume one includes twenty interviews including the special presentation by Roger McPherson. Nineteen of these were presented on the Alaska Gold Trails Radio Show while the interview with Duke Kilbury was conducted privately in Ketchikan, Alaska. The following sketches provide a brief introduction to each interview.

Jim Binkley was born in the year 1920 in the little town of Wrangell, Alaska. He has enjoyed a fascinating life centered around riverboating. Jim reminisces about life on the river: *"You know, the hours alone in the wheelhouse, way up high like that, particularly up in the Arctic, where at midnight the sun is right on the horizon and it's putting those purple fingers out through the trees, and the snow on the high mountains having those purple shadows coming down and the power of the boat going against the current and that total peace that's involved there. It's a life that's* *hard to describe unless you've experienced it.*" In an easy yet enchanting manner, Captain Jim Binkley describes how sternwheel riverboats were piloted through the rapids of the Yukon River, around the sandbars of the Tanana River and along the Chena River to Fairbanks. Jim relates his early adventures, the respect he has for the proud people of Alaska and how he acquired the skills of riverboating.

Mary Binkley was born in Oregon in 1926. She was attracted to Alaska for the adventure of seeing the frontier and to attend the University. Mary relates what her cousin, a music teacher at the University, told her about Alaska: *"the adventure and the cold and the beauty of the snow in the winter, the northern lights and the bright moonlight, and dog teams and friendly people. It was even more than what she told me."* Mary found adventure when she married Jim Binkley and together they raised their family and worked to preserve and share their riverboat experiences. Mary describes, with charming clarity, the history of the riverboats that were the precursors to the sternwheeler, *"Discovery III,"* which currently carries guests on excursions and acquaints them with the history of sternwheel riverboating in Alaska.

Robert Charlie was born near Minto, Alaska in 1927. He is the grandson of Chief Charlie. Robert describes the nomadic way of life in a remote native community: *"the fall season, like right about now, is berry-picking time. We gather all sorts of berries for the winter and store them away in birchbark baskets. The birchbark baskets were made by family members. Mostly mothers and/or older daughters helped put these baskets together while the men would be busy out hunting moose."* With clarity and precision, Robert shares with us his life in the early years as he grew up in Minto. It is an exciting experience to follow along with Robert's recent efforts to relocate the many out-camps and preserve his heritage for the benefit and education of future generations.

Doug Colp was born near Petersburg, Alaska, in 1914. He was raised on a fox farm, where he lived until 1935, when he came to Fairbanks, attended the University and obtained a professional degree in mining engineering. Doug describes his first job with the F.E. Company, that at the time was operating bucket line gold dredges in the Fairbanks area: *"In the Spring of 1936, I applied for work with them, and after about a two week wait going through their long lines of people wanting work at that time, I finally got up to the window and the employment man at that time says, 'You're on. Have your sleeping bag here next Monday morning. You're on for a week. We're going to put you on the point field driving cold water points 65 feet to bedrock.—So thats how I got my start."* In a delightfully light and often humorous way, Doug shares with us his vast background and history with the bucket-line gold dredges that operated in Alaska. We are mesmerized as he clearly explains how the frozen ground was thawed and how the dredges worked to process the gravels and remove the gold.

Tony Gularte: Roger McPherson, an Alaskan frontier history buff, recognized the valuable contribution Tony Gularte, a well-known Alaskan Pioneer could make to Alaskan history. As a result he taped Tony's description of the adventures of Johnny Beatin and his prospecting partner, W. A. Dikeman. Johnny Beatin tells Tony the story of how he advised a young man against prospecting a particular creek because he didn't think there was any gold on it. All the other creeks in the area were being tested and the young prospector didn't want to infringe on anyone else's ground. So he told Johnny he was going to test that creek. The way Tony tells it: *"So he sank this hole. He got a two and a half dollar pan. So he comes down Flat Creek, and he goes up Otter Creek, and he says to Johnny Beatin, he says, 'Johnny, I thought you told me there was no money on that creek.' Johnny says 'yes.' Well he says 'Here, look. It's a two and a half dollar pan.' Tony goes on to say, "Johnny said, "You know I slapped my head, you know," he says, "and I walked away from it."* In an entertaining way that only an early Alaska frontiersman could tell it, Tony describes to us, step-by-step, the colorful and exciting sequence of events that led to the discovery of gold in the creeks of the Iditarod on Christmas day, 1908 and ultimately the beginning of the Iditarod gold rush.

Cliff Haydon was born in 1910 in Spokane, Washington. Cliff appeared on five Alaska Gold Trails shows telling in great detail the colorful adventures surrounding his travels and life in Alaska. It became clear during the first show that Cliff was a young man searching for adventure. He found that adventure in the frontier of Alaska. He tells the story about working his way up to Alaska on a cannery tender and how the boat named *"Fidelity"* was renamed the *"Infidelity"* because of its rotting condition. Cliff clearly describes the stormy sea and events as they crossed Dixon Entrance: *"All at once the fellow that was down below, he came running up yelling, "We're taking on water." So the captain said, "Hang on to the wheel, Haydon, and I'll go down." Well, what had happened, a wave, when he quartered around, had hit one of the portholes just right and the old rotten iron around it dumped the whole thing right in on the floor in the engine room. So, "Well," he said, "We've got to quarter the other way for awhile now, and we gotta patch that hole." What are we gonna do?* Cliff went on with the story: *"And so, of course, I was along for the adventure, so I said, "I'll go over."* You will not be able to contain your laughter as you follow through with Cliff Haydon and learn why it took him three years to get from Spokane, Washington, to Fairbanks, Alaska. The excitement grows as Cliff explains how he turned an operating fishing boat into a doughnut shop right before the captains eyes. As one caller said, "This is better than a novel."

Orea Haydon was born in the year 1922 in Fairbanks, Alaska. In 1942 Orea met a dazzling young man by the name of Cliff Lloyd Haydon, and they eloped. The clips that follow describe the events that led up to her marriage to Cliff: *"I told my stepmother, "Cliff and I really want to get married."———— And she said, "No, you can't." ———— So one day I just couldn't take it any longer. We went down and got our license. ———— While I was getting my clothes, first of all I wrote a note out saying what I was going to do, and in the meantime my stepmother drove into the yard and I knew she'd find the note.————So I went out the back door, running with an armload of clothes, down the street. Cliff came up First Avenue and he saw me running with all these clothes and he said "Well come on.———— So we went over to his house and put my things in the trunk, and we were getting ready to leave, and here comes my stepmother down the street. She spotted us. ————Here she comes. Here she comes."————and off we went. Well, the light was in our favor* (only light in town). *So we got across the bridge safely and she had to wait for the light. We got way away from her, because our pickup was newer than hers. So she never knew whether we went to Livengood or Circle Hot Springs."* In a charming presentation Orea shares the events of her life with us, beginning with the 1922 flu epidemic in Fairbanks when she was born, She tells about her early years in Washington and her return trip with her younger sister by way of the Alaska Steamship Company and the Valdez Trail when she was thirteen. She weaves a fascinating tale about how Livengood was named and how she mined gold there during her summers as a teenager. And finally, she gives a detailed description of her courtship and marriage to our young adventurer, Cliff Haydon.

Juanita Helms was born in Chicago, Illinois, in 1941. Juanita came to Alaska in 1950 after her father answered an ad for a engineering position with the Army Corps of Engineers. In 1952 her father was awarded the concession to run the hotel at Mt. McKinley National Park. She indicates that her time in McKinley Park was one of the most memorable periods of her young life. This story demonstrates why. *"My brother and I were walking up a small hill, and at that time we didn't know it, but a bear was coming up the other side, and we all met at the top. Well, the bear ran down one side and my brother ran down the other, and I stood up there screaming and waving my arms, and my father was a little upset because we'd scared the bear away and he wasn't able to get a good picture of him."* In a good natured and often humorous approach, Juanita shares the exciting events of her life in Alaska, including her adventures in Mt. McKinley National Park during the early 1950s, her school days in Fairbanks and her summer employment as a car-hop, the unorthodox proposal and courtship by Sam Helms, and her years as Fairbanks North Star Borough mayor.

Duke Kilbury was born in Spokane, Washington, in 1911. Duke's adventurous spirit took over at age 18 when he hitched a ride out of Seattle to Ketchikan on a trolling boat. He recognized early that there was no where else he would rather live. Duke relates many of his favorite frontier stories and in this case why he built his cabin on pilings: *"Be safe, yeah. That's why the cabin on the lower river is up on pilings. The floor of the cabin is a good eight feet up—there's lots of bear walking up and down the river there. I had built that cabin up on pilings, and I got a ladder up onto the porch which we pull up every night. Because I wouldn't like to wake up with a bear's bad breath in my nose."* With precision and clarity, Duke relates some of the more colorful experiences he and his friends have had during their prospecting adventures in Southeastern Alaska. He explains with detailed descriptions how to prospect for gold in alpine glacial streams, how he set up his mining operation and why it is so successful.

Don May was born in North Carolina in 1930. He had always been interested in Alaska and, as many others, was attracted by the adventure. He arrived in 1950 and began carving a life for himself and ultimately his family in gold mining. Don relates some of his early adventures in trapping and hunting and how he tried to live off the land in the Circle Hot Springs area. He describes the hospitality of Mrs. Leach when he and his partner, Joe would make their monthly visits to the hot springs for rest and recuperation. *"'Come on in, boys. Have a cup of coffee or a cup of cocoa and some cookies', you know, and after what we'd been facing for the previous month it was always so much of a relief to come in and spend time there. But I would never advise anybody to go out and try to live off the country, Jim. It's a hard thing to do. We ate all the squirrels that were in the trees. We ate all the porcupines that were around, and we had some moose there. We ate three moose that we had, and we were just continually hungry."* In his natural easy going manner, Don shares his adventures of trapping, hunting and gold mining with us and describes in vivid detail how he and his family created one of the largest and most successful placer gold mining companies in Alaska.

Don Nelson was born in Minneapolis, Minnesota. He came to Alaska in 1956 as a missionary. He indicates that he was continually tested in many ways. He relates a story that occurred in Cantwell. *"We would go down and talk with the people of the village at night. It was one of those occasions that I went down to Westneys, who was a miner and a very old man at the time. If I was ever tested to find out if I was a real Christian, that was the test, because he brought out fruit jars full of gold. I'm not talking about little bottles, I'm talking about fruit jars. And they weren't* *just a little bit in the bottom of various kinds of gold, they were fines in some jars and coarse nuggets in other jars but full jars of it, you know, and they were heavy. You can imagine what a fruit jar full of gold weighs. And he was showing it to us and he was handling one and he handed it over to me and I looked at it, and he said, "You know something? I'm a very very old man. You can see I'm kind of crippled up and I have difficulty defending myself. And nobody knows I got this gold. You could either hit me on the head and take it or you could just walk off with it. How could I stop you? Here you have all this gold." And I can't remember the exact words that he said because I must confess it kind of shocked me, you know. I thought, "I wonder what made him think I would be tempted," is what kept crossing my mind."* In an exciting and sometimes humorous way Don describes in colorful detail the events and stories told him by the old timers in the many towns and villages of Alaska where he served as a missionary.

Jeannette Therriault was born in Pincher Creek, Alberta, Canada. She came to Alaska after catching one of those Alaskan Yankees as he was passing through Pincher Creek. Jeannette describes Fairbanks when she arrived in 1951: *"The pavement was Second Avenue and about from Fifth Street down Cushman. The Post Office was there at the intersection of Cushman and Second Avenue. That was the only traffic light in town. I remember walking to the bus depot on Noble Street in the old Greiman Building, I believe it was, and it was wood sidewalks."* Jeannette shares her adventures of driving the Alcan in the 1950s, living in a tiny house trailer at the end of the airstrip at Eielson Air force Base, and adapting to life in Alaska, and how she and her husband developed a successful business, which serves the placer gold mining industry.

Hector Therriault was born in the year 1920 in Pincher Creek, Alberta, Canada. Hector first came to Alaska in 1947 after being convinced by a neighbor who had visited the territory, that as a welder he would have no difficulty finding work. Hector describes his first day in Fairbanks: *"It was very much a frontier. I don't know, it seemed like everybody knew everybody, but you knew they didn't, you know? Myself, I came in here, there wasn't a hotel room to be had, so I was walking down the street and I asked where I could find a hotel room and they said, "Well, you should contact Eva McGown." So I went to the old Nordale Hotel, and there was Eva McGown sitting there behind the desk, and she found me a bed under a church, let's see on Noble. The church was on Noble, and the pastor had some beds under the church there, and he'd rent them out for $2 a night. Very nice beds. They were clean and everything, but that's what it was. I was lucky to get a bed."* Often with guarded humor, Hector describes his experiences when he arrived in Alaska, how while visiting in Canada he met his wife, Jeannette, and how together they returned to Alaska and worked to develop Hector's Welding and ultimately the "Hector Box" that was so successful in the Alaskan gold mining industry.

Rudy Vetter was born in 1917 in Roof, Washington. Rudy was drawn to Alaska by the lure of gold. He tells of the effect the yarns the "old timers" spun had on him: *"Their stories about the gold and gold mining in Alaska intrigued me and this is, as I said before, why I came here to do prospecting and mining."* Rudy Vetter is a legendary Alaskan prospector with a rich background filled with prospecting and gold mining adventures. He tells us in vivid detail how he and his brother Adolf searched for and discovered several significant gold deposits. With an inviting flavor he openly shares with us his methods and colorful history in Alaska hardrock and placer mining.

Doris Vogler was born in Oklahoma City in 1919. Doris visited Anchorage right after the war then came to Fairbanks on an employment assignment in 1948. She explains her view of Fairbanks: *"I loved it. Everybody was friendly. My gosh, people spoke to you whether they knew you or whether they didn't know you. You'd go into a store and they'd welcome you with open arms. It was just wonderful."* She described the conditions of her employment: *"I came back* (to Alaska) *when Vince Monten out of Oklahoma City contracted to build the utilidors out here at Ladd Air Force Base, in '48, '49, '50, I believe. But anyway, I got a job, but I was only supposed to be here for a month. Two years later I went home and got the rest of my clothes and came back."* In a humorous and colorful presentation, Doris shares the events of her life, how she met Joe Vogler and their rather unique courtship. In a lively way she tells us of the events surrounding the Winter Carnival, living in the Historic Rose Building, and what life was like in Fairbanks in the late 40s and early 50s.

Joe Vogler was born in Barnes, Kansas, in 1913. Joe came to Alaska in 1942 on a job assignment with the Sim's Great Puget Sound Bridge and Dredging Company, which was among the consortium of companies that were building the Naval facility in Old Woman's Bay outside of Kodiak. From that time Joe worked on a number of construction jobs where he did anything and everything. This background gave him considerable experience with equipment and mechanics. In 1951 he quit his job and became a full-time gold miner. Joe tells us how he prepared the sluice box for his first gold mining operation: *"We built a sluice box out of wood. I remember putting that together right there on the ground — 2 by 4's and I think 1 by 10 planks. We found a couple of old truck beds and made a slick plate to doze onto, and the slick plate channeled the gravels to the wooden sluice. They were using that method up on Mastodon Creek, and I got to take a look at it, constructed ours, and then began dozing away with the Cat."* In an alluring fashion, Joe Vogler tells us his story and simultaneously, through his experiences, reveals the true character of mid-twentieth century Alaska as he worked his way through and explains the purpose of various construction projects around the country, entertainingly interprets the early mining history on several of Alaska's most famous creeks and clearly describes his successes and failures at gold mining in Alaska.

Ernie Wolff was born in Minnesota in the late 1910s. He came to Alaska in 1938 to go to school and get away from the depression. Ernie describes Fairbanks when he arrived: *"It had gravel streets or no streets at all, or no gravel at all anyway. Dirt streets, pretty muddy at times, pretty dusty at times. There were a great many boardwalks in evidence, but it wasn't a wild west town by any means. In fact it's probably one of the most peaceable places that I'd seen. Naturally, a lot of young fellows a long way from home, you would expect a lot of fights. Well there weren't that many fights, compared to other places I've been. I think people were working too hard to make a living to cause much trouble."* In an easy, good-natured and often charming way Ernie Wolff, through his experiences, provides us with a clear picture of his adventures as he traveled to Alaska and, with precision, describes the frontier character of Fairbanks, its blossoming mining industry, and its developing University. Simultaneously, in a lively fashion, he weaves in a tribute to the people that were responsible for pioneering the Alaskan frontier.

Dr. William R. Wood was born in Illinois. He came to Fairbanks, Alaska, in 1960 because he was offered a job as the President of the University of Alaska. Following 13 years of service, he retired and, because he liked Alaska so well, he just stayed. Dr. Wood describes why he felt the conditions at the University of Alaska were ideal for him: *"The one place which had everything to do was Alaska. And since my interests are always to explore and to try to find new ways to do something to create, to build, this was simply an ideal chance."* He goes on to conclude: *"I came not only because I was asked, but because it was a job that was to me the finest job in all higher education in North America."* Dr. Wood carries us with him as he travels through the episodes of his career in education, his retirement in Fairbanks, Alaska and his time as mayor of Fairbanks. His unbounded energy and resultant achievements in every activity, from professional basketball player to coach, teacher, university administrator and city mayor is overwhelming.

Shorty Zucchini was born in St. Louis, Missouri, in 1911. Shorty indicates that he came to Alaska in 1947 because it was a call to freedom. He relates his experience: *"I got a round-trip fare just in case things wouldn't work out. But I knew that I hit my high peak in life just after I landed here and met these wonderful Alaskans. I don't know why the people are different, unless it's putting snowshoes on and knowing what 60 below is* *and dark nights or freezing my feet, or having these daggone mosquitoes bite the hell out of me. You know, when you put all this together, it changes your life, Jim. "* In an honest and often emotional way Shorty brings to life his experiences with the people and the environment of Alaska. He explains in often interesting terms some of his prospecting and mining adventures. But most impressive, is his genuine respect and love for the people, environment and adventure he found in Alaska.

Paul McCarthy came to Alaska in 1964 from Syracuse, New York. He came because he was offered a position as a librarian at the University of Alaska in Fairbanks. In the early years Paul worked primarily with the archives. Paul was not a stereotype archivist, but rather a successful prospector in his own way. He explains what an Alaskan Archivist does as he travels down the Yukon River in a canoe. *"The trip that the caller just referred to was a trip that was suggested to us in 1966 or '67, of going down and trying to survey the historical sites along the Yukon and to retrieve any records that were abandoned and to document that part of Alaska's history. "* Paul's colorful adventures as an archivist—gathering, salvaging and preserving documents and materials—took him to many parts of the state. He relates these meaningful adventures in an entertaining yet informative manner. Paul's clear explanation of the nature of the University of Alaska archives and how useful they are as a resource for research material provides a welcome mat of opportunity to the general public, students and visitors in search of historical information on Alaska.

Paul McCarthy was the last Alaskan Gold Trails guest. At that time (Nov. 30, 1989) he was presented with a full set of 96 Alaska Gold Trail cassette tapes for inclusion in the University of Alaska Fairbanks Library Archives.

Part III

The Pioneers

Jim Binkley
with
Jim Madonna
May 25, 1989

Jim M: Our guest today is Captain Jim Binkley of Riverboat Discovery fame. Welcome to Alaska Gold Trails, Jim.

Jim B: Jim Madonna, I'm delighted to be here.

Jim M: Well, Jim, immediately, we have a call, and I think one of your friends might like to talk to you.

Jim B: Sure.

Caller: Captain Binkley, I've been waiting for your show. I have a couple of questions for you. Hope you can make a comment and explanation.

Jim B: Surely.

Caller: And this has to do with aspects of steamboating on the Yukon. The first question that I want you to address is the procedure of grasshoppering over shallow places with the big poles like stilts in front, and the second one is could you address and maybe comment and explain winching up through Five-finger Rapids?

Jim B: Surely. The phrase you used, grasshoppering, well that's sparring off, when one is stuck on a sandbar. There are any number of ways to attempt to get off. The sticking on a sandbar can be a pretty serious thing, because you lose a lot of time for the company you're working for, and, of course, that relates to money. So the sooner you can get off, the better. Ordinarily you're pushing a barge, or two, or even three, and the boat usually comes off first. Then you can help get the barges off once you've got the boat free and up against the riverbank. But the procedure of grasshoppering that you are talking about are the two big spars, which look like big utility poles, on each side of the boat, for example, the steamer *Nenana*. Those were lifted and dumped over the side, sticking down in the sand, straight upright. Then a tackle was attached to the deck, and using the winch you would actually lift the bow of the boat, and while you did that you gave the engineer a ring and told him to give it a shot of power, and he would give it a kick with the sternwheel, which of course is above the bottom of the boat, so it pushes the boat ahead. So you've lifted the front of the boat, only the stern is sticking. The power of the wheel gives you a shot and you move ahead about six feet. Then you retrieve those spars and put them upright again, lift yourself another time and push yourself ahead. Tremendous amount of work for the deck crew. Didn't always work, but when it did work, it was terrific. Winching through the rapids was something we had to do occasionally when we didn't have power enough to push up against the current. So we'd run a small boat ahead, take out a line, fasten it to a convenient tree or trees, if necessary, bring that line back to the boat, put it through what we called the fairlead, out in the front, so that we'd have the line coming straight to the winch. Then the pilot or the captain, whoever was steering, would hold the boat offshore in a convenient place, then you start to pull. So you'd winch yourself up through the swift spots. At Five-finger Rapids that you talked about, it's a little different there, because they had a cable already fastened to the rocks above and below the swift spot. The cable had a lot of slack in it. When you came up alongside on the downstream side and picked up the cable, put the slack on deck, wrapped it around your capstan, and with the steam pressure against the capstans, you would take a tight pull on the line, thereby pulling the boat up through the swift spot. When you got to the point where the boat had sufficient power to push against the current, you'd unwind the cable from the capstan, throw it over the side and continue on your way. So that covers those two.

Jim M: Jim, our caller referenced Five-fingers Rapids. Are we referring to that part of the Yukon River between Whitehorse and Dawson?

Jim B: Yes. Five-finger was the most dramatic one, the one that got the most publicity, because it looks so difficult. It wasn't all that tough. Rink Rapids, just below Five-finger Rapids, destroyed several steamers in the early days. As a matter of fact, my Dad had some very harrowing experiences in Rink Rapids back in 1898-1899.

Jim M: Did your father travel all the way down from Lake Bennett?

Jim B: Well he started at Lake Bennett. He walked over the White Pass when he was just a young man and carried two thousand pounds of gear on his back. Took him about a month to get up there, and he built a boat at Lake Bennett out of wood-sawed lumber, like so many did. But he had an advantage because he had been trained as a pilot on the Ohio River. He was born in Indiana, on a farm, but he was always attracted to boats and machinery and that sort of thing, so he trained as a riverboat pilot. He was a cub pilot on the Ohio. He heard about the furor in Alaska and he headed out toward the Pacific coast, arrived in Seattle in 1897 and made a stake and got himself the gear, put himself on a boat, and off he went. He began the Yukon Journey at Lake Bennett, in the spring of 1898.

Jim M: Your father, then, had first hand experience through all the rapid areas, including Miles Canyon, Whitehorse Rapids and the rest.

Jim B: Miles Canyon was probably the most dramatic one. Those people who have seen it know that it is a pretty dramatic canyon, where all the water from the lakes, that comes down that side of the watershed in Canada, gathers up into Marsh Lake, and Marsh Lake empties out into what is now the Yukon through a canal of rocks. Maybe in those days it was as much as 150 feet high and probably not much wider than that. So it was really a flume of highly turbulent water. Many miners were lost in there. Some of them didn't want to take their rafts through, so they would portage around it, which was expensive and difficult. But my Dad would charge from $25 to $100 to take rafts through. He got the money to build his first steamboat that way.

Jim M: We have a caller Jim. Hello, welcome to Alaska Gold Trails, you're on the air with our guest Jim Binkley.

Caller: Yes. I was on the phone just a few minutes ago and I had one more question that Captain Binkley brought up, and that has to do with where the Yukon River starts. The first trip I ever made over the highway, the river running out of Marsh Lake was the Lewes. My question is, how did they pronounce it? Was it the Lewes or the Lewis.

Jim B: It was the Lewes River at that time, and the beginning of the Yukon listed at that time was where the White and the Pelly Rivers came together. That was officially the Yukon. But then, in the days when we had visitors coming up here, they wanted to see the Yukon and Whitehorse wanted to take advantage of that, so they just extended the source of the Yukon up to Marsh Lake—took away the sign that said "Lewes" and then called it the "Yukon". You're right on.

Jim M: Where was it that your father was running the river in 1898?

Jim B: It was the Whitehorse-Dawson area, Jim, that he was running in those days, and there were plenty of big steamboats on the river hauling freight to the miners, and he discovered that he could do better by working on the side streams. So he met one of the men who has become a very famous Alaskan character, Sid Barrington, who is my godfather, by the way, and he and Sid became partners, and they built small boats and operated on the side streams. They followed all the gold strikes. Whenever there was a strike, they were right there with their small boats. In order to get up some of these streams they had to use a propeller boat, instead of a sternwheeler. My Dad did not invent the idea, but he built the first tunnel—stern boats west of the Mississippi River and they were successful in hauling tons and tons of freight up the very shallow side streams to the mining sites. And in those days they got paid off in gold dust. They carried gold scales right with them.

Jim M: Jim, perhaps we should start at the beginning. Many times we get ahead of ourselves on the show and everything gets so interesting some-how we forget to ask such questions as where and when was Jim Binkley born, and what kind of life has Jim Binkley had?

Jim B: I was born in Wrangell, Alaska, in Southeast Alaska, about halfway between Ketchikan and Juneau, little lumber town, fishing town, mostly fishing in those days. I was born in 1920 and my Dad had established, with his partner, a business on the Stikine River, hauling freight to the miners up in British Columbia. They had, incidentally, been on the shores of Ship Creek, at a place that eventually was called Anchorage, where they were bringing surveyors in to survey for the town, and also up the Susitna River to survey for the Alaska Railroad. Then the government took over and they had to move, so they moved to the Stikine River and started there, and that's where I was born. My Dad died when I was just very young, and my two uncles, who were river men, took over my river education. I spent three years in high school in California, staying with my maternal grandparents.

Jim M: Did you have your introduction to riverboats and riverboating be-fore you went to high school in California?

Jim B: Well, to a certain extent, yes. I wasn't getting paid for it.

Jim M: Was it an exciting introduction to your future career?

Jim B: Absolutely. My first real experience came after I got out of high school and got serious about it and decided I wanted to follow that ca-reer, because to me it was a family tradition. You see, my paternal grand-father had logged and rafted logs on the Ohio River also, which was one of the ways my father got started, so to me it seemed like a family tradi-tion. And it's an exciting business. I wanted to get into that wheel house as fast as I could, but, of course, I spent plenty of time in the engine room and plenty of time in the galley and plenty of time on deck before I finally got up there and became a pilot.

Jim M: Tell us about what you do in the engine room. What kind of engines drive the boat?

Jim B: Well, two different things. We had internal combustion engines that were running boats in those days, and also the steam powered, and I was fortunate in getting started in the very earliest days with steam, when they were still burning wood, here in the Interior. I left Wrangell in late '39—early '40 to come to Fairbanks to attend the University, and of course, got a job right away because I'd had some river experience and it was what I wanted to do. I worked for the late Captain George Black, who operated out of Fairbanks for years. I operated three years between Fairbanks and Dawson on the mail run—two thousand mile round trip. We'd sometimes turn around at Eagle, sometimes go on up to Dawson.

That was an exciting period where I got my first sternwheeler piloting experience. During World War II, I was really very fortunate, because I was moved from boat to boat—got the kind of experience it would take a person a lifetime to get, really in just a few years. I followed it from small tugboats with a two-man crew to the big steamer *Klondike* out of Whitehorse, with a 50-man crew in those days. During wartime they put on extra help and we carried huge loads of freight down the Yukon to Circle, which eventually came around into Fairbanks. That extends the type of experience that I've had. But probably the most glorious of all to me was those earlier days, from 1940 through the beginning of World War II, here in the Interior. I developed a tremendous admiration and respect for the many cultures here in the Interior. Watching those self-reliant proud people in the early days and the way they carried on. Their families, their family associations, the trapping that they did, and the villages in those days to me were just a great delight.

Jim M: It is clear that you developed a first-hand feeling and understanding for the nature of the country and it's people during that time , Jim.

Jim B: Oh, my, I should say so. You know, the hours alone in the wheelhouse, way up high like that, particularly up in the Arctic, where at midnight the sun is right on the horizon and it's putting those purple fingers out through the trees, and the snow on the high mountains having those purple shadows coming down and the power of the boat going against the current and that total peace that's involved there. It's a life that's hard to describe unless you've experienced it.

Jim M: We have a caller, Jim. Hi, welcome to Alaska Gold Trails. You're on the air with our guest Jim Binkley.

Caller: Hi. I know you brought *Discovery III* up on a barge to the mouth of the Yukon, sunk the barge and drove the boat up here under its own power. How were the old ones brought up into Alaska?

Jim B: That's a neat question, because that in itself is a real Alaskan story. Many of the boats were built in Seattle in knocked down condition, shipped up by barge, and assembled at Unalaska and also right near the mouth of the Yukon, St. Michael, where they were put together. Some were built by the Moran Company in Seattle in the earliest days and they came up under their own power. The attrition rate on those was pretty high. But some of those earliest boats were built at Whitehorse by old Scotch shipbuilders and I used to take great delight in watching, in springtime, as the boats were being fitted out and readied for the summer. Some boats were built here. The earliest one built in Fairbanks I think was about 1910 or something like that, the steamer *Idler*, which I served on in 1940, and the wheelhouse on that boat is now the wheelhouse on *Discovery I*. So we've been able to preserve a little bit of that history. *Discovery I*, of course, we built in our back yard, right here on University Avenue in 1955, and *Discovery II* was the steamer *Yutana* that had belonged to the Captain George Black estate, and we took it and converted it. It looks nothing like the original boat, but some of the original material is still in it. That's a bit of Alaskan real history there.

Caller: So we can safely figure that taking a sternwheeler or a riverboat across the Gulf of Alaska was not a low-risk project.

Jim B: Indeed. As a matter of fact, we gave serious consideration to running *Discovery III* up here under her own power, and that is possible to do, but the expense involved was greater than transporting it on a barge, and the insurance premium on bringing it up under its own power as opposed to barging was terrifying—more so than the conditions.

Caller: OK. Thank you.

Jim M: Another caller, Jim. Hi welcome to Alaska Gold Trails, you're on the air with Jim Binkley.

Caller: Yes. When you're running down the Tanana, a lot of times you'll send out a pilot boat and find the bars and the channel and put buoys out next to the sandbar. What side of the bar does the buoy go on, or does it change if you're going up or down stream?

Jim B: It depends on the conditions. If you're coming downstream with a load of freight, there are points that you simply must cut very close, without sticking the barges, as they are loaded with freight. The buoys are placed at a particular point to give the pilot a reference for turning and thereby marking the channel in the best position for the boat. Coming upstream we rarely put out buoys. Most of the time it was going down, and then we would retrieve them, because that buoy might be on dry land on the return trip which might be as much as two weeks later. The position of the buoy was determined by the pilot and the man in the sounding boat, as to what they wanted as a reference place, where they had to turn so they wouldn't be swept down on a bar. So it was a matter of just making up your mind right on the spot as to what was the most favorable spot for it.

Caller: Well then, the channel wouldn't necessarily be on the right or the left.

Jim B: Not at all. And the wave conditions are something else too. You see, those boats are subject to wind, which is a tremendous factor to a pilot, because there's a small amount of boat in the water and a tremendous sail area up above. Now when that wind hits, it is important to determine just how much power must be put against it, and then if the wind suddenly dies, the pilot must be prepared to reduce power right along with it. That marker would depend on the combination of current, the bar and the wind.

Caller: We were coming up last year and you were going down, and the first two markers you had out, we got on the left side and we thought we had it made. The next one we cut on the left side and we were high and dry. So I thought maybe there was a system.

Jim B: No, the only system is the one that's determined by the two pilots that are guiding the pilot boat and the steering, at the time, to their best advantage.

Caller: Well, with the radio communications you can figure it out easy enough. OK. Thank you, captain.

Jim B: You're sure welcome.

Jim M: We have another caller, Jim, Hello, welcome to Alaska Gold Trails. You're on the air with Jim Binkley.

Caller: Yes. One more question, Captain Binkley. You were in the transition period between steam and internal combustion engines. Would you comment on the handling characteristics, all other considerations aside, of steam versus internal combustion?

Jim B: Sure. The steamboats were very large, because the wheel had to grow in size as the power of the boat was increased. With an internal combustion you merely added more propellers and more engines and you had the same small crew in a relatively small boat. So the steamboat, the more power you had the bigger it got to contain the wheel and the power applied to it. So the difference was that the big boat was very very difficult to handle. One characteristic that was terrific, it has tremendous backing power, which is what you need when you're handling freight going downstream on a tough river like the Tanana, for example. And that, to me, was always a joy, because you could back it in either direction, with the big flanking rudders that responded to the reverse power of that wheel. With the propeller boats, though, you had differential power, where you could use one engine and go ahead and another one in back, or any combination of several. So I guess the difference was that there was a lot of romance in the steamboat and a lot of hard work in the propeller boat, but I like them both. I think I have a more nostalgic feeling about the steamboat, because it was just so much fun to be in that part of Alaska's and United States' history. A tugboat is just a tugboat, no matter what. You get a good feeling for it, but the old steamboats are just something in your mind and in your heart that's so much different than a regular tugboat.

Caller: Perhaps I phrased my question wrong. I was just wondering in terms of the paddlewheel boats. Were you on the transition in them from steam to combustion?

Jim B: Personally making the transition? Yeah, a little difficult. Not all that bad, though, because fortunately for me, I got to move around a lot. Ordinarily a person would be a pilot then a captain on a boat, and it could take almost a lifetime, and a mate could be waiting for years to get to be able to handle a boat and become a pilot, but in the utility role that I played, I just moved around from boat to boat and it really wasn't too difficult for me to make the transition from a big steamer down to a small tug. Relatively easy, although I must confess, to answer your question, some of the fellows did have a lot of trouble doing that. Somehow it was relatively easy for me, because the whole thing was just a lot of fun, no matter what I was doing.

Caller: Well, I'll phrase it one more way. In terms of steam, you've got maximum torque and zero r.p.m., whereas internal combustion engines are different. And I was just wondering as to the responsiveness of steam versus the internal combustion.

Jim B: No difference. Because internal combustion is applied several ways. Internal combustion engine can be applied to run a generator which runs an electric motor which could turn your paddle wheel. Or a hydraulic system could turn your paddle wheel. Or a direct connection. And the response was just as fast as steam. Although I must say I missed the smell of cylinder oil and steam. I used to take a piece of hookum and stick it under my pillow at night.

Caller: Thank you.

Jim M: I'm getting confused here. There are all kinds of wheels on these boats, Jim. They've got them on the sides and they've got them on the back. Tell us something about that.

Jim B: Well the sidewheelers were never successful here because of a few reasons. One, you couldn't work as close to shore as you want to in these rivers, where you want to get in tight to save time. You get right into the brush. With the paddlewheel way behind you, back there, it was in the safest position. And the sidewheeler, if you had listed over to one side, you'd lose power on the other side. So the sternwheeler was more successful. With a propeller boat you had the propellers underneath the hull, up in a tunnel, and you had the small propellers and you had to be more careful of those in the snags and sticks and trees that you went over, than you did with the sternwheeler. So you had three types—the paddlewheeler with the side wheels, the sternwheel, with the rear wheel, and then the regular propellers on a boat you would visualize today. Did that help?

Jim M: That helped a great deal. We're starting to get this cleared up. What did you do in terms of developing *Discovery* through the years.

Jim B: I've got a little story that will go with that other one, too. I had a big twin-screw propeller boat that I was operating on the river, and the military had one of the old time mates come over and work with me, and I asked if he wanted to stand a shift, and he said, "Sure." So, he was accustomed to a paddlewheel, and of course we had none on that boat, and he couldn't remember for sure what power he was applying to the engines through his signals, so he said to one of the deckhands, "Hey, run back and see which way the wheel is turning," and the deckhand came back and he said, "There's no wheel back there." That transition was a little difficult for him.

Jim M: I'll bet you have hundreds like that, Jim. Maybe some more will surface as we start the adventure with your romance in riverboating.

Jim B: Well, it started with the *Godspeed*. That was our first small boat. Sternwheeler romancing, yes, *Discovery I* was the genesis of that. The *Godspeed* we purchased from the Episcopal Bishop here in Fairbanks, and that's the way Mary and I got our start. What we had was a 25-passenger boat. We could see immediately that we were going to need a larger one. So I had a friend of mine, who was a professional architect, help me design *Discovery I*. It was constructed right in our back yard on University Avenue, and launched in the Noyes Slough in 1955. At that time it carried 49 passengers, and again, the same situation. Business was growing, so I cut it in half and stretched it out, made it longer, and then we got up to 80 passengers. Then I wanted twice that many later on, so I widened it out eight feet and made it again a little bit longer. That accommodated 150 passengers. When we got up to the point of talking to the Coast Guard about making it larger again, they said, "Hey. Hold up, here. You can only go so far with that." So we purchased the old boat from Nenana that I had worked on years ago, that traveled so many thousands of miles of the Yukon. We purchased it from the George Black estate and we converted it to what is now *Discovery II*. I went through the same situation there. We made it wider and longer through the years, until we could no longer do that. Then our family made the decision to build *Discovery III*, which has been just eminently successful. A beautiful beautiful boat. Probably the most sophisticated sternwheeler boat ever built, and still an old fashioned sternwheeler.

Jim M: You had quite an adventure bringing that up. You had somebody actually do a video tape of that entire trip, didn't you?

Jim B: Yes. We did. As a matter of fact, Princess Tours sponsored that, and they hired a Hollywood crew and really a fine professional gang to come up with it. And the photographer who did the photography, Bill Farnsworth, is a well-known Hollywood cameraman, and the young guy who did the story line of the whole thing is an advertising person. One who incidentally worked for us years ago. Neat young man, whose father is an advertising man in Hollywood. And they did a superb job on that, just grand. They took it from the time that it came off the boat, and then they did their research on the old days. And what they did was to interview people along the river and get their impressions about what has happened since those earlier days—the old folks, particularly, and the way they were feeling seeing this big sternwheeler coming up the river. They interviewed kids and older folks, the Eskimo cultures on the coast and the Indian culture as they came close to the Interior, and then of course the arrival in Fairbanks. Incidentally, I had no part in that. I turned that over to our two sons, oldest and youngest. Number two son and daughter and Mary and I ran the operation here while they went down to the mouth of the Yukon and with their crew, took the boat off and brought her all the way home. Really an outstanding accomplishment, to do that. Just the trip alone, 3,500 miles by barge, was quite a situation. We had to put it on the barge ourselves and cradle it, and number one son schemed all that out, did the whole works.

Jim M: When you came up to Nenana things became more interesting, you actually had to hinge the stack over didn't you?

Jim B: Let me tell you how that occurred. I had made that run years ago. I've run all the way from Dawson, clear down to the Bering Sea and almost all the side streams in between, through the years, and I felt it'd be a great adventure for two of the boys, at least, to be able to bring that thing up here. And they can encounter the same kinds of things that I did, have the same surprise and marvelous feelings that I had. And I'd done it already. Why should I do it again? So I briefed them. We sat down and we took my old charts and so on, and we took every portion of the river—what they were likely to encounter. Of course, many changes since those years. But as we did that, we got to Nenana, and I said, "Wait a minute. We've got to go under two bridges here." And then I recalled that the steamer *Nenana* had to do the same thing. So the boys went down, and actually there are records about the height of the bridge above the water, but we wanted to know exactly. So they went down and they dropped a plumb line down and actually, on the ice, measured the exact height above the ice line. They compared that to the water records at Nenana, so they knew at any given time how much clearance they would have. So we had to hinge that stack, take the whole thing apart, and there are four exhaust pipes that come up through there—it's actually a functional stack. So the exhaust system had to be modified to take that too, but it worked very well. Below Nenana they just took the bolts loose and lowered the stack. And the beautiful thing is, they went under the train bridge at Nenana at exactly the same moment a train was going south across the top of the bridge, and that's part of that film, "Path of Gold," which incidentally has played on PBS. Marvelous marvelous film.

Jim M: We've heard a lot about your adventures as a riverboat captain. How about your private life. You talk about your sons. You talk about your wife. Perhaps we should go back maybe a couple of years here, anyway, to the time when you met Mary. Would you discuss that a little bit for us, Jim.

Jim B: Sure, I'd be delighted to. There's an interesting story that goes with that, if we have time to go through it here, Jim. After I was discharged from the service, in January of 1946, my mother and my stepfather were living up above Eagle on the Canadian border. I could hardly wait to get up there, and incidentally, by that time I had piloted boats in the Bering Sea, in the Gulf of Alaska, in the Aleutian chain, on the Yukon River, all of Prince William Sound, the whole works, during the period that I was in the military. I gained tremendous experience on a variety of vessels—small troop ships right down to the biggest riverboat in the business, at that time, the steamer *Klondike*. However, I never had that privilege of running the *Nenana*, but I worked alongside it for a long time. Well, when I was out of the service I wanted to get home and I flew up to Eagle with a bush pilot—this was in 1946—and I borrowed a dog team from an Indian friend of mine at the Eagle village and mushed on up to see my parents—my mother and my stepfather. And unbeknownst to me the weather was changing—a cold front was moving in, and as I left Eagle it was about zero, but I hadn't been out but an hour before that cold weather began to creep up on me. It got down to about 48-49 below. The dogs wouldn't work and I didn't know enough to slow down. I was excited anyhow, and I breathed in so much of that dry cold air that I actually did what they call "freezing your lungs," which is merely a dry pneumonia, where all the bronchia in your bronchial area collapse, and it's a very serious situation. Fortunately for me, my mother is a nurse, so when I got to the camp she immediately saw that there was something wrong with me, the way I was breathing, and the dogs were OK because they just wouldn't work at all—I did all the pushing on the sled (musher's are usually the hardest working dog in the team anyhow). But at any rate, I was becoming cyanotic—my lips were blue and my fingernails—and I just was absolutely struggling for breath. And she gave me injections of adrenaline to dilate my capillaries, but she'd have to give me so much that it would make my heart skip a beat, so they had to get me out of there in a hurry, and the Indians from the village and the villagers cleared off a spot where a bush pilot friend of mine by the name of Johnny Lind, in those days, flew in an old Ballanca and flew me out. I was in the hospital here in Fairbanks for about a month, and they gave me penicillin and this sort of thing. Finally I went back to the University and stayed with a friend of mine who was the superintendent of maintenance there, and that's where I met Mary, while I was convalescing from the hospital and living with my friend Jack Sullivan, who was the engineer. And she would come with another girl and clean the apartment there periodically. So I spotted her at the bottom of the stairs and I said, "Hey, my prayers have been answered." I suggested to her a few days after we had met that it would be appropriate for us to get married, and by gosh it took me about a year to talk her into it. I was in a veterans' hospital in Portland, Oregon for several months as a result of that, and she's lived in that area.

Jim M: For some reason, she found her way down to that area during that period of time.

Jim B: Yes, indeed. Somehow our paths were parallel.

Jim M: What a coincidence.

Jim B: Indeed it was. Well, anyway, so finally she succumbed and said, "OK." And I, of course, had visions of our living in a log cabin with a pitcher pump and an outhouse and that sort of thing, but it simply didn't work out that way.

Jim M: You got some new directions, did you?

Jim B: Yes I did.

Jim M: That was quite a story. Tell us about your children, Jim.

Jim B: We have four. We have a daughter and three sons.

Jim M: And they're all interested in riverboating?

Jim B: Yes, All working at it. Our daughter, handles all the marketing and sales and our gift shop on the boat. And Jim handles all the personnel and the cosmetics. And Skip handles all the mechanical details. And I'm now chairman of the board and he is president of the company. Our son John, who works with us in the summertime, is a state senator. He will be working with us in the summer and we'll have everybody, including our ten-year-old grandson, our oldest of eight. We are all uniformed these days in our tourist business, and our grandson who works on board has a uniform with a half a stripe.

Jim M: A half a stripe?

Jim B: Absolutely. You gotta start somewhere.

Jim M: Jim we have a call. Hi. You're on the air with Jim Binkley.

Caller: I'd like to ask Jim what he has planned for tomorrow for the senior citizens of Fairbanks? I'll hang up and listen.

Jim B: I'd be delighted to answer that. Tomorrow's a very special day. As you probably realize, we haul literally hundreds of little school kids in the spring time, as kind of a nice treat for them, and we just love to do it. And we have a special one that we're doing tomorrow at 1:30 for the physically challenged at Denali Center, the Pioneers Home, the seniors from the Senior Center at Fairbanks, Nenana Seniors, the North Pole Seniors, and the Fairbanks Native Association Senior Center, and this will depart tomorrow at 1:30. So all of the folks who are aware of that, check with the senior centers and they'll give you all the information. This is a time of year when we try to do as much as we can for the local people who wouldn't have that opportunity otherwise before we start our regular season, which incidentally begins on Saturday. We have a trip this afternoon that I will begin right after the show. We have Friday, the senior citizen group and the physically handicapped, and then on Saturday we start our regular 8:45, 2:00 PM double trip day all summer long.

Jim M: Jim, give us a little information. You said you have *Discovery I*, *Discovery II* and *Discovery III*. Where is *Discovery I* right now?

Jim B: *Discovery I* is on our dry dock right now. We have our own dry dock, one we built from surplus 48-inch pipe, and we're doing some changes and repairs on it. We must have enough back up for the big boat that we never interrupt our schedule. Discovery II, for example, made over 4,000 consecutive voyages without five minutes delay, which is a pretty remarkable record for any piece of mechanical equipment. However, if we are going to keep a schedule and accommodate all of our visitors here, and our obligations, we must have backup, in the event that we have a mechanical problem. So *Discovery II* and *Discovery I* are backups to *Discovery III*. There's something else I'd like to say while we still have the time here, Jim, if I may, about the steamer *Nenana*, in town. That really is a treasure, and I have much admiration and respect for Jack Williams and his group that's doing the work on that steamer, and the effort that's being generated by the school kids on that marvelous old vessel. I enjoy listening to Gayle Malloy in the morning and the young people who are asking these trivia questions and so on, the answers to which I know very well and I'm always tempted to punch the button and call in, but I know that I shouldn't do that.

Jim M: No fair, Jim.

Jim B: Sure. But really, it just thrills me to see that steamboat coming back alive again.

Jim M: The trivia question this morning was: "What was the hogging system?" What's a hogging system, Jim?

Jim B: Well, Sagging is when the boat sags in the middle. Hogging is when it falls down on each end, sags on each end. So you put a big post in the center and run cables out to the ends to hold it up. You've got the machinery on one end and the boilers on the other, so it's liable to sag down there.

Jim M: All right. We've got the answer. We have a caller. Hi, You're on the air with Jim Binkley.

Caller: Hello. I'd like to ask Jim a question please. Jim, I remember you in Nenana, the fall of 1945. You were in the service. What boat were you on?

Jim B: On the *Hazel B. II*. I was captain of that vessel, a 110-foot 2-inch-screw tug that carried 35 passengers, and it could push about 250 tons of freight.

Caller: Yeah, I remember you well.

Jim B: Oh my. Well, those were glorious days and I have a lot of very fond memories of my times in Nenana and down to Galena, even clear down to the mouth and clear up to Eagle.

Caller: Yeah, I'm going to be on your boat tomorrow.

Jim B: Wonderful. I'll look forward to it.

Caller: Yeah, my husband and I, I don't know if I'll get to see you, but we'll be on board.

Jim B: Well, if you're on board, you come and talk to me. I'll be there. Thanks for calling.

Caller: You betcha. Bye.

Jim M: Jim, when we walk onto *Discovery III*, what do we see there? What will we be able to see? Will we see an engine room?

Jim B: The engine room is pretty well sealed up, but we have a film that we show, and incidentally we have television on that boat. We have seven big monitors on there so that people on all decks can see anything that occurs. The commentator, for example, is seen on all decks on this big video screen, and then you can see things ashore that we show with that. We have seating area with unlimited visibility—unobstructed. All three decks. One deck is in the open air, with a Texas deck up there and a little shelter up on top, seating all around it. That boat is licensed for 1,000 people, however we never carry more than 750 because we feel that we can entertain 750 in the manner that we want to. Any more and it becomes a little crowded.

Jim M: You have a gift shop on board?

Jim B: Yes. We have a fine gift shop and we have two snack bars. It's big, it's comfortable and it's safe. Our sound system is terrific, and the video is good, and the crew just loves to do it, and we have about 35 people that work with us. The village where we stop is an exciting place and it really takes you back in time to the era that I've been talking about, when I first got started here.

Jim M: It's been a real pleasure to have you here. Thank you, Jim Binkley.

Jim B: Pleasure to be here. Our boat sails in about three minutes, and I'm going to be on it. So thank you, Jim. I've enjoyed being on your program.

Mary Binkley
with
Jim Madonna
May 11, 1989

Jim: I want to welcome Mary Binkley to Alaska Gold Trails. How are you today, Mary?

Mary: Oh, just great. Love this beautiful early summer weather in Fairbanks.

Jim: It's been a little unpredictable to this point, Mary. We don't know if we're in summer or out of summer lately. Mary, since you came to Alaska have you seen some variations in the weather that were particularly outstanding, in terms of the winter extending into the summer farther than it is this year?

Mary: Well, I probably have. I've been here, it will be 45 years this summer. So I've seen quite a few changes, but I'm not sure that I remember anything outstanding. I do recall the spring of 1948. Jim and I were living in Nenana. We'd just come back from the Seattle area. And that's when Nenana had a flood, and Fairbanks was flooding, and they shipped all the women and the children out of Nenana on the train. We arrived here in Fairbanks and were taken up on the University campus hill. That was quite an exciting time for Nenana—everything under water except a little bit of gravel around the depot station, but the train could still get in and out. Fairbanks was flooding also at that time, down by the hospital and the railroad area.

Jim: Following the 1948 flood, we had another disastrous flood in Fairbanks. Do you remember when that second flood occurred, Mary?

Mary: I think everybody remembers that—1967. There were many other floods here too, but those were outstanding ones.

Jim: Mary, tell us, where were you born and am I out of order asking what year that might have been?

Mary: Well, it sets all right. I don't mind telling. I'm not old, I'm just young— young at heart anyway. I was born in Oregon. I'm the only one in our family who's a non-Alaskan by birth. And I was born about around 1926.

Jim: Around 1926. Well, that's a fair answer. And tell us, where did you go to school?

Mary: In Oregon, in a small little community northwest of Portland, about 60 miles.

Jim: What kind of environment were you in. Were you in a farm, industrial or just a small community?

Mary: It was just a small community. We lived on the edge of this little town. It had about 1,600 people, and still has about 1,600, although the population type has changed. It was a sawmill, lumbering area, logging, and now it's a retirement area more than anything else.

Jim: I see. And you went clear through the full 12 grades, is that right?

Mary: Yes.

Jim: When did you come to Alaska, and what was the reason?

Mary: Well, I arrived in Alaska in 1944. I was 18 and had just finished high school. I came up here with my first cousin, who was a music instructor at the University. So I came up to attend school here on the campus. I had heard about Alaska from her the year before, and I was in love with what she had told me, and it lived up to every expectation.

Jim: What did she tell you?

Mary: Oh, about the adventure and the cold and the beauty of the snow in the winter, the northern lights and the bright moonlight, and dog teams and friendly people. It was even more than what she told me.

Jim: Back in the 1940s, when you first arrived and saw the northern lights, were you fascinated by the color display of the lights?

Mary: Oh, definitely, and I still am. When I see them now, I run outside to look, every once in a while in the winter, to see them, and I still get excited. It's just such a wonderful phenomenon.

Jim: When you came to the University of Alaska, what was it like? I've heard a lot of stories about how people traveled back and forth from the University to Fairbanks during the wintertime. Did they have a train that went back and forth from town to the University at that time?

Mary: I don't believe so, not when I was going there. Just the bus, and that was operated by Paul Greimann, and he was always dependable. It was always pretty much on time. We all knew by heart the schedule of the buses into town, and the roads were not the best. The old College Road was the way we went, and at least during breakup time—all during the month of April—it was pretty hectic getting to town on the bus, because many times there had to be a bulldozer to pull the cars and the buses through the really soft permafrost areas.

Jim: I have heard stories about how the buses would get buried to the axles and they had to get the Cats out to pull them through. Changing direction here a bit, how big was the University and what was it like back in the early 40s?

Mary: Well, it was pretty small. There was one nice dormitory, three stories, Harriet Hess Hall. That was the women's dormitory. And then there were two wooden ones, the main dorm and the club dorm. And then Unit 5, which was sort of attached to the Eielson Building, was where some of the men stayed.

Jim: Was the Brooks Building there at that time?

Mary: No, none of those buildings. It was the Eielson and the old building that was the library and the gymnasium. The wooden building now called Signers Hall. That was the gymnasium and the library was up above on the second floor.

Jim: It was kind of small in comparison to what it is today, wasn't it?

Mary: Very much so. That first year that I was there, there were less than 100 students that lived on campus.

Jim: Less than 100 on campus.

Mary: I think that was the total enrollment—in fact, less than 100—and there were 13 new freshmen that year. I was one of the 13.

Jim: Is that right? Tell us, did they have kind of an introductory festivity for entering freshmen each year, and if so, what would that be?

Mary: Well we did have, and I think any of the people who went to school here in the earlier years of the University of Alaska remember the traditional bonfire. Dr. Bunnell, of course, was the first president, and still the president when I was going to school in the 40s, and every September, usually mid to late September, the freshmen would gather all burnable material that they could find—old boards and logs and old tires, anything—and build this huge bonfire right on the hillside where the old main building used to be. I think Bunnell Building is more or less in that same location now. And then we built individual bonfires around that, and that evening, a Saturday night, when we'd have the bonfire (and we'd have to protect it ahead of time, so the upper classmen and the sophomores wouldn't come and start it before the big bonfire night), and Dr. Bunnell always talked to the students in a more serious vein about education, the importance of it, and this big central bonfire signified the fire of knowledge, and then our individual bonfires, we'd go around to the main bonfire after it was lit, and have a long stick, and then we would take that fire of knowledge to our own little individual bonfires and light them. And it was quite symbolic and a wonderful tradition, but as the University grew that became sort of an impossible thing to do, to continue, as the freshman classes grew to hundreds and hundreds.

Jim: We've got a call, Mary, but a quick question before we speak to our caller. Were the upper classmen ever successful in lighting the fire before the night of the festivities?

Mary: I think there were a few years when they did that, and I don't know if it all burned down, but there were times I think when that did happen.

Caller: I'd sure like to have Mary explain a little bit of the riverboating on the waterways of Alaska here, and also maybe she could expound a little bit on the four pretty wonderful children that she's reared in this town that she should be very proud of. And with that I'll let Mary maybe expound on her family life and summarize the Riverboat Discovery business.

Jim: Thank you. Do you know this person, Mary?

Mary: Well, he sounds familiar, but I don't know who it was.

Jim: Well, he certainly knows and respects you and your family. Please answer his questions, Mary.

Mary: OK. Well on the riverboating, I don't know too much about the early early riverboating, just what I've heard and read from others. My husband started in 1939 in Wrangell, Alaskan riverboating, and then came to the Interior in 1940, worked for George Black and for Clyde Day, and then operated boats for the military during World War II. He had quite a bit of background in it by the time we were married in 1947. And then, in 1950 Chuck West, who had a travel agency locally and wanted to have something more for people to do in Fairbanks than just a city sightseeing encouraged us to buy this little surplus boat that the Episcopal Church had for sale. It was called the *Godspeed*. It was a river cruiser. And so my husband rebuilt it, expanded it during the winter of '49, spring of '50, and had it operating and authorized and inspected by the Coast Guard to carry 25 passengers. So we started with the little *Godspeed*, going from down on the lower Chena River, on down the Tanana quite a ways, visiting some fish camps and old timers along the way, and sometimes had five and six hour trips. And then we made our payments that fall and had maybe one or two hundred dollars to spare, which seemed like a great second job for us. My husband was working nights at the powerplant at that time, and we continued doing it as a summer second job and bought the boat ourselves. And then I think in late 1954 (that might have been the last year that the Alaska Steamship Company was carrying passengers) we were really outgrowing the little *Godspeed*, making a morning and an afternoon trip. So we decided to build a new boat that was more Alaskan looking, so my husband constructed *Discovery I* in our backyard in 1955. It looked considerably different, and carried 50 passengers, twice that of the little *Godspeed*, and we thought, "Boy, we're set for many years now." And before long we were cutting *Discovery I* in half and adding ten feet to it and widening it by eight feet and adding a new larger stern wheel, and it grew.

Jim: Ultimately, how many passengers could it accommodate?

Mary: One hundred and fifty on *Discovery I.*

Jim: Earlier we were discussing your education at the University of Alaska, and before we jump too far ahead, there were a couple of comments that you may still like to make regarding the University. I understand that you went to the University of Alaska for two years?

Mary: Yes.

Jim: What was your major?

Mary: Well, it was fisheries, or pre-fisheries.

Jim: What did you do following the two years of education?

Mary: Well, then I went back to Oregon and worked for my brothers at their cannery. I had three brothers, living on the coast of Oregon who were commercial fishermen. They had helped me with my expenses at school. It was very difficult for girls at that time to be able to work in the summer and earn enough money to pay for all of their school year. I worked during the time I was going to school, but it was nice of my older brothers to help financially.

Jim: I understand that you also spent some time in Ketchikan?

Mary: Oh, the summer of '45, during my freshman and sophomore years, I was on a fellowship at the fisheries laboratory at Ketchikan.

Jim: What was your participation in the fisheries laboratory?

Mary: I was a student learner. Various people—some of the chemists and the home economics majors—were working on various cannery products and fishery products, so I worked a lot with them, and I did work with a project of my own of gathering kelp and using some old Russian recipes made kelp pickles and kelp preserves. They were like watermelon rind preserves, and they did try to do that commercially a few years later, but this was just all experimental. It was a wonderful experience.

Jim: And following that period of time, did you go back to Oregon?

Mary: No, not until 1946. I'd been here two years. I just went to Ketchikan for the summer and then right back to school again.

Jim: In 1946 back to Oregon. How long did you stay in Oregon before you returned to Alaska?

Mary: Well, close to two years—a year and 3/4. I went to Oregon State that fall for the first term, and by that time my savings was all used up, and I had met Jim in the meantime and so I took a job in Portland to earn some money for my upcoming wedding.

Jim: What year was that again?

Mary: Well, let's see. I met Jim in 1946 on campus. He'd just gotten out of the service, and I was finishing my sophomore year. It was my 20th birthday and I thought he was very nice—tall and handsome and had a big smile—and the special thing that I was interested in was that he was a riverboat pilot—that was a little bit influential anyway—and my girl friend Beverly and I were going back to Oregon that summer and we had talked about trying to go on the Yukon River to Whitehorse or to Dawson and then fly from there. We thought it would just be a great adventure to be on the Yukon. And we'd heard of George Black, so when I met Jim, he mentioned that he was a pilot, and had worked with George Black and knew him, so that really caught my attention. So I was getting all the information I could about that.

Jim: Let's carry that a little bit farther. You met Jim, and before we continue on with that story tell us a little about Mr. Black.

Mary: Well, I found out that Mr. Black, George Black, never took passengers on his boats; they were strictly freight boats and they didn't have facilities. But it was worthwhile checking on it. Then Jim and I dated for about six weeks before I went back to Oregon, and then he came down to Oregon later that summer. So we weren't too far away. He attended school that fall in Portland, and I was going to school in Corvallis at Oregon State that fall.

Jim: Wait a minute, where was Jim?

Mary: He was in Alaska, but he came out for medical reasons that summer to Portland. I was in Newport and then that fall I started to school in Corvallis at Oregon State, and he stayed in Portland and went to school in Portland.

Jim: And you visited one another.

Mary: Oh yes, and wrote.

Jim: I just wondered how far apart these towns were, about 300 miles?

Mary: Well, maybe less than that, maybe 200.

Jim: So we can see what was developing here. And you got married the next year.

Mary: Yes, In 1947. We stayed in Seattle, where he was working at Boeing. Then in the spring of 1948 we came back to Alaska. When we returned Jim started working on a riverboat down in Nenana. Then during the flood of '48 we had to leave Nenana. Our oldest son, Skip, was expected that fall, so Jim got a job here in Fairbanks, so he would be here during the summertime and not on the river. We lived on campus. He was working at the University power plant that late summer of '48.

Jim: You talked about the little riverboat that you had in the beginning.

Mary: The *Godspeed*.

Jim: Also, there is a book out that was written about your family and the riverboating that you've done. Who wrote that book?

Mary: Kent Sturgis did, and it was published last summer. Called *"Four Generations on the Yukon."*

Jim: I wonder what inspired Kent to write such a book. He must have recognized your colorful life and the many contributions you've made to Alaska.

Mary: Well, we've known him for many many years. I think he went to school at the same time our oldest son Skip did and was a good friend. Then he made the trip up the Yukon in the summer of 1987, when *Discovery III* was making its maiden voyage up to Fairbanks from St. Mary's. It had been built in the Seattle area, Whidby Island, and then came on a barge up to St. Mary's. It was towed up. And then under its own power from St. Mary's to Fairbanks. So Kent was familiar with the boat, and he reported on its construction in Whidby Island and its journey up the Yukon . So he just had an idea that it would make a good story.

Jim: Talk a little more about *Discovery III*. We have *Discovery I* and we have *Discovery III*.

Mary: Well, there's *Discovery II* in the middle there.

Jim: Well, let's talk a little bit about *Discovery II* before we launch into *Discovery III*. When did it originate?

Mary: Well, it was built here in Fairbanks, about 1953, I believe, by George Black. He was the river freighter, very colorful fellow, nice fellow. This was his first sternwheeler that he built. It was all steel, and he operated it until he drowned a short time later. He fell off of one of the barges down at Minto, and they aren't sure if he had a heart attack or what, but they never did find his body. The boat carried freight, and then it was used as a ferry down at Nenana before the bridges were built going across the Tanana River. It had some hard use. We purchased it in 1968, and then we were going to make a barge from it, but Jim thought it was too good, and so he worked on it through the winter months and by 1971 had it all re-done—new superstructure, new decks and all—and made it into a passenger vessel. We started carrying passengers in July of 1971.

Jim: Since 1971 we've seen a lot of things happen in the state of Alaska. We've seen the pipeline. Near the end of the '70s we saw a mini-gold rush here in Fairbanks—a lot of people came up when gold reached the height of $850 an ounce. Did your business prosper during those years, and did you feel the increase in population?

Mary: Well we did. I think that tourism was a steady increase, just because it was a new industry and more people were becoming aware of Alaska.

So tourism, which is the industry we are in, was growing during those years. But during the pipeline there were definitely more people here. There were a lot more charters—a lot of weddings on the boat. Expense was no deterrent to some of these people. Money was easy to make and they spent it very easily. So we certainly felt the effects of the oil pipeline.

Jim: From 1980 until present have you noticed a dramatic increase in tourism?

Mary: Definitely. A big growth since 1980. We were just operating *Discovery II* and sometimes *Discovery I* as a backup, and there would be times in the '80s when we would go out with two boats in the afternoon. But very definitely big growth patterns, and we could see it coming, so we had to make plans maybe two years in advance before we ever started construction of *Discovery III*. It was too large to construct here during the winter months, and too cold, so we had to have it built in the Seattle area.

Jim: We have a caller, let's let them have the next question. Hi, you're on the air with Mary Binkley.

Caller: Hi. I want to ask Mary, when did she first meet Merty Boggin?

Mary: Well, Merty Boggin was a very dear friend of mine, and I think we built on University Avenue about 1951. The Wilcoxes lived in their house, had the property at that time, and I think the Boggins might have moved down there in the mid-'50s. It's really hard for me to remember, but that's when I first met her, was when she was a neighbor. They lived right on the river of University Avenue, and that's before the bridge was built. University Avenue was a little dirt road and it ended, and you knew all the neighbors.

Caller: Yes. That was the good times in Fairbanks.

Mary: Oh it really was. Really nice. She was a very special person.

Caller: Yes, she was. I knew her quite well too. Thank you very much.

Mary: You're welcome.

Jim: Mary, there was a tape made of *Discovery III* and how it made its way to Alaska. Tell us where we might obtain that tape. I saw it presented on television; it was the most marvelous adventure. Where can the people obtain that tape?

Mary: Well, we have it for sale on the boat and at our office. I don't think it is sold any place else, but it was produced by Princess Tours. They commissioned a young fellow that was a deckhand for us for a year, a junior cub deckhand when he was only 13, and he's grown now and that's his business—doing videos. They did a very professional job. It's the story of the boat coming up the river, really. It was brought on a barge to St. Mary's, then that barge was sunk so the boat floated free, and then under its own power, our oldest son Skip and our youngest son John brought it up.

Jim: Our time has come to an end. Mary, thank you for joining us on Alaska Gold Trails today. It's been a pleasure.

Mary: Oh, it was a fun time. Thanks, Jim.

Robert Charlie
With
Jim Madonna
September 7, 1989

Jim: This afternoon, our guest is Robert Charlie, Robert Charlie is an old time Alaskan. We will let him tell us the story. Welcome to Alaska Gold Trails, Robert.

Robert: Thank you.

Jim: Robert, tell us, when did you come to Alaska?

Robert: 1927.

Jim: In 1927. Where did you come from?

Robert: I was born in the Minto Flats area, just outside of Old Minto—New Minto now.

Jim: Give us a little bit of information about Old Minto and what it was like as you grew up here in Alaska—something about the community, something about the trading post, if you would.

Robert: OK. The community of Old Minto was founded in the early 1900s by Chief Charlie, who was the traditional chief back in those days. There's a lot of history in Wickersham's notes. Chief Charlie met with one of the chiefs who met with Wickersham over some land issues back in 1913, and before the settlement of Old Minto, people just were living in seasonal camps and just sort of migrating with their subsistence type of food they could gather.

Jim: When you say seasonal camps, Robert, but before we get into that, Chief Charlie and Robert Charlie, how are they related? There seems to be a name connection here.

Robert: There is some relationship there. He's my grandpa, on my Dad's side.

Jim: OK, now that we've got that connection established, the next question is, you talked about these camps, and the people were a bit nomadic in that they traveled from camp to camp. Was this because of the availability of food at different localities during different times of the year?

Robert: Yes. That's what we call seasonal camps.

Jim: You were following the game. Just how did that work in terms of the kind of camp. Was it a camp that, for example, one camp would be preferred for the moose population and another because of a different kind of animal population, and so forth?

Robert: Yes. Back in the year I was born, it was in the spring of the year and we were out at a muskrat hunting camp, there in May. And back then my parents traded muskrat fur for whatever their needs were, like food and hunting gear and stuff like that. That season lasts about two months, and then we go into the summer season, which would be the salmon fishing season. It's either done on the Tanana or back in the Lake Mintos for pike, whitefish and other freshwater fish. And the other season, the fall season, like right about now, is berry-picking time. We gather all sorts of berries for the winter and store them away in birchbark baskets. The birchbark baskets were made by family members, mostly mothers and/or older daughters helped put these baskets together, while the men would be busy out hunting moose. From stories I hear, moose weren't that plentiful back when I was a kid, so it was kind of hard to get a moose for the winter. And then you would go into the winter, which was the season for trapping (and some hunting, but trapping took up most of our time) and we had to spend a lot of time in the camp cutting wood and taking care of daily work chores to keep the camp up. That would continue until around February, and then the beaver season would take place, and people began trapping beaver through the ice. And that takes about another month.

Jim: Robert, let me just ask a question regarding the seasons. This all took place back in the 1920s, is that correct?

Robert: Yes.

Jim: OK. That was really a season, not a law-type governed season, but a season that you established as the main time for collecting beaver, is that correct, because of their pelts and so forth?

Robert: Yes. I remember back when we were moving around these camps, the only law enforcement would be a federal game warden, and he is a person to be expected at any time, at any place. And although he doesn't get out there very often, he does show up, and everybody always keeps an eye out for him, although there was no problem keeping within the law, because what they were doing was the type of living they always did, you know.

Jim: Strictly subsistence.

Robert: Yes.

Jim: I want to go back just a little bit, and talk about your birth place. You said you were born in a muskrat camp. You weren't born in Minto, then, you were born in one of the outcamps.

Robert: Yes. I was born outside of where New Minto is, about four miles up the Tolovana River from New Minto, in the spring of the year.

Jim: OK. Let's talk about Minto. What type of structures were around Minto? I mean what kind of housing facilities, dwellings, did you have in Minto, during those early years?

Robert: Well, from stories that's been told to me, when Chief Charlie founded the village, at first there was only two cabins. They were built out of logs and had board flooring and some type of window, and that was their house. They had sod roofs and that type of material.

Jim: It seems to me that I just heard from a friend that they used to strip the hides off some of the animals very thin and use that thin hide as windows. Did you ever have that experience?

Robert: No, ever since I can remember they had glass.

Jim: Minto, then, built up from the two log cabins. Did they continue with log structures, or did they put in frame structures, or just how did it develop?

Robert: Well, Old Minto, they started with the two log cabins and then eventually people started building cabins, and then up to the '30s, 1938, there were probably around 20 or 30 cabins in Minto. That was the year they built a school down there, the first BIA school, and it took them two years to build that school, and it's still standing up and it's still usable.

Jim: In regards to the community, then, let's see if we can't build the atmosphere and the character of the community. Did you have a trading post and a church or something of that nature?

Robert: Yes, before they built a school, there was an old two-story log house that was built by a well-known craftsman, I believe his name was Chappell, and he would awl those logs into three-sided logs and put them into place until he completed a two-story building. The two-story building was a neatly constructed building, and he also built a church, and the church is still standing there in Minto (the same craftsman). And we had a community hall which was built by the public people in the village, all hand work, and then this store that was established by Johnny Campbell, it was two miles down river from Old Minto. Now this guy was really a gentleman. He was there for a purpose; he put up what he wanted to, and he wanted to see that the people got food year round, and he just lived there with the people and he knew everybody in the village—kid's names, everybody. And he was really a character because he loved people, and he did it not only for profit, but he did make very little profit, but he did it mostly for the service in the community.

Jim: He came there to "live," in other words.

Robert: You bet.

Jim: And become a part of your community. So then we've established that you did have a full community in terms of a church and a school and a trading post nearby, within two miles of the village. Tell us the variation between the outcamps and the village of Minto. What were they like, were they cabins or were they just small shelters that were put up for a short period of time?

Robert: Some of the outcamps would be trapping cabins, but most of them would be tent-type camps.

Jim: So the outcabin would be the central point, then. Would it be a log cabin set at the site and then more tents brought in as the people came in? I guess I don't quite understand.

Robert: The trapping cabin is the cabin way out there where one would be trapping from, and that would be the central place for trapping, but from that cabin you go out far enough one day, then you would have to put up a tent, which would be your trapping tent. Let me take you back before the settlement of Old Minto, and I think it was the same system all over the Interior. That was back when the missionaries went to these camps, when they were all spread out, no central settling community; everybody was, in their own way, moving around, following the game, or doing their subsistence activities, seasonally. So, back then they were all using tents, and a lot of times, back before I was born, back in the 1800s, they were probably using fur like hides for their tents. Back before the settlement of Old Minto, it was more like the minister's job to get to these people and tell them that they needed to start changing their ways, because their children will have to go to school one day. So they would have to settle into one large community. Then everybody moved back to this community so the kids could go to school. That way it would be easier for the minister and it would be easier for a lot of things. It took them quite a while to get the idea of what this minister was talking about. Back when I was a kid, I remember when my family had to move around during the winter, that would be when school was on, they soon got the idea that this teacher was going to teach the kids how to read and write and how to spell their name, and even count numbers, and that was all great. So they began to realize that they were heading into something new, and then they began sending their kids to school. Finally, they got the idea that every year they had to come back and start their kids to school. But that didn't stop the parents from doing their subsistence food gathering. They would leave their kids with some family member and then go out and do their subsistence hunting and gathering to make sure they got enough food for the winter.

Jim: Robert, tell us a little bit about how it was, growing up in a small village, like Minto. How many people were in Minto, as you grew up? How did the population increase and what did you do for entertainment and excitement?

Robert: The population was much smaller than it is right now. We have about 300 members in Minto, today. At the time when I was a kid, there was probably 75-80, and there wasn't too many kids. I think by the time I was going to school, there must have been about 30 of us, and we all had one little classroom that we were going to.

Jim: One-room classrooms are fun. I went to school in a one-room classroom. Everybody was in the same room; you never knew if you were getting eighth grade stuff or first grade stuff.

Robert: You bet. And it was really, come to think of it, it was kind of funny for me to look back and think about school, and it was great, you know, back then, to me, it was new.

Jim: What kind of games did you play in school? The traditional games that we think of, or did you have some native kind of games that you played?

Robert: No, we just had traditional kind of games. Our teacher just thought of whatever he could come up with, you know, like football and baseball, and play games and that kind of thing.

Jim: And so, you went through all eight grades right there in that school?

Robert: No. I got out when I finished the sixth grade.

Jim: What other activities did you participate in? Did you collect wood? Did you trap in the outcamps and so forth, when you were at a young age?

Robert: Yes. Of course, even right now they practice that a lot. Many of the kids in a family have to take part in chores around the house, so during our school years, we'd have to chop wood at the school, bring some water, clean up. The girls would clean up the house and kitchen work and that kind of thing. And you mentioned radio, I remember my brother bought the first radio from Sears and Roebuck, and it was one of those big radio types with a heavy battery, and it was in the '30s, I guess. We were catching KFAR then and listening to that station all the time. I think it was educational, because a lot of us kids back then started speaking English pretty good by listening to radio.

Jim: This is, I understand, the 50th year of KFAR.

Robert: Yeah, it was in the 30s when we got our radio.

Jim: So, you did participate in the outcamps and so forth, as far as your duties were concerned. Did you have dog teams and sleds? How did you get from one point to another? Did you walk, dogsled, or was there another mode of transportation? When did the snowmachine come into effect? Can I ask you a few more questions here and confuse you all at once? Did you use dog teams?

Robert: Yes, we had dogs. The dog team was the major part of our transportation.

Jim: How many dogs to a team, generally?

Robert: Well, each family will have to justify the number of dogs according to the size of the family, because dogs run pretty expensive for subsistence food. It would require more work to get food for the dogs also. So they didn't have too many dogs. I guess the most dogs a family would have might be 14 and they would be all good working dogs.

Jim: It was a family team, then?

Robert: Yes, It was just a family team.

Jim: And anybody in the family could drive the team.

Robert: Yes, as long as it was for a good purpose.

Jim: Sure. Meaning simply, that if you were going to the outcamp, you could drive the team, or your father or brother could drive it if they were going. Do you have any brothers or sisters?

Robert: Yes, I have four brothers and two sisters.

Jim: You came from a relatively large family, then. Is that generally the size of the family at Minto, or were they smaller or larger?

Robert: Well, back then it was about the size of families.

Jim: Robert, we have a couple of minutes here. Tell us briefly what you've been doing out at Minto at this time and what you hope to achieve and accomplish through your efforts.

Robert: OK. This past spring and part of last winter we did some planning for this summer, and one of the projects that we were doing, that we got some grant money for, was to identify some sites in the Minto Flats area that were used by our ancestors, and which are used yet today. And then we got into another project where we were going to go to these sites and take videotapes of people having tea, telling stories about the site and putting all that together for future reference for our children who, in maybe ten or twenty years, might want to know about these things. Me and my wife are going to put a map together identifying all these historical places on the map and identify them, along with the names of lakes and the streams that run into the Minto Flats area. There are several projects being done in that regard, but nothing that shows up well enough to catch the eye of students and the public. So what we want to do is put a map together that'll benefit the students, the elders and the young people in Minto, where they can see this map and say, "Oh, yeah. I know this lake. Now, let me find out the name of it in Athabascan." That kind of thing. Along with that, we are trying to revise Old Minto back into active status again, by putting a cultural training camp there. We had a very good summer this summer, and it was very excellent. We got a lot of support from individuals in Fairbanks, and everybody was supporting us from Minto, and in Nenana. We hope to continue this project. Hopefully this winter we will be making more plans for next summer.

Jim: Well, Robert, thank you very much for sharing this time with us on Alaska Gold Trails, today.

Robert: Jim, I want to thank you and the audience, and I hope you all have a nice day. Thank you.

Doug Colp
with
Jim Madonna
December 18, 1987

Jim: Our guest today is Doug Colp, a well known mining engineer and placer miner. Welcome to Alaska Gold Trails, Doug, give us a little background. I understand you were born in Alaska. Is that right?

Doug: Yes sir. I was born in Southeastern Alaska. Therefore, you might say I didn't have any choice in the matter. The year was 1914, and I was raised on a fox ranch down there within five miles of Petersburg. That's where I spent my boyhood. Among the foxes and fishing fleet, logging camps and canneries. After I graduated from high school and fighting the battles of the fishing industry and the logging camps, I figured there should be an easier way of making a living. I decided that maybe I wasn't as smart as I thought I was, so I decided to come on up to the University of Alaska. That was in 1935. I came up to Fairbanks and attended classes for four years. I guess I've completed my four years, but I'm still hanging in there.

Jim: You're still studying, is that right?

Doug: I'm still studying, learning every day.

Jim: And you got your degree in what discipline?

Doug: I got my degree in Mining Engineering.

Jim: What year was that, Doug?

Doug: 1940.

Jim: What was Fairbanks like in those days?

Doug: Fairbanks was larger than Anchorage at that time. We had about 2,000 people here, and 12th Avenue was the end of town. It was all the way from a half hour to an hour and a half to make the five mile trip to the University by bus, because during the snow storms, especially by the old Creamers Field, located about two and a half miles out on the College Road, many times we had to get off the bus and shovel our way through or wait for one of those snow blowers to come along to open up the road so we could get through. The bus and the railroad that ran a car back and forth were the only two routes we had to commute between town and the University.

Jim: How big was the University at that time, Doug, do you recall?

Doug: It was around 300 students at that time. I graduated in 1940 from a class of 17.

Jim: 17 people. Well, that's quite a difference from what today's graduating class would be isn't it? Was that 17 people from the School of Mines or was that from all the disciplines at the University.

Doug: That was all the disciplines at the school.

Jim: At that time, was the school still divided into the Agricultural College and the School of Mines?

Doug: No. 1935 is when they changed from the Agricultural School and School of Mines to the University of Alaska.

Jim: What did you do for employment during the time that you were attending the University of Alaska?

Doug: Well, Jim, the old F.E. Company, which is a subsidiary to the U.S. Smelting, Refining and Mining Company, the big company here at that time, was especially good to us university kids. They went out of their way to hire as many as possible. So in the spring of 1936, I applied for work with them, and after about a two-week wait going through their long lines of people wanting work at that time, I finally got up to the window and the employment man at that time says, "You're on. Have your sleeping bag here next Monday morning. You're on for a week. We're going to put you on the point field driving cold water points 65 feet to bedrock. Some referred to it as a point field and some referred to it as a thaw field. So that's how I got my start. I spent all that summer of '36 driving points to bedrock in the thawing process of placer gravels.

Jim: Tell us, Doug, how many thaw points did you drive? Were you responsible for a number of thaw points or just how did that work?

Doug: Yes. The lines were different for each unit, but my particular unit for most of the summer was about 65 points, and I was driving about 65 feet. When those points reached bedrock, they were allowed to sit there for ten days or two weeks, and after that period of time the ground had thawed out from bottom to top, and with the cold water running through these points there's about a ten-pound pressure, which resulted in the whole field being thawed. Once it was thawed, the points were pulled and another unit set up to one side.

Jim: A lot of times in classes I've been asked why they use cold water over steam to thaw the gravels. Doug, do you have any answers for that kind of question?

Doug: Yes. The cold water under low pressure, thaws the same area on the bottom as it does on top, as opposed to steam. Steam thaws a kind of pyramid shaped thaw—nothing on the bottom and wide on top—which is not good for thawing a whole field where you have to have the same thawed area at the bottom as at the top.

Jim: So the frozen wedges down there at the bottom, extending to bedrock would probably damage the dredges as they floated into position and began processing the gravels. Is that correct?

Doug: That's correct. Those pyramids are impossible to dig, and of course if you can't dig bedrock you cannot recover the gold. Dredges were not made to dig frozen ground.

Jim: Doug, did you ever work directly on the dredges?

Doug: Yes, I had a lot of experience on dredges. The second year with the F.E. Company I was on the thaw crew and the stripping crew and working on the clean up crew on the dredges. Then in '38, '39 and '40 I was at Manley Hot Springs on a dredge where I worked in all capacities, including the thaw crew, strip crew and on the dredge crew. That of course started my dredging career. In 1940 I helped build a dredge up on Caribou Creek, which is a tributary of the Salcha River, east of Fairbanks here. Then the war came along, and of course they shut the gold mining industry down until 1946. So during that time I worked for the Army engineers, either in or out of uniform, all over Alaska. Then in '46 I went up to the Kobuk River and the Koyukuk and worked in the placer mines up there and on the dredges—on the dredges on Cleary Creek and the tributary of the Squirrel River, on the Kobuk, and I worked three years at Livengood, '51, '52, and '53. I've spent my time on these dredges. I think Dredge 8 was probably the first dredge I was ever on—that was in 1936. Regarding fine gold recovery, dredges are noted for their efficiency. They are about 85% efficient. The bucket line brings the pay gravels on up to a rotating trommel screen with a series of holes in the screen tapering from small holes, say 3/8 inch to begin with, down to 3/4 inch near the end of the sluice. Then the last two feet is a screen that has larger slots to allow the larger gold pieces to come into what is called a nugget sluice. But the upper part of the screen is small to large, and the screen is used as a washing mechanism as well as a classification method. So everything that passes through the trommel falls onto a stacker belt that delivers it to the tailing pile behind the dredge. Everything that falls through the holes in the screen goes through a distributor into lateral sluices or tables, as they are referred to on the dredge, and the fine gold in the upper part is caught in the riffles of the primary tables, which extend perpendicular from the rotating elongate, trommel which extends from the head to the tail of the dredge body. These flow into longitudinal sluices that also have riffles in them and the oversize or the waste from those sluices dropped into the pond behind the dredge. So they're really an efficient unit.

Jim: I'll say you've spent your time on these dredges. You have worked in gold mining as much or more than anybody in the State of Alaska, Doug. In addition to your gold mining activity on the dredges, did you ever enter into gold mining on your own, as strictly a private adventure?

Doug: Yes, I did that. I mined three years by myself. I took a lease on a dredge up on the Kobuk River for three years during the early '60s and operated the dredge during the summer months.

Jim: In addition to the dredges I understand that you entered into placer mining by open cut mining methods. Can you give us some information about how the open cut mining developed here in the State? What is open-cut mining? Does it include using Cats and loaders and equipment like that?

Doug: Yes. Any mining that's done from the surface is classified as open-cut—even dredging actually is an open-cut method, but we refer to that strictly as dredging. But open-cut you can use Cats and draglines and so forth for all open-cut methods. Backhoes are used too. Front end loaders and so forth. But normally it's a Cat operation that you're usually speaking about when you say "open-cut."

Jim: Have you been involved in open-cut mining over these past two or three decades then, Doug?

Doug: I've been involved with open-cut mining and all phases and types of placer evaluation, drilling and prospecting prior to developing the appropriate mining methods.

Jim: Doug, where have you mined in Alaska, using the open-cut mining method?

Doug: Well, it's hard to remember all the spots, being here so many years, but probably the most important to me was the Chistochina. In 1973, I did the evaluation down there, and it was determined to be economic. So we set up a mining plant there in 1979, and it operated for about five years at a profit. Before that I was up in the Koyukuk operating open-cut placer mines up there in the Wiseman area and on Gold Bench and the south fork of the Koyukuk. Then over in the Seward Peninsula. More recently, since the 80s, I've been mining out at 104-mile on the Steese Highway in what's called Eagle Creek area. We are looking at a piece of property in the Toftee area now and it will eventually be a good sized open-cut mine. Also, we're evaluating another piece of ground up in the Candle area, in the Kualik Flats.

Jim: Doug, tell us a little about your mining operations up in the Central area. You were still mining in Central this past summer weren't you?

Doug: Yes, we made a short season of it this year with the possibility of being shut down the summer of 1988. We made a decision to move our big outfit from the Eagle Creek area to the Candle area, which is a 600 mile move, so we cut our mining season at Eagle this year to about 96 days. And then we freighted everything—washing plant and all the conveyors, the dozer, camp and all the Cats and the pumps and the pipe and buildings and so forth. Freighted them into the Fox turnoff to the Livengood road, then out the Livengood road and out the Dalton Highway to the Yukon River bridge, and there we put everything on a big barge 180 feet long by 60 feet wide. We got our whole camp mining outfit on the barge and headed down the Yukon River with the barge and tug, and 16 days later and $135,000 difference, we arrived eight miles from our destination on the Kualik spit, near Candle, and there we offloaded all our equipment. Next April, when the ground is frozen to the maximum depths—hopefully four or five feet—we'll freight our equipment the last eight miles into the mining site.

Jim: Doug, our time has come to an end. Thank you for joining us on Alaska Gold Trails and good luck at Candle next year.

Doug: Thank you for inviting me, Jim.

Tony Gularte
with
Roger McPherson
December 24, 1987

Jim: *The following interview was done between Roger McPherson, a local frontier history buff, and Tony Gularte, a well-known Alaskan pioneer. It deals with the Iditarod Stampede. That's the gold rush that was initiated on Christmas Day in 1908. Roger taped the interview years before it was presented on Alaska Gold Trails.*

Roger: Tell us the story about the Iditarod gold rush, Tony.

Tony: When Johnny Beatin and Diteman left Fairbanks to go to the Ophir Stampede, you know where Ophir is on the head of the Anoka. Well, that night, on the Anoka River, now I got this story from Johnny Beatin himself. This is not second hand. I knew Johnny Beatin very very well. He was a very nice little man. He was a Scotchman. And when he and Diteman were camped across from the Iditarod, which they didn't know that the Iditarod came in there, there was a trapper came out of the Iditarod and he saw their campfire. Well he was in the Iditarod country for three years, but he got sick, so he had to come out, and he had a whole load of fur in the boat that he built. Well he saw their campfire when he came out of the Iditarod. So he goes over there and here's Johnny Beatin and Diteman. They were camped for the night you know. And they had a little boat with a little boiler in it and it had a little steam, and had two sidewheelers, see? So when they were going upstream they could cut wood and use steam to use the little sidewheelers to help them go up the river.

So he got over there talking to these guys, and he told them, he says "You know, I've been three years up in this country and I've been panning the bars," and he says "you know, they pan good on this river," way way up. He told them how many miles he figured it was. So, now he says, "If you guys go up there, why," he says, "you stake me in if you go up there." Well they changed their minds that night and they goes up the Iditarod, and they got up to where he told them where the swift water was and they start panning the bars, well then they begin to get a few colors, and he had told them, "Now," he says, "you know, when you get above this creek, I call it Otter Creek, because I caught so many otter on it, why," he says, "it don't pan above that." But, "he says, "Otter pans good." And that's how it got its name "Otter" from this old man, and they just called it Otter from then on see.

Well, when they went up there and they got above Otter Creek and they ran out of the panning, so they dropped down see? But they couldn't get up Otter with their boat because Otter Creek was too small for their size of boat. And they had a two-year supply in that boat, see. Them days you had to take plenty of supplies with you. And then there was a lot of boys in Fairbanks that would stake. They'd give them a hundred dollars, you know, and to give them a power of attorney to stake for them if they hit anything see? So they goes up the Iditarod and as I say they got above Otter Creek, so Johnny Beatin walked up Otter Creek and he got up above this mountain here (Roger and Tony are looking at a map). This mountain faces Otter Creek, and when he got above this, he climbed this mountain and got up on top of it, to see where the Iditarod came the closest, see? And he found out it came the closest in this big bend. And that would—instead of walking up through the flats, which would be hard walking all the time, you know, the swamps and all that. So they went back and they drifted down until they came to this big bend. Then they parked their boat. Then they could take the ridges to Flat (Otter?) and that would be easier walking, see, because it was up high and dry. They got up above Granite Creek and the pay on Otter, where the trapper said it would run out, so they kept dropping down, and they got down below Granite Creek, there they began to get a little pay.

So, on Christmas Day, they struck the pay, in 1908, on Otter Creek. So Johnny Beatin and Diteman, they were partners in the boat, they were partners in the grub, they were partners sinking holes, but when they come to staking, they staked individually. In them days, you could stake eight claim associations, see? So Johnny Beatin, if he took the left limit, Diteman would take the right limit. Then they would crisscross. And they done that all the way down below the mouth of Flat, which I would say, maybe four to four-and-a-half miles that they staked, 'cause they had so many power of attorneys too, you know.

Well, then they had to hike to Ophir, you know. And so they went up Otter Creek and took the ridges all over until they came out to Ophir. And they recorded. Then on their way back, there was three or four boys that wanted to come with them, or maybe more, I don't know. Anyway when they got back to Otter Creek it was staked. So these guys, one would take Slate Creek, one took Black Creek, one took Granite Creek, one took Glen Gulch, and before Johnny went to Ophir to record, he walked up Flat Creek, and right at the head of Flat Creek, and you go right up on the top of the summit, there's three great big granite pillars, all granite boulders, sitting right on top of each other. They're still there. And he looked up there and he decided that there was not any money on Flat Creek.

See, Nome don't carry granite, Fairbanks don't carry granite, the Klondike didn't carry any granite. Iditarod was the first outcrop of granite that these old timers run across that carried gold, see? So he walked away. He come down, went back to camp, then they started over to record at Ophir. And as I say, these boys came over with them, which they asked them if they could come with them, and they said "Yeah, sure, there's plenty of country over there, and it needs prospecting." So this one guy was left, see? And Johnny told him there's no sense going down to that creek 'cause it had a big granite outburst, or blowout, I should say.

Well, he says "Johnny, I don't want to infringe on these other guys," he says, "I'm going down there and I'm going to sink a hole on that creek." So he went down there and you know you always go up to the head of the creek to sink, because you figure it'd be shallower ground than at the mouth. So he went up, right to the butt of the hill, going up in the upgrade, and he set his tent up, and he started sinking a hole, which was then maybe oh 12, 14, or 16 feet deep. So he sank this hole. He got a two-and-a-half dollar pan. So he comes down Flat Creek, and he goes up Otter Creek, and he says to Johnny Beatin, he says, "Johnny, I thought you told me there was no money on that creek." Johnny says yes. Well he says "Here, look. It's a two and a half dollar pan." Well at that time a two and a half dollar pan would be about $17 a foot, see? Well, that's awful good money. If it was only $16 an ounce. Johnny said, "You know, I slapped my head, you know," he says, "and I walked away from it."

Roger: Tony, that was a great piece of Alaskan history. Thank you so much for the interview.

Jim: *We want to thank Roger for recognizing the valuable contribution Tony has made to Alaskan history and the colorful sequence of events which led to the discovery of gold in the creeks of the Iditarod on Christmas day, 1908.*

Cliff Haydon
with
Jim Madonna
(first show)
January 5, 1989

Jim: Hello, ladies and gentlemen, today our guest is Cliff Haydon. Cliff, welcome to Alaska Gold Trails.

Cliff: Thank you.

Jim: Cliff, tell us a little bit about, well, we better ask the first question, right? How old are you, Cliff? You're pretty young.

Cliff: Well, now, when did I get into mining? Or when did I get to Alaska?

Jim: No, when did you get into the world?

Cliff: Oh. Well, now that's a little embarrassing, but that was June 19, 1910, in Spokane, Washington. I wasn't too large when I was born—four pounds. And to be born four pounds when all of the other members of both sides of my family were six feet plus—my father was six four and 240 pounds. He looked like me, only I'm just a little tiny guy. So, my mother was rather, well, she didn't care to display me too much to the friends when they came up to see me, but her aunt did not have any children, so she was tickled, because she figured that I would be her boy and there'd be no arguments whatsoever. Well, the aunt was known for being very very strict, and when my uncles went to visit her, why they didn't want to stay. Oh, Aunt Ellen was a little bit rough. But with me, well, from the moment I could remember, it was Aunt Ellen. And she kept me and took care of me. She had a hotel downtown there in Spokane, and I think she had one maid hired to do nothing else but look after me or run me down. And then we had a great many miners staying in the hotel, and previous to that time, she had made herself a nice little bit of money. When the miners would come there some of them had run out of funds, so they'd say, "Ellen, can you let us have a little money to grubstake?" And she said, "Yes. Certainly." She'd do that. And she was never mistaken as far as their character. When she began staking these miners, was at the time the Coeur d'Alene mines were starting to be discovered, and many of those miners hit it rich, but they wrote her down as a partner. And so then afterwards they'd always come to her hotel and they'd well take me out for a walk, or in the perambulator, and so sometimes I'd get into a little trouble over it, because, well...

Jim: You were mischievous, is that what you're trying to say? A little bit mischievous, when you were a young lad?

Cliff: Just a little bit. I grew out of that rather rapidly. But one time they had me down for a little ride in the perambulator and there was a fellow who had what they called Jimmy Dirkin's Saloon, to be honest with you, and these miners they wandered in there, and of course, they had me along, and Jimmy Dirkin, he was just a little tiny guy but he had known my aunt's hotel and my aunt, you know, through business dealings and whatnot—so he'd grab me and sit me up on the bar, and say, "Just a small one here for the lad's kidney." And this one time, I think they put me up on the bar once too often and when I got home, why the maid wasn't watching me too close and my aunt always had this big silver bowl of walnuts on the table in the parlor, and I peeked out the window and I could see somebody coming along close to the window there, so I said, "Oh boy." I went and I got this tray, and instead of dropping one nut, I dumped the whole thing on that fella. Well, it was just about ten seconds 'til I could hear somebody a'comin' up the stairs, boom boom, and screaming for Ellen, and here she come on the run, and she says, "Officer, what is the problem?" "I caught that little angel of a laddie of yours this time myself. He dumped a whole bowl of walnuts down on my head. Now he has to go to your sister Martha's down on the farm, about 30 miles from Spokane, and stay there 'til he gets civilized. And that parrot of his, that Barnacle Bill, his vocabulary is nothing but embarrassing swear words, and he's got to go in the river." So I went to the farm.

Jim: Did the parrot go to the river?

Cliff: I never seen the parrot again. So, Aunt Ellen, about a year later, she came down to the farm—in those days you had to hop on the train and come down, and she came down to the farm, and she took me in the back room and had a little chat. "Now," she says, "Buster, you've gottin' to be a big lot." And I was five years old, "So now, you know the difference between right and wrong, and I'm not going to have the maid watch you all the time. So, remember, I'll give you one more chance." And I knew that's what she meant. "And I'll take you back up to the hotel, but if you make any more mistakes, back to the farm you come forever." So, I tell you, I was very careful, and of course I think the word got out that I wasn't to go down to Jimmy Durkin's to have anything else for my kidneys, but the miners then they had a lot of fun as they come in there and they started teaching me about mining. Just a little tiny kid. How they took the ore out, you know, and drilled the holes, and how they sunk little shafts, and they even taught me to pan a little bit. And then as I grew older, why they kept coming to my Aunt Ellen's and kept filling me in. My Aunt Ellen, though, insisted that if a boy came and started to hit me, I wasn't to run. She just set me right back there. "Put your chest over and let him hit you on the chest a little bit. But don't you run." Well, she gradually had some of the fellows teach me how to box, and so I didn't like it 'cause they'd hit me pretty hard sometimes. "No, you go right back in there. Now you know what you're going to do. Don't worry about what you're going to do. Just watch that other fellow." And so this went on until I was a young man. I had to go, among other things, and keep up with my boxing, which I'd'a gladly given up at any time.

Jim: Cliff, tell us, after you got to be a young man, did you go away to school?

Cliff: Well, she insisted. She thought it was better that I didn't go too much to school within the city of Spokane, that I should go down to the country schools around Sprague, Washington, where my grandmother was. As I got to be about 16 or so, well, she thought it would be nice if I went down to Walla Walla, Washington to the high school there. They had more to offer. They even had geology in high school there. That I loved. But anyway, so finally I graduated from high school and then I went over around Montana School of Mines. I met Dr. Thompson, who was the head of the mines there, and they were very very nice to me. I had just nicely got started to going to school there and I took sick with the influenza. And so Dr. Thompson said, "Well, you have this semester in kind of a bad way. I think you better take that over." Some of the other fellows in Butte, that were going to school there, said they had met a man from the Mohave Desert, and he was trying to promote (that's got to be in the fall of 1930) a hard rock prospect he had down there, and invested a lot in it, so he could sell it. And it was about oh, 10, 12 mile on Cockin's Hill from the little town of Mohave. So I talked with him and I went with him down there and spent the winter, and I learned practically everything, as far as hardrock mining. We didn't have a shell or anything like that to hold a jackhammer. We had two jackhammers, an air compressor and everything like that, but you'd have to hold it in your arms, and I was taught how to put in the rounds and blast. We had two old time shifters from Butte and the mines around in California, and at 60 years old they considered they were getting too old for these large mines, and we were fortunate to get them to come to work with us. So they were a very big help for me. And one thing they liked about me, they thought, well, I'd run the hoist or something like that. "Oh, no," I said, "I'm not going to do that." And so I'd get right down in and muck, or whatever, or drill. And fortunately, around oh before the first of April, a man came along one Sunday—we never worked on Sundays, even though we were working for ourselves there—and he was interested in the mine. He was a radio announcer in Los Angeles, and he had a charming wife with him. And I was the only one at the mine. Oh, I sharpened the picks and worked on the compressor and things like that a little bit on Sundays, so he said, "Is there any gold here?" And I took him to where I knew there was a real rich little string, not much bigger than an average pencil, of ore coming down, and I knew if I dug that out, I figured he'd be smart enough to know I might salt him, so I said, "Here, you do this. Dig that out, put it in a pan." We took it outside, we had a little piece of railroad iron and a hammer, and beat it up, and he put the sample in his pan, and we had a little tub of water there. And holy smokes, I don't think we ever got a better showing of gold than that time. And he was real excited. He done that a time or two, and he says, "You know, my father-in-law is in real estate and promoting, over at Bakersfield." And he said, "Would you mind if during the week sometime that we come over and visit you?" And the boss man, my partner, that had the mine, why he was there, and right away quick, before they left, they worked up a deal to buy the place because, "Oh," he said, "you bring people out here and they see gold like that..." And that was after the price of gold came up you know, to $35 per ounce. Anyway, so I had then a little stake of my own, from that time on, without digging into family reserves or anything. So that made a big difference, and then I came to Southeast Alaska. But in the winter I'd go back out for a while and then I went back to Butte again, and Dr. Thompson said, "Listen, Haydon, now there's no use of you even trying to go to school. You've had a lot of experience and what not, and you won't stay away from Alaska." And I hadn't even got to Fairbanks yet. And so he said, "There's a man by the name of Jimmy Evans, who graduated from Montana Mines a little over 20 years ago and he worked for Colonel Perry down in the African gold mines, and he's here and he's been sent back to prospect for placer in Montana. And he's looking for a helper." Well, Jimmy Evans was one of the swellest little Scotchmen you ever ran onto, and he took me along as a helper, and we went to towns and then even over around Jackson, and then we went up north in northwestern Montana. I normally would go and help Jimmy, going from mine to mine where he had three different outfits of prospecting. I'd get down in the holes there and, of course, I learned how to crib up the holes in wet ground and what not, but he was very patient and he had wonderful books and stuff as far as gold mining. That's what he was trying to teach me for, placer work. And now we can get back to getting to Alaska.

Jim: Well, we've got the background down, Cliff. Tell us about your adventures as you came to Alaska.

Cliff: Well, I was working in Spokane and staying with my Aunt Ellen, and finally I got, well, uneasy, and I wanted to come to Alaska. I had been interested from the time I was in the fourth grade and seen these pictures of Alaska—Fairbanks area. Here in the summertime there's strawberries and raising grain and all this, and then in the wintertime the buildings were practically all buried with snow. Now this was hard for me to quite understand, the conditions, you know. I just figured that Alaska was just nothing but ice and snow. So I gave my boss, where I was working, a month's notice and he about fainted. He said, "You've worked up a bit with this organization and you're luckier than most; you have a car and all this and that. Why quit?" "Well," I said, "It's one of those things I wish to do." And so he thanked me. And anyway, well, I decided that sometime in March I would head for Alaska. I was so anxious to get to Alaska. I'm not kidding you. I spent some of my hard earned money on an airplane ticket, on old Northwest, to get to Seattle. I wasn't running from anyone now, I want you to get that straight. And so this was a tri-motored Ford, and talk about a noise. We even had a stewardess on the plane, and there's maybe 15-20 people, and her job was to run around first and give you lots of cotton to put in your ears, and chewing gum. And they also gave us ice cream containers, empty ones, and she says, "Now don't be embarrassed if you have to use the thing." Well, we had a pretty rough trip getting over to Seattle, but we made it to Seattle, and I went down right quick and I got a ...

Jim: Question here, Cliff. What about the ice cream container?

Cliff: Fortunately... I felt like it a time or two but I didn't. One or two of the men did. There was nothing but businessmen or salesmen or something like that on the plane with me. We got into Seattle at night and the next morning, bright and early, I was down at Alaska Steam, and I got a ticket to Seward. So, oh about the last week in March I got on the old *Victoria*. Now, that was an ancient ship, belonged to Alaska Steam. Not too large but it was a sturdy boat. And so away we headed for Alaska. Well, everything was going along fine, as far as going to Seward, but on the boat I met a family who were going to Petersburg, and they said, "Look, man, you don't want to go into Fairbanks at this time of year. It's too early. Stop off at Ketchikan 'til the next boat comes along, but when you get to Petersburg, stop off for a week." Well, I stopped off at Ketchikan for three days or so, 'til the next boat came along, then when I got to Petersburg I went to the hotel and got a room for a week. And being used to getting up in the morning, I got up early the next morning and I went down on the dock and I seen a fellow sitting there with a steaming small paper bag, and he's taking something out of it and shelling it like peanuts, and I said, "Man, what do you have there?" "Oh," he said, "that's some of Earl Ohler's shrimp here at Glacier Seafoods, and you can get a bag like this for 25 cents. You got 25 cents?" "Yes." And I went over and I got a bag and I was sitting there eating them and here came a tall man with a kind of an engineering outfit on and a big, you know, say a forest ranger type hat, boots, and he came over and sat down and started to talk to me, real fast like, and so he says, "You're new in town." And I said, "Well, that's quite apparent." And he said, "Have you ever been out on salt water?" I said, "Nope. Only on the *Victoria*, and then the other boat I got on coming up here." "Well," he said, "You say you have a week's time." "Yes." "And you have friends here." "Yes." "Well," he said, "contact them and tell 'em you'll be back in a couple of days." I said, "Whataya mean?" "Well," he said, "You see those two shrimp boats sitting down there? Well, one of 'em is going over to Thomas Bay to pick up a raft of logs." And he said, "Right now, we're just loaded up with shrimp here, so you can take a ride with them and go over to Thomas Bay after the logs." "Well," I said, "it'd be a lot of fun, all right, but I don't know anything. What can I do to pay for this?" "You don't have to do anything. You just kind of give 'em a hand, as a deckhand or something." So he takes me over to the boat, and we get on the thing, and so this man introduced me to two fellows and he said, "Now this one skipper, the skipper of the *Louise*, the one that's going over there, is Harry Colp. He's been with me for a long time."

Jim: Was that Doug Colp's father?

Cliff: That's Doug Colp's father, yes. So him and the other captain, from the other boat, why, "Yeah, come on man, we'd like to have you go along. You have a bedroll?" "Oh," I said, "Yeah, up at the Steadman Hotel." And so, "Oh, come on. Come on. We got to leave pretty quick. You know the tides are getting about right." I says, "Will I need anything else? A few groceries?" "No, no, no. You don't need anything like that." So I went on over and I told them at the Steadman I was taking off, going with Colp and so forth after these logs, and I dashed back and jumped on and away we went. Along with us, the funny thing was, is a young college man in his early twenties. He come arunnin' with a pack on his back and hopped on the boat. Oh, they said, this is so-and-so's son, the man that runs the logging outfit over in Thomas Bay, and so we headed out. We had a nice trip going over there, real nice, and, of course, we got in there when it was dark, and so Harry Colp said, "So-and-so (that was the young man, the son of the logger) let me get a skiff overboard and Jackie and I'll get it over and take you around to the house there." "No. No." this fellow said. "You telling me? I was born in this country and around these logs. I don't need any boat to get over there." And he had his cork boots on by then, and he put his pack on his back and he jumped in. Holy smokes, I couldn't believe it. I kinda thought maybe that looked like a monstrous big piece of bark off of a log. And he went straight through it. Splash. And Colp and Jackie, they didn't get excited. They got some pike poles, and first Colp hooked on to this young fellow and Jackie reached in and got his pack, and of course the young man he was highly embarrassed, but that is just one of those things—typical mistake a fellow could make like that. So, anyway, we were around there for a little while. And when the tide was right we pulled out and we went back. And it took us all day to get back over to Petersburg. But it was a fun trip, but oh they had an awful lot of fun with me because I had never been around salt water before. So then, when they got back to town, they all wanted me to hang around. They said, "There's opportunities in Petersburg for you." Here I wasn't even a Norwegian, but there's opportunity. So then I went up to the office of this man that had wanted me to stop in and spend a week in Petersburg, and he happened to be the superintendent there of Pacific American Fisheries. His name was George Ringstad, and he had two beautiful daughters and a nice wife. Anyway, he said, "There's a lot of opportunities here for you." "Well," I said, "I don't know anything about this. The extent of my experience is with Colp on the *Louise*." He said, "That's all right. I'll give you a job." "Oh, no, no," I said. "I want to get on to Fairbanks." He said, "Listen. You're here, and have an opportunity to go to work." And he said, "I know what's the matter. Just because you know the girls, you don't want to work for me." And before I could say anything else, he was a ringin' on the phone and he got a fellow by the name of Oscar Nicholson that had a little cannery down at Scow Bay in Wrangell Narrows, a few miles from Petersburg. And he said, "Oscar, I have a real nice young man." Oh, he was spreadin' it on. "What can he do?" "Oh, he can do anything." Well, he said, "Oh, yeah, sure. He can cook. He's a good cook." And here, he didn't know a thing about me. He turned around to me and he says, "Hey man, can you cook anything?" "Oh, yes. I can cook a little bit." "Well," he said, "don't worry. The captain has ulcers, the engineer has ulcers, and the heck with the other guys." And so they had this little boat they called their flagship, the *Ira II*. Just like that I became a cook on that. And one of the things I could cook up and the other fellows seemed to like was donuts and coffee. And so, anyway, I spent the first summer in Petersburg doing that. I had no intention of staying in Petersburg at all.

Jim: You were a cook on the fishing boat, then.

Cliff: Yes, I was the cook on the fishing boat.

Jim: All summer.

Cliff: All summer, yes. That was my job. Then at the end of the season, Oscar said, "Hey, would you please come back next year." He said, "I know you don't really care to cook and you can do other things, but I'll have another job." He said, "I kinda wanta get you off as a cook because you turned the *Ira II* into a donut and coffee shop."

Jim: Cliff, we have a call. Hi, welcome to Alaska Gold Trails. You're on the air with Cliff Haydon.

Caller: Well, I was just wondering if you could have Mr. Haydon come back another time, 'cause it sounds like he's gonna run out of time and I'm interested in what he has to say.

Jim: You know, I was thinking exactly the same thing that you're thinking. We better invite him back on the show so he can give us the rest of the story, don't you think?

Caller: Yeah.

Jim: Well thank you for the call. Did you have anything else?

Caller: No.

Jim: Did you hear that, Cliff?

Cliff: No.

Jim: You didn't hear that the listening audience would like to have you come back on the show?

Cliff: You mean somebody wants me to return?

Jim: Well, we've only hit on a little bit of the story, but I would like to very quickly, in one or two minutes here, find out, did you ever make it to Fairbanks?

Cliff: Ah, I tell you. 1938, when I came back through Petersburg, with a ticket, that time I wouldn't even poke my head out the porthole, because I knew if I had, those Petersburg people treated me so very very nice that I'd be stuck there forever. And I didn't know it at the time, but those young Norwegians, anything they didn't want to do, they taught me how to do it.

Jim: Now Cliff, after your experiences as a cook, did you go back south? Did you go back to Seattle?

Cliff: Each winter for a while. Each winter I went back down south. The first time I went back because my mother at that time wasn't too well, and so I went back. But by the way, my mother is still healthy, happy and 95 years old.

Jim: Oh my goodness. That's remarkable. Tell us. 1938? Is that the year...

Cliff: 1938, in about the middle of May, 10th of May maybe, we hit Valdez. And then we came on in. It was kind of an interesting start. There was a group of us fellows together, and it's kind of interesting in a way, the things that happened to us, from Valdez on in.

Jim: You came by the Alaska Steamship Company?

Cliff: Yes. Unfortunately, I got on the *Yukon*, coming across the Gulf.

Jim: That was the shaky boat?

Cliff: No, no, that was the Alaska Steam *Yukon*.

Jim: I see. Well, look, we haven't gotten to Fairbanks, yet, Cliff, and we're going to have to hear more about that in the future. So, we're going to set a date to have you back on the show to tell us about your experiences in Fairbanks, Alaska. And I want to tell you right now that we appreciate you appearing here on Alaska Gold Trails, and we hope to be seeing you here soon, very soon, in the near future. Cliff, thank you.

Cliff: You're welcome. Thank you, Jim.

Alaska Gold Trails, February 2, 1989, Cliff Haydon with Jim Madonna (second show)

Jim: Today, ladies and gentlemen, our guest is, once again, Cliff Haydon. Of course, as many of you know, he was on with us a couple of weeks ago, and as far as we got with Cliff was up to Petersburg. We spoke about his life and the fact that he had spent a lot of time in and around Washington and then ultimately arrived in Petersburg while on his way to Interior Alaska. For some reason he got stopped in Petersburg and spent three seasons there working on a boat. Cliff, tell us, what kind of work did you do on the boat?

Cliff: Well, I had no intentions of staying any length of time down in Southeast Alaska, and originally I'd had a ticket, when I left Seattle, for Seward. But some charming young ladies from Seattle wished me to stop off in Petersburg and visit their folks, so I did. And so I visited this young lady's father in his office. His name was George Ringstad and he was Superintendent of Pacific American Fisheries for the fishing industry along the coast of Alaska. So, he said, You don't want to go on into the Interior. Why there's plenty of work here. I'll give you a job." I said, "Oh no. I wish to go to the Interior of Alaska." And he said, "Just a minute. I know, just because you know my daughter you don't wish to go to work for me." So he grabbed the telephone and he rung up a little place down along the narrows, the Scow Bay, and he had Oscar Nicholson, the man who owned the Scow Bay Packing Company, on the line. He says, "I have a young man here that needs a job. He can do anything." Well, Oscar apparently said, "The only thing I have open is I need a cook for the *Ira II*." So, after working around Petersburg for a week or two, why I went down and got on the *Ira II*, and I spent that summer working on the little *Ira II*, as a cook. And I got a lot of help, but I became famous because I could make fair doughnuts. Well, one of my regular customers there was some young mining engineer. He went up to the University, and his name was Douglas Colp, and he was a regular customer there. And I guess doughnuts weren't too bad because Douglas is still fairly healthy. But after spending one year on the *Ira II* as a cook, why, the owner of the cannery said, "Haydon, I want you to come back next year, but so help me, you're not going to be the cook on the Ira II, because you just turned it into a doughnut factory. I went back the next year, and the funny thing was, everybody told me before I even got off the boat, "You don't look like a Scandinavian to me." And I said, "That's one thing I'm not." "Well, you'd just as well not stop off there, because 98% of the people are Norwegians from the old country and they're kinda clannish," and this and that, and so I just didn't pay any attention to this talk. I'd heard talk like that before, but I never met a group of people that were so much fun and I was so happy with them. They were very cautious. Even though they were all from the old country, they'd never speak Norwegian in front of me; if one would make a mistake, the others would say, "How would you feel if you were in Haydon's position and everybody spoke a different language?" But, of course, they overlooked it with the oldtimers, and so I kept atellin' 'em, "Well, next year, I'm going to Fairbanks, because I've been wanting to go to Fairbanks ever since I was in the fourth grade. In my geography book there was a picture of them threshing hay or grain with an ancient threshing machine—that was in the summer—and then in the winter there was 10 foot of snow on the buildings, and I thought, "That's where I want to go." I got ready to head to Fairbanks in '37, but I got a call from some of my friends—I was living in Spokane that winter—and they said, "Oscar says he has a first class ticket for you to go, at a certain date, back to Petersburg. Now, come on and go back." So, back to Petersburg for the third year I went. It seemed like, as years went by, these young Scandinavians would teach me to do anything around on a boat. Anything they didn't like to do, they tried extra hard to make certain I could do it, whether it was working in the top loft or the piledriver, or anything like that, they would make certain I was good at it. "Oh, Cliff, he is real good at it." So, I did work on the top loft and the piledriver, and so Oscar Nicholson, the owner of the cannery, he'd get out on shore, he'd say, "How does it look?" He'd yell at me, "Should we go a little one way or the other?" and "Don't you think it ought to go a little port or starboard?" And I'd say, "Yes, I think so, Oscar." Then he'd say, "Well now, doesn't that look about right?" "Yes," I'd say, "Sink her, boys, sink her." And when the end of the season came, he said, "Cliff, I couldn't have done a better job myself." So, we got that job done.

Jim: That was the end of your third year in Petersburg, Cliff?

Cliff: Yes. Oh, but then there was something else came up. They were having a good run of fish down off of Cape Yulitna, and they was going to send two cannery tenders down there to buy them. So, one day Oscar came to me, when they got about ready to go, and he said, "Cliff, would you go with Brand X, Johnny so-and-so, on his boat, to bring my boat home?" I said, "What's he for?" "Well, oh he is awful good at getting in the areas; everybody knows him and they like him. And so then you do the counting of the fish and things like that, and if some poor little fellow is just getting by with a small boat, give him a few extra clicks on the counter. And that all helps, ya see?" So I said, "OK." So I go down there, and I'm not kidding you, we load that old boat up and get the hull full and then put canvas over the hatch, then we'd even throw them on deck and I'd keep awatchin' for the water to come over the deck. And in the meantime, Danny and some of the fellows were having a little toddy in the galley, and so Danny would say, "Well, now look, I've got to take a nap. You can go home the shortcut that I came down on, or you can go clear out around and come up by Warren Island and come in through that way. And I said, "Look, I'll see for certain, by the time we hit Wrangell Narrows, you're out of bed." "OK, OK." Well, how I ever got that boat up to the southern end of Wrangell Narrows, I don't know, but anyway, I got there. And we had a little Philipino cook, and everybody had confidence in me except the little Philipino cook. Of course, that time of the fall we'd been having fog, and it was night, you know, so I'd have the window open, apokin' my head out of the pilot house, and here was this Philipino cook back there with a weird little mandolin, going "Clinkity, clinkity, clink." And I put the peg in the wheel and I went back and I says, "Cookie, you go on back in or go down below and go to sleep." "No, no, no." I said, "You do, or I'll throw you overboard." He said, "Go ahead and throw me overboard. At least I'll die on the surface of the water." So that got us to Wrangell Narrows.

Jim: Cliff, tell us, what did you do after you threw "Cookie" overboard and finished your third summer in Petersburg?

Cliff: I had many friends throughout Montana, especially around Butte, Montana, where I'd gone to sign up to go to school at the Montana School of Mines. In the fall of '37, I went back again to the Montana School of Mines to go to school. "Now," Dr. Thompson said, "Come on, let's be realistic. You're not going to spend a whole year here. But there is a gentleman by the name of Jimmie Evans," The Evans brothers are twins, one of them had the Apoma Hotel in Butte, Montana, but Jimmie had gotten a job with the Colonel Perry Mining Company and went down in Africa someplace to mine diamonds. But by the fall of '37, the price of gold was up to $35 from what it had been, and the Colonel Perry Mining Company sent Jimmie back to Montana to go over these old placer fields to see if he could find a deposit of gold that would be worthwhile to mine, that had been overlooked or, at $28 an ounce, wasn't rich enough. Anyway, Dr. Thompson said, "Let me give Jimmie a call, because he's looking for somebody that can be a handyman, that had some experience in all types of mining. But he said, "He's a wonderful fellow to work for." So he gave him a call, and I went up to the Apoma Hotel and he signed me up to go along as his handyman. And I went all around, from towns in Montana to Jackson, Wyoming, and then we came back to western Montana and went up nearly to the Canadian border. He spent a lot of time going over the way he had been taught, from his experience in mining. I stayed with him until December, then I returned to Spokane. I says, "This time, come the first of May, I'm going to be in Seattle, armed with a ticket from the Steamship Company and this time I will go to Seward. And so now I'm at the New Hungerford Hotel, if you drift back down Memory Lane with me, first of May, 1938. In the place that a number of Alaskans hung out. As soon as I got there I met with some of my friends I'd made in Southeast Alaska, and of course one of the first things they wanted to do, after they got all lined out with their tickets or with their fishing bosses to go to Alaska, well, "How about us going down to Ballard?" Now Ballard Way had some nice Scandinavian restaurants, they had hangouts where we went down there to visit, 'cause we always got good food and there was friends down there. So we were in this Scandinavian restaurant, having a good time, and along comes a little old man—to me he was old, he was 65 I'd say—and a lot of these young fellows knew him, and they said, "Are you going back up north?" "Yes," he said, "but I have a little problem." And they said, "What's your problem?" "Well," he said, "An outfit I know from off of Kodiak bought a boat, a big cannery tender, and they want it taken to Kodiak, but," he said, "my problem is this. I have a good cook and a good young diesel engineer, but I have six college boys, relatives of the people that own this cannery in Kodiak, and all of their experience has been in pleasure boats on Puget Sound." And he said, "If I could get somebody that knew how to watch that compass, where I could lay down and take a nap 'til these boys get used to being out on salt water and so forth and handling this boat," he said. "If I could just go to Ketchikan." And of course he talked to some of the fellows he knew. "No, no, I'm going with so-and-so. I'm already signed on," and this and that. And they said, "How about Haydon, here? Why, he's been in Petersburg area for three years, and he even was out with a fish buying outfit last fall off of Cape Yulitka, and he can handle a boat." So the fellow says, "Well, how about it, Mr. Haydon?" I said, "Look, I have my ticket, and this time I'm going to go right out of here to Seward." "Well," he said, "I'm in a bind. Can't you help me?" "Oh," I said, "All right, I'll go." And so I went and cashed in my ticket and made arrangements that if, Lord willing, we made it to Ketchikan or Juneau···I wanted to go on up to Juneau, so I had my ticket fixed to a certain date from Juneau. So in about two or three days, why, this outfit that had bought this boat to go to Kodiak, they sent a rig to pick me and my things up and take me down to see this boat, and oh, it was a beautiful big white boat, trimmed in green, and on it was the word *"Fidelity."* So, I says, "By golly, this here has rooms so the crew can have plenty of space to get around, a nice big galley, and I got in there and I met the cook and he was a very pleasant fellow and then they took me on down to meet the young diesel engineer in the engine room and left me to talk with him for a while, and I said, "Say, was that one of the first diesels ever put in a sea-going rig like this?" And the engineer laughed and he said, "I don't know why I signed on this rig. Man, it is, I think, the first diesel engine." And I got to looking at it a little bit and I said, "Gee, it's all painted up nice." And he says, "That's the problem. They covered everything up with paint. Looks to me like it's going to be a rough deal. Anyway, well, he said, we'll make it somehow. He said, have you ever been up in the interior before? And I said, No. I tried to three years ago, but I got stymied in Southeastern." And he says, "I have a brother that works in a place in Fairbanks called Model Cafe." Well that helped a little later on in the year. So, anyway, the fellows all got aboard, and a nicer bunch of fellows about 25 years old, college men, you'd never have met anyplace. But they were all happy go lucky, and so finally we took off on the tide and we headed for Alaska. Well, I don't think we were eight hours away from Seattle 'til these young men re-named the boat the *"Infidelity"* They found so many things wrong, and the doggone fuel line started to leak, going to the engine, and oh, they had to have one man down there with the engineer at all times. So, that left the captain and me in the pilot house a lot. So then we got up along the coast and we were sailing along fine one night. So the captain said, "I'll have one of these young men take over. He's pretty sharp on this. And you lay down. But don't go below or anything, just lay down on the bench here and if he needs you he'll shake you." And after a few hours I woke up and I looked out the window of the pilot house and there was rocks and trees not over two or three hundred yards on each side of us, and looking ahead it looked like we were going into a blind alley, up a dead-end cove. And I run back and I shook the captain and he was tired and he says, "Haydon, you're getting too nervous." I said, "You'll be nervous too when you take a look out the pilot house window." And he dashed in there in his longjohns and he rang the bell for the engineer to throw her in reverse or something. Well, the old man had a good sense of humor. He said, "Everybody's gotta learn." To this young man he said, "What happened? You were right on course for a long time." "Well," he said, "I saw something interesting, over to the port or starboard, so I looked back, so I had to compensate for my mistake."

Jim: Cliff, don't quit, tell us a little bit more about your adventures of getting the *Infidelity* up to Ketchikan.

Cliff: The *Infidelity.* Well, we went for a long ways without having any problem, and we got up to, oh, quite a ways up along, and the skipper found a sheltered cove he knew of and we went in there and spent about 12 hours while the engineer was checking the boat over, and everybody rested. Then we took off and we headed up and we got to Queen Charlotte Sound, and the skipper says, "Haydon, you familiar with Queen Charlotte Sound?" "Yes," I said, "I have brought some boats down last fall from Petersburg to Seattle for repair work, some cannery tenders." So he said, "I'm going to lay down and take a nap." So, by golly, when we got to Queen Charlotte, I pulled way out into the ocean and I headed out there, then I was going to whip back and around, and I was way out there and all at once the diesel engine quit again. And the minute it quit, the captain he jumped out of his bunk and come out of his quarters. "What's wrong now?" Well, there is something wrong with the fuel oil line. We gotta repair that. That'll take an hour maybe. And the captain looked at where I was and he said, "What in the world is the matter with you, Haydon? You're way out in the ocean here." "Well," I said, "Tommy Sather of the Scow Bay Packing Company, whom I was with when we came down last fall, he recommended to me that you always should pull out and then if anything goes wrong you're not in against the rocks. "Well," he says, "maybe that was a good idea." So we got the fuel oil line patched and we were maybe a quarter mile off the rocks when we got going again and we headed on and we had good luck until we got to Dickson's Entrance, and we just nicely got out there and I tell you, that was one of the roughest spots I've ever seen in my years around salt water, and here we were on the *Infidelity*. But this old skipper, I'm not kidding you, he was second to none as far as being a boat skipper in Alaskan waters. So he kind of quartered into the waves good and everything and we was going along pretty nice, but all hands were in the pilot house and an extra man with the engineer, and all at once the fellow that was down below, he came running up yelling, "We're taking on water." So the captain said, "Hang onto the wheel, Haydon, and I'll go down." Well, what had happened, a wave, when he quartered around, had hit one of the portholes just right and the old rotten iron around it dumped the whole thing right in on the floor in the engine room. So, "Well," he said, "We've got to quarter the other way for awhile now, and we gotta patch that hole." What are we gonna do? Well, we had a case of kerosene, and the captain said, "Take and dump the kerosene overboard, take the cans and the boards, save the nails, and we'll call for volunteers to go over the side. But," he said, "don't trust the handrails on this thing, why they might do you in." And so of course I was along for the adventure, so I said, "I'll go over." And the young fellows were fighting over who was going over, so this one smaller fellow, they decided he'd go over with me, then they'd put a line around him and one around under my arms and let us go overboard, and the captain wanted these big fellows to have the other end of the line in through the window of the pilot house, because they didn't want to trust anything, because everything we took ahold of seemed to come apart. So we went over the side and we took and we put a bunch of stuff into the hole, then we took the boards from the box, nailed them over the hole, with the nails from the box, then we took the tin from two five-gallon cans and put a double layer of that over and nailed them down good, then we found some more material and nailed it over the inside. So, away we went again. And by gollies, it bounced around a lot, but that old skipper, he got us to Ketchikan. Unfortunately, there were two or three boats (nobody lost their lives) that were put up on the rocks in a spot or two. Who did we see when we pulled in to anchor up in Ketchikan? Here was the mighty *Carla*, the pride of the PAF cannery tenders. It had been everyplace. She was the unsinkable. And who was the engineer on the thing, but a fellow that I had known for three years in Southeastern Alaska by the name of Curly Mills. He was a good engineer and good diesel man and he came over and he said, "Haydon, were you on that wreck last night?" I said, "Yeah, we had a little problem." He said, "You know, that handsome young skipper on the *Carla*, he believed what the salesman told him when they got this boat new, you couldn't sink it, and he headed right into one of those waves and we all thought the wave was going to take the pilot house off. He said, "I know it stretched the tie-down bolts because I can see a crack around there. Boy, that young skipper really got a lesson there." Well, anyway, here I am at Ketchikan, and I met a lot of old friends. I stayed around for about a day, but didn't have too much time to lose, so I thumbed a ride to Juneau on a shrimper.

Jim: You went to Juneau on a shrimper?.

Cliff: I did. But first I asked, "But you're not going to stop at Petersburg." "No," he said, "Why? Don't you like the people there?" I said, "Too well."

Jim: Did you stop at Petersburg?

Cliff: No, thank goodness, the skipper on the shrimper kept his word. I made it to Juneau. I'm in Juneau sitting there waiting for three days for the steamship *Alaska* to take me on up to Seward, but it took me 40 more years to get to Seward.

Jim: Sorry to say, we have come to the end of our time, Cliff. Thank you for joining us on Alaska Gold Trails. Maybe next time we can get you to Fairbanks. But, the way we are going you'll probably get stuck in some small nice little town or village along the way.

Cliff: Thank you for inviting me, Jim. It's been a pleasure.

Alaska Gold Trails, March 30, 1989
Cliff Haydon with Jim Madonna
(third show)

Jim: Cliff, you know, we've been trying for two shows now to get you all the way from Spokane, Washington, if I'm not mistaken, when you were a young lad, to Fairbanks, Alaska. Well, we might not even make it today, but we'll make it before many more years pass, won't we?

Cliff: Well, I hope we make it today, because your customers are gonna listen, but they'll get off the air if they get tired of my voice here.

Jim: Oh, a lot of them told me they never get tired of you, Cliff. They love to hear your stories. You were talking to some people about a boat ride in Ketchikan. Tell us about where you were regarding that boat ride.

Cliff: Well, there was a number of us fellows that were in Ketchikan there in the hotel restaurant. In fact, there was a number of young fellows that I had worked with and known there, and they were trying to get me to stick around in Southeastern. I said, "No way, man, I'm going to Fairbanks. I've had a wonderful time down here and it is quite an experience riding on the *Infidelity* from Seattle to Ketchikan, but I have a ticket from Juneau to Seward, but I've got to get over to Juneau. And so right at the next table from us, dining, was a halibut fisherman and his crew, and they got to talking with us and he said, "Say, I heard these fellows saying that you knew a little bit about cooking and we had one of these men that's a fair cook, but he doesn't want to cook, he wants to be a plain halibut fisherman." I says, "Well, that's enough of that. I'm not interested in any more cooking, and I know halibut fishing is a good occupation. But I wish to be a miner." "Well," this owner of the halibut boat said, "we'll take you on up and drop you off in Juneau." So later, when the tide was right, we threw my equipment onto the halibut boat and we headed out, and this fellow said, "Now are you sure you don't want to stop and say hello to the fellows at Petersburg?" I said, "Man, that's the last thing I want to do." He said, "Are you wanted there?" "No," I said, "not that. Not that I know about." "Well, don't you like the people?" I said, "That's the problem right there. I like them too well. I stopped off once for a week and I made it my headquarters for three years, but I want to go to Fairbanks." "Well," he said, "we'll get you on up to Juneau." And I got into Juneau and went to the hotel there, and I discovered that the boat that I'd intended to cross the gulf on, I think was the *Yukon*, wasn't scheduled and we ended up, us fellows, getting onto the *Alaska,* which kinda dipsy-doodled across the gulf. But while we were sitting around a couple of days or so, waiting for the *Alaska* to come along, we got acquainted. There must have been at least 20 fellows there, going to Fairbanks. And they was nice young fellows and most of them had some college education and they were like me, more of an adventurer and wanted to see Fairbanks, and planned on getting some work in '38 and then stay the winter and then work in '39 and head back south again. So anyway, finally we got on the *Alaska* and headed out across the gulf, and so we started discussing it, "Well, hey, how about eight or ten of us guys get together and it'll be on a kind of economy deal, because if we get a room, like housing in Fairbanks, well we'll all kind of help each other along." And I said, "Well, that sounds like a good deal to me." And so we bounced on across the gulf, and oh about the day before we docked at Valdez, here comes a young man, and oh, that fellow had a personality plus, and he had an eye for business too. And so, he introduced himself, and he said, "Now, my brother has, among other things, a transportation outfit—the General Transportation—in Fairbanks—the largest in Fairbanks. And I've been down in Seattle area, stateside, going to school, and so he's having me bring a brand new stake bed truck, fair sized, up to Fairbanks, and the thought came to my mind, "Well, why not get some fellows going in for the first time and make a real adventure, and take them across the trail—the first people over the trail in the spring." And we listened to him. You couldn't help but like the character.

Jim: What was his name, Cliff?

Cliff: Oh, Bill. Yes. And so, he said, "Now listen, like everybody else, going into the Interior for a year or two, you have your things, quite a bit of supplies, clothes, and other things to take along," and he said, "I decided, for $20 apiece I'd take you from Valdez to Fairbanks and take all your equipment—don't care how much equipment you have—and we'll make plenty of stops." And he said, "I can contact the roadhouses a little bit ahead and line up the meals," and he said, "They just put the food out and I don't care whether its breakfast, dinner or supper, why it's family style and it's excellent food." So we said, "OK, man," and we planned on leaving next morning out of Valdez. We rounded up a room the minute we got into Valdez, so we could stay overnight there and get up and take off the following morning. We lined out the room, came back down on the streets. Holy smokes, here came friend Bill, galloping and yelling and a-waving his arms and "Where's the boat? Where's the boat?" he kept yelling. "Well, there's the boat, out in the middle of the bay. Why?" "I just got word from the road commission that part way from here to Fairbanks there's a giant washout, and it'll take them at least a week to fix it." Well, we were a little perturbed with him right then, and the fellows all had a pretty good sense of humor. "Oh, well, we can find something around here to do for a week. "Are you sure that they can get this straightened out in a week?" "Oh yes, sure," he said. So then some of the fellows said, "Well, we agreed that, even though we have a few dollars, to kind of stretch them, so let's look around and see if we can find kind of an old cabin or a house where we can stay there, cook up and go out and around and look the country over here. So, by golly, here comes the city marshal of Valdez, down the street, and one of the fellows stopped him and told him what we had in mind, and he said, "You're in luck, fellows. There's a woman that is a cook for some mining outfit, and she has a nice little two-room house and one big bed and a couple of couches and cooking utensils, and each year for a number of years, she's had me rent it out a week at a time or whatever we could rent it out for," he said, "so I know it'd be just right for you fellows, and he took us and showed us the house. And it was a very nice little house.

Jim: What did she do, Cliff?

Cliff: The woman? She was a cook out in some mine, out from Valdez someplace in the summertime. So it was immaculate, and it had everything we needed for cooking equipment and reading material on Alaska. She had a great big bookshelf there and it was loaded down, and so we proceeded to have fun, and if the weather was a little bad we stayed in and we read and everybody pitched in with the cooking, and then we figured the meals out and somebody would go over town and get what we needed for groceries. We ate a lot of stew and hotcakes and bacon, and some sandwiches too. Anyway, our friend Bill, he came by to visit us every morning, and so did the town marshal. That was his duty, was to make certain that nobody got out of hand as far as around the house, and we kept it clean as she had it and chopped extra wood and sawed and stuff, and then we'd hike. And we were blessed with a great deal of good weather.

Jim: What was Valdez like in those days? What kind of community was it?

Cliff: Well, it was a place—a fishing village—and there's some miners and there's some hard rock out there, I was told. I didn't go out to the hard rock mine; it was out a ways. But then, of course, that was the end of the trail where an awful lot of trading was done, for the Interior of Alaska. Many people had trucks hauling materials to the Interior. Well, anyway, this went on for about a week. So, our friend Bill, he came in one evening, so we wanted to know what was taking place, because we'd been to Valdez, and if nothing else we wanted to move on out away from Valdez, maybe a hundred miles or so and get an old cabin, and shucks, he could sit around there and enjoy himself too. "Well," he said, "I'll go call Max." So he called up his brother Max and they had an idea, "Well, now the fellows have been patient and you want to get in too, but we can't get that truck in for a while, so how about you bringing them up to the wash-out and I'll drive down with an old stakebed, and pick 'em up. They can walk around the washout, and there's already a little Cat there and a doggone stone boat to haul stuff around, and they can haul their stuff around with the little Cat." That sounded good, so the next morning we got up and told everybody around that we'd met there "Goodbye" and headed out. Bill said, "Now listen, don't eat breakfast before we leave. That way we can leave pretty early. We drove quite a little before we stopped for breakfast, but it was a nice place. I'm skipping ahead here. We must have gone up over Thompson Pass before we ate. When we went up there, oh, the snow must have been 10-12 feet deep up there and they must have had a rotary or something to blow the snow out of that pass and it was quite a thing for everybody, even though they'd been around mountains and a lot of snow. It was a beautiful day. So Bill put the truck right over against the snow bank and by getting up and walking up on the stake sides they could crawl up on the top of the snow and take pictures around over the country, and it was really a beautiful viewpoint. And so some of the fellows did that, but there was a kind of a heavy-set young man there and he kept looking at me and looking at me and I thought, "Wow, man, that man looks familiar." But gosh, you know how it is, you see a lot of people in your travels. But finally this fellow came over to me and he said, "Say, aren't you Buster?" Well, when he mentioned my name as Buster, I knew that he had to know my personal family real well or had contact down where my mother's family had a farm out of Spokane, Washington about 30 mile, and I said, "Yes. You look very very familiar." Well, he says, "I'm George Smith." He said, "I, for a couple of different years, went down in the summertime and worked on the farm for your Uncle Jimmie McClaig." And he said, "One day in the Spring of '36, you had a buddy of yours bring you down from Spokane. You were getting ready to take off for Alaska and wanted to visit with your Uncle Jimmie. So, anyway, it was raining, and your Uncle Jimmie, he always looked for any excuse to go fishing, and it was raining, so we weren't working the field with the teams. And just as you pulled in they were getting their fishing tackle out and they have nice fishing tackle and I don't have any fishing tackle and they said they'd cut me some willows and I'd probably catch more fish than they did with the willow." But he'd said, "I just kinda don't feel right, you know, with a willow," and I reached over and I patted him on the shoulder and I said, "Don't be concerned about that." And I went over to the fellow's car, the man who had brought me down from Spokane to the farm, and opened up the rig and pulled out a big box of fishing tackle and a nice pole, maybe offhand in those days, $25 worth. "Well, what are you going to do with this?" And he says, "I don't have any money. I can't afford to pay much." And I said, "It's yours." And my Uncle Jimmie said, "Yeah? How come you have that fishing tackle?" Well, the man who took me down said, "Well, we stopped in for a little bite of breakfast on the way down, at the outskirts of Spokane, and this restaurant had a bunch of big punchboards there. And you threw down 50-cents and punched out that much money in a couple of punches and you won all this. And they said, "Yeah, sure." So my Uncle Jimmie explained it to us that it was a golden rule by my strict great aunt and my grandmother that you will have bad luck if you ever keep unearned wealth. Now, it's fine for us to give it to George. So, anyway, that's how George got his fishing tackle for that day. So we get back up there on the pass, and George made me acquainted with his brother, who had been working in a hard rock mine out of Valdez, I believe. And so then we went on to a roadhouse and had a nice breakfast and headed on. It was a beautiful day. We saw a lot of animals along the road. Shucks, I think the first thing we saw in good supply was the coyotes, and then we went a little farther and by golly, here we saw caribou and moose and bear—not many, but just a few. And even a wolverine. But as I say, we stopped at this roadhouse and we had a very very nice breakfast, and then we traveled on towards where the road was washed out. Well, we got there, and here was the truck over on the other side and Max had his truck over there, this big old stakebed. And here was the little tractor with the stone boat, and the fellows were loading on their things and I think I put everything, including the packboard on it. Most of the fellows did, but George he hung on. He had a bedroll and a suitcase, a little suitcase, and we were walking along the edge of where the road was washed out and the next thing somebody yelled, "A man just went into the water." And we looked and here George had slid off and he was about up to his armpits in this water. Well, it had just washed out in there, there was no real current, but oh it was a cold muddy mess. So, there's always somebody right quick thinking and they got some poles and they pulled George out and his suitcase and his bedroll. So the next thing we knew we had to do real quick was build a fire and we called a halt to the operation as far as we were concerned and got a fire to going. Some of us fellows went over to our equipment and got some GI blankets and we got them and had some fellows stand around the fire holding up these blankets so George could get warm, and we shared our towels, and there's always somebody in a group like that who has some extra large... George wasn't that extra large but he was a plump sort of a guy. So they helped him rub down, and of course he was ashivering and the teeth were chattering, but pretty soon he started to laugh. And he just couldn't quit laughing. It seemed funny to him that here he slid down, we forked him out and had all this stuff up around him and everything. And so one of the older fellows along with us said, "Well, that guy is a happy-go-lucky cuss." So from then on, as long as we knew George, or any of us fellows that was on that trip, it was Happy

Smith. So, then we headed on. We didn't have quite as nice a truck to ride in, but it was adequate and it run, and we bounced down the dirt road. They had a little gravel here and there all right, and Max was real nice about stopping if there was something we wished to take a picture of, and he never never missed any type of a roadhouse, even if they had nothing more but coffee there, why he was faithful to the people along the road.

Jim: Cliff, tell us some more about your adventures during your trip from Valdez to Fairbanks. Did anything more exciting happen enroute?

Cliff: Well, after we got George Smith all dried out and were on our way again, there wasn't a great deal, other than the beauty. It was a beautiful day, and so we finally ended up at Rapids Roadhouse. And that was a sight, in those days. Not only the roadhouse was something nice and different, but the Black Rapids Glacier. The people there were quite concerned that it would come down and cut off the river and flood the whole area out. And to me that is just absolutely unbelievable the way that glacier stood up there.

Jim: We have a call, Cliff. Hello, welcome to Alaska Gold Trails, you're on the air with Cliff Haydon.

Caller: I just called up to say this is better than reading a book. I'm really enjoying the story, so just go ahead with it. It's just wonderful.

Jim: Thank you for the call. OK, Cliff you heard the lady, go ahead with the story.

Cliff: For people to just look at some of the pictures and read about the glacier, it couldn't compare to the way it was when we were there right when it had gotten down as close to the river as it ever did, and it just stood right up and it was really a beautiful sight.

Jim: We have a call, Cliff. Hi, you're on the air with Cliff Haydon.

Caller: Hi. I hate to interrupt him. I'm really interested in this. I was just calling about the Black Rapids. Driving by today you can see all the stuff that the glacier pushed over there and it's a classic example and something to see if you understand how those big piles of stuff got out there.

Jim: Well, you know, it is interesting. What Cliff is saying is the glacier was much more prominent when he came in 1938.

Caller: That's what I was going to ask, I didn't realize what year you were talking about.

Jim: Want to comment on that, Cliff, the change in the glacier between 1938 and today?

Cliff: Well, it's very unbelievable, to be honest with you, because it was just the ice sticking up there and pushing stuff ahead of it, then a short time later it started to recede.

Jim: Today you can look out there and actually see the moraines that have been left behind by the glacier.

Cliff: Yes.

Jim: Is there anything else you'd like to say to Cliff today?

Caller: No. I think it's very interesting. Keep it up.

Jim: OK, Cliff, we were at Black Rapids, so let's talk a little more about that.

Cliff: Yes. So we decided to spend the night at Black Rapids, which we did. But we got in there and it was the time of year that people were coming and going and they really didn't have room for us. But they made us welcome if we wished to roll our bedrolls out on the floor or in the dining room or anyplace around in there. They really did everything to try to make us comfortable, and some of us had a real good supply of bedding along and some of the fellows didn't. Well, just like George Smith; well, his brother Dave was there, and he had quite a supply but he isn't sharing it with George, and we gave him a little extra blanket. And then there's a guy and his wife back in a kind of a storeroom, but they was having a hard time, so we shook everybody down for a couple or three blankets for them. But we spent the night there and got up and had a nice breakfast.

Jim: Cliff, when you left Black Rapids, you say there were a lot of people there. Were there a lot of people going down to Valdez?

Cliff: They were coming and going both ways.

Jim: The road had just opened at that time then.

Cliff: Well, they had the word that in a day or so, by the time they got down there, why it'd be opened up.

Jim: What time of year was that Cliff?

Cliff: It would have been the latter part of May, because, now when we were at Black Rapids, we came on in that day, and that was the first day of June, in '38, that we pulled into Fairbanks.

Jim: You mean to say that the first day of June, 1938 you pulled into Fairbanks, Alaska?

Cliff: That's right.

Jim: Well, Cliff, I wanted you to know that on this radio show, Alaska Gold Trails, we finally got you from Washington to Fairbanks. It only took us three shows. Now, what we have to do is think about the future. We have to know what Fairbanks was like when you came, and we have to know what you've been doing for the past 50 years, since you've been here—what kind of activities you've been engaged in. It looks to me like we've got at least another three shows to go before we get you up to this date, don't you think?

Cliff: I'm afraid you'll get me back to cooking again, if you do that.

Jim: Cliff Haydon, thank you so much for joining us on Alaska Gold Trails today.

Cliff: You're certainly welcome, Jim.

Alaska Gold Trails, July 13, 1989
Cliff Haydon With Jim Madonna
(fourth show)

Jim: Well, our guest today is, once again, Cliff Haydon. Cliff, welcome to Alaska Gold Trails.

Cliff: Thank you, Jim.

Jim: In summary—and correct me if I am wrong, Cliff—you have been here with us on the Alaska Gold Trails show three times in the past. We covered your travels up from Spokane to Petersburg for three years then ultimately into Alaska, at Valdez, and across the Valdez trail to Fairbanks. You had quite a journey and all our listeners enjoyed all the spectacular events that took place with you during the journey. Now that we have you in Fairbanks, finally, we want to know what happened to you after you landed in town. Cliff, how about it. Tell us a little bit about what Fairbanks was like when you arrived here.

Cliff: Well, I arrived in Fairbanks on June 1, 1938, and it was in the afternoon, and I'd say about two dozen or better of us fellows were down in Valdez and we had made a deal with the General Transportation Company here to ride in the back of an open stake-bed truck. Well, you know, we had a few little problems, but all-in-all it was really a nice and unusual trip and we got into town late in the afternoon, and the owner of General Transportation Company said, "Now, we're building this Miller Apartments here, and so you could go in there and roll out your bedroll, and I recommend if you don't have friends or arrangements here, to do that for tonight, then get up in the morning and go look the town over." So, anyway, why we did that; and that evening we strolled around and we noticed all these board sidewalks and these different stores. One thing, the town was small enough at that time that if anybody new came into town, they knew you had just arrived, and it was surprising how many people came up to you and wanted to know what part of the United States you came from and all about your trip. And so, as I say, we got a good night's sleep, and the next morning I went looking for some fellows I'd known down in Southeast, near Petersburg, where I'd spent three years. So, I finally found one young man. He was working for a cab company, and so he wasn't busy with his cab right then and his boss said, "Go ahead and take your friend around town." Well, it didn't use up too much gas, 'cause the town wasn't that large, but he stopped along the way and made me acquainted with some charming young ladies, and I guess I looked pretty bushy to them, because they still remember me, the ones that are still around. Then the next thing, this friend of mine from Petersburg says, "Well, what do you plan as far as housing, or have you lined out some work before you come?" and we said, "No." The fellows I was traveling with were from farther east, and they were young college men, and they said, "There's eight of us, including Haydon. We're getting something with a roof over us and there's a bed or two in there. We'll draw straws to see who gets the bed." Well, in my associations with them from when they arrived in town 'til September, whenever I was in town, I slept on the floor. Now, this was a fairly large old frame house, of all things, and so one night, we hadn't been there very long, and there came a big heavy shower or downpour of rain and one of my buddies on the floor he said, "Get up. The river's overflowed, or something. There's water several inches deep on the floor." Well, I reached around, splash, splash, and discovered that the roof leaked and the center of the house, well, it sagged about four or five inches anyway. So, that was that part of that story. As we went out and around town and went into the stores, the folks could tell that we were new in town and all of 'em was getting in a little pinch. Well, now if you need anything and you go out in the creeks anyplace, why, "Here, give me your name and where you came from and whatnot, and you know the policy is, if you go out on the creek, send in with some of these pilots or the truckers for what you need, and then in the fall you can pay up and we'll get ahold of you then." We went in the N.C. Company and it was the same story there. "Well, if you're going out, even not too far from town and you need something, well..." And that was certainly different than what I'd ever been used to before. So this one fellow from northern California that was in our group, why when I started out to look the town over, about the second day we were around here in Fairbanks, he said, "If you don't mind, I'll hike along with you." And I said, "I thought you had that buddy you grew up with." "Oh," he said, "I grew up with him next door." And he said, "I wanted to associate with someone a little different." And so, fine, his name was Brenton Dipple and so, he's an unusual young man, and to be born in northern California, why you'd 'a' thought he was a real outdoorsman. But he didn't happen to be. There was many things he was outstanding in, but he couldn't cook a meal for himself, and when he went to chop a tree down, you had to watch that there wasn't something gonna fall down on top of him. We were hiking around, and saw a man trying to repair an old house, and his name was Charlie, and we get to talking and sure, he knew we was new in town, and he said, "Say, you lads wouldn't like to have a little work at a dollar an hour, and some days I'll have a full day and other days, not." So we said, "Sure." He said, "Well, I'll give you some gloves. Let's go right to work." And so, anyway, we came to the weekend and he said, "I have a little homestead out on the end of Badger Road, about eight miles from town, where my cabin is." And he said, "How would you like to come out there. I got a big ol' log cabin. It's a new one, and you can roll out your bedroll, and I have some extra bunks for friends." So, out there we went Saturday night, and we met the old timers. I don't mind telling you the old timers that were out on the end of Badger Road in those days. One was Jack Horne, you would never never meet anybody nicer than Jack. And I met a lot of nice people. You could meet some as nice, but not nicer. And Harry Badger, the strawberry king. And he had a little friend by the name of Walter Creek, and he was fairly well stiffened up with arthritis, but he could still do a lot of work, and one thing, little Walter was very interesting to us because when he first came to Alaska, he went over on the Russian side of the straits up there, and he worked for a few years, and he said he was doing real good until the darn Russians found out he was there. So he had to get out quick. But then, as I say, Charlie had a cabin and there was one other fellow, a young man that had a cabin across the slough—Badger Slough, or Piledriver, or whatever you want to call it—from Jack Horne's, and he was a surveyor and a photographer, and he had been doing work for the government in McKinley, they called it in those days. So anyway, we spent the night there with Charlie, When we first got there, why he said, "Hey, you fellows get that old ladder there that's about 20 feet long, and hold it." We did, and here he came out he'd been to one of the cafes downtown, and he'd gotten big chunks of bacon rind. And he goes up this tree and he takes big roofing tacks and he nails that on that darned tree. And so, by golly, we said, "What's the idea?" "Well, just wait an hour or so. We'll go back in and have some coffee in the cabin." Pretty soon we heard a lot of growling and a woofing out in that yard, you knew it was those darn black bears really woofing and a fighting to get up to the tree, to get that bacon rind. And he goes out there with his camera, and Brenton, he gets out there too, and they took some pictures. And that was that part of that story for that day. And then Charlie said in the morning, Sunday morning, he said, "Now when we stopped and visited Jack that was the fellow with that log cabin there that I introduced you to, I told him we'd be down for breakfast, because Jack Horne can make some of the finest sourdough hotcakes." But he said, "When he gets that great big kettle out there, don't pay any attention to that two-inch thick hard dried up lining of that pot. The sourdoughs wouldn't be too good if he cut that out of there." So, when we got there at the appointed time for breakfast, maybe around 7:30 or so, and here Jack had things agoin' and he had everything, hotcakes, all about ready to throw on, you know, and the bacon and egg apiece. So anyway, before we got to Jack's, Charlie says, "Now look. Don't tell Jack that I nailed those bacon rinds in that tree a quarter of a mile from his house, or he'll run me out of here, 'cause that just, as you've seen, brings the bears in." So then, anyway, we had breakfast there and talked with Jack and he said, "Why, you boys ought to homestead some ground around here or something. There's lots of it. Out at the end of the road here, there's a whole new ground with I think three or four titles. Get in on that first half dozen." So he did convince us that, "Well, if you don't wanna homestead, I'll tell you where to get a woodcutting permit for it." "Yeah," Jack said, "that would be good. That'd really be a good deal to get a woodcutting permit." And, oh, Charlie thought a lot of that, because in the wintertime he hauled wood, and there's a few drawbacks in the old system in that woodcutting, inasmuch as you cut the wood, and the top price for cutting good spruce and piling it up, after splitting it, was four dollars a cord. But then you had to take the chance that there wouldn't be a buyer coming through the country. There wasn't much thievery, but it had to lay there a full year, before the fellow cutting the wood could get his money. Well, we ended up with 54 cords, in our spare time. We'd go out there during the summer. So that was the situation there, and then we spent a lot of time helping Charlie and picked up quite a bit of money that way. But we did have time off to take little trips here and there and go out and look the area over.

Jim: By the way, Cliff, didn't you attend college here at the University of Alaska?

Cliff: I went the winter of '38 and '39, as a special student. I carried four subjects, out at the University

Jim: Were you working at that time?

Cliff: Well, this is embarrassing. I studied many trades and too often I ended up cooking. I'd even go out, sometimes, to a mine or a logging outfit here in the Interior. There was only one or two up here. And they'd say, "Well, we have this opening, but if the cook gets sick, then you will have to take over." Well, so that was part of it. Well, along the latter part of the summer they had a C.C. camp, and maybe if you are familiar with the Conservation Corps, that was started out by Franklin Delano Roosevelt. And so the young forest ranger from down in Oregon, at Oregon State, came up here early in the summer, not long after we got here, and established a C.C. camp. They had to build the buildings and everything, and so he could get anything, practically. He had two or three assistant forest rangers—I believe Maury Smith was one of them for awhile. But they had planned on getting a professional cook. As far as the head of the forestry outfit back in Washington, D.C., they said, "You should be able to get an old cook around there and then train them to get by." I think we had a 40-man camp, normally with about 30 living there, but they filled up the rest of the capacity with young unemployed men that didn't have a job, and they had the privilege of eating in the camp and so on. So, anyway, this Virgil Heath, this young forest ranger, he came out to our little woodcutting shack out on Badger Road, he said, "Listen, Haydon, how about cooking for the C.C. camp this winter? I can't get anything from out of headquarters back in Washington, and these young fellows around here say that you can cook." "Well," I said, "I never cooked for a bunch of men like that. I made a donut factory out of Oscar Nicholson's *Ira II* in Petersburg, and he gave me a different job the next year, but no, I..." "Well," he said, "Won't you try it?" But I said, "I want to go to school." "Well," he said, "Arrange your hours so you can slip away, and we'll get a lot of help." So that is what I ended up doing. We called it the Chena Country Club. The oldtimers remember it, maybe with fond memories, and some not too fond. But I finally found a few fellows that had helped their mama cooking at home or something, and they were anxious to get in and give a helping hand and make a success of the camp, and so I detailed myself to doing the baking and writing up the menus and ordering the groceries. So, from the time the camp was completed late in the fall, until the first of April, that's what I did that first winter. But as I say, I went to the University as a special student. Now, how did the University impress me? Well, the first Sunday we were in Fairbanks, my group of eight took a notion we'd hike out to the University and look it over. Well, we got out there and here was a fellow in slouchy clothes, going around working on the flowers and raking trash around the building. This was the summertime there. So, he noticed us walking around and staring, and we thought he was the roads and grounds man. Why, that's not what he really was. He came over and he said, "Boys, I'm Doctor Bunnell." Well, that meant nothing. He said, "Now, I know that doesn't mean anything to you, but I happen to be the president of the University." Now, I'd known some presidents of small universities before, but I never did see them out doing the grounds work like that. So he said, "I'll take time off from what I'm doing and show you through the school." And the buildings weren't too large, and I can remember the old wooden hall that they had there, that the men lived in for their barracks. Well, it was adequate, and that was all that was necessary. Now, he said, "Do any of you boys intend to go to school here this winter?" Well, all of us but one said yes. But one young man said, "Now look, I got through high school and I didn't flunk anything."

But he said, "I didn't consider myself an adequate student to go on to college." Dr. Bunnell said, "Let me tell you something, young man. If you just come to school and sit in class and behave yourself and listen, and don't say a word, then enough will rub off on you that the government will be well paid for you to come to the University." So even that fellow went to school there that winter. Now that was Dr. Bunnell's attitude. In those days, I believe that there was 35, maybe 40, maybe not that many, in each class. Now, like the freshman class I believe, the first year I was there, was around 40. One other thing, high school fared a little better downtown, I think between the years '38 to '42, they had 42 students in the class. Now I got to add one other thing that impressed me. When school started I hung around up at the University, and the teachers impressed me very very much. They'd come up here and they'd work for years, and you didn't want to be surprised if you met up with a couple of high school teachers out here working like at Circle Hot Springs and down, another place was at Mt. McKinley, or Denali, as they call it. I even ran into good ol' Annabeth Rainey down in at Denali, and I know over at Circle Hot Springs. And they didn't go Outside—I don't know whether they figured it would take too much of the payroll—and they stayed here year after year. Then the college professors were exceedingly good. Most of them were fairly young, but there was like the anthropology teacher, Dr. Ranig Bront. Well, I tell you that he went on and he was really a very outstanding professor. But all of them, they were really good. And here, you've practically got individual attention in some of these classes. As Dr. Bunnell says, it'll rub off on you, because they take time and explain.

Jim: I think you can still get that at the University of Alaska, Cliff, especially in the Mining Extension program. By the way, didn't you take a class with me, in Mining Extension, up at the University?

Cliff: Yes, and I'll tell you, I have about 20 certificates in those special classes. Yes, I have at least 20. I think I had one or two and it was not only enjoyable but enlightening, because you went to all the trouble one time, when the environmental stuff started up, of getting people from both sides, and sometimes you'd have a person that was against the environmental issue, and some from the other side, and they sat there and they were all ladies and gentlemen and kinda poked fun at one another a little bit, but you learned a great deal, and I really got a lot out of that class.

Jim: Carry on with your story, Cliff.

Cliff: I have something else that impressed me very much when I came here. It was how good the businessmen treat you, not only the businessmen but everybody. In 1940, when I flew in from the Fortymile country, working out there in Upper Wade Creek, why the next day I went to work for the Department of Defense at old Ladd Air Force Base. I said, "I think maybe I'll stay another year or two and I need a little transportation. So I looked around and there's a car manufacturer I'd dealt with a great deal down in the states. Why I walked down the street—I didn't have to walk too far in those days—and I walked in and I asked them, I said, "How much does a pickup run?" Well, the one I chose, they said, "Now, that costs $1,000, laid down in Valdez." And so the man and his brother-in-law owned this outfit, said, "Wait just a minute. Early last spring, an old sourdough that had made some money contacted us from Seattle and said that he was bringing a young relative up and they wanted to spend the summer driving around the roads in Alaska, and they needed a pickup and he'd pick it up in Valdez. And now that summer's over, well, he wants to sell it. And he has a lot of extras and he took good care of it and it's like new, and he has a couple of spare tires and tools and everything, and he'd sell it for $1,000. And I said, "Fine." So they called the man up and he brought this blue pickup over there and it was a pretty little shiny Chevrolet. So I handed him $1,000, and by golly a young man run over to me and he said, "Say, Haydon." He knew me by name; everybody by then did, you know. Now, he said, "I've talked to my father and uncle and I want to get into business and make a little money of my own. These other guys, they get out and do this and that." And I think he wasn't over about a freshman in high school, but anyway his name wasn't Robby, it was Bobby.

Jim: Bobby who?

Cliff: Bobby Ginther over at Tip Top Chevrolet.

Jim: Well, that's quite a testimonial, isn't it? A family business through the years, is that right?

Cliff: I know we are running out of time but remind me, if we get a chance, to tell you about Bobby Ginther when he was in high school and first went into business.

Jim: We sure will, Cliff, but once again we have run out of time. Thank you very much for joining us today on Alaska Gold Trails. It looks like you and I need to have another session.

Cliff: To get me out of Fairbanks?

Jim: To get you doing something here. We haven't traveled very far. It's a slow but, oh so interesting journey. Folks, I want to take a minute to thank Cliff Haydon for joining us here this afternoon and I want to thank you, the listening audience, for joining us and for participating in our show. Join me right here on KFAR next week.

Alaska Gold Trails, October 5, 1989
Cliff Haydon With Jim Madonna
(fifth show)

Jim: Cliff Haydon has given us an exciting recap of his life and the adventures he's had in not only coming to Alaska but some of the lifestyles he's had here in Alaska. Cliff is going to be here with us today in about 10 minutes to once again give us some of the adventures that he has participated in, here in Alaska, mostly centered around mining and his earliest years in the Fairbanks area. For those who are not familiar with Cliff's activities, he came out of Washington in the early days. He came up by a variety of extremely interesting boat trips that ultimately landed him in Juneau, then he came by Alaska Steamship Company to Valdez and then traveled the Valdez trail to Fairbanks. He had quite a few adventures along the way. And of course we're going to hear some more of these adventures in just a few minutes. You want to keep in mind, and it's kind of humorous, that we had Cliff on the show three times before we ever got him to Fairbanks, and this time, finally, we're going to get him to start telling us about his life in the Fairbanks area and all his wonderful adventures here. But you must remember now that Cliff was a cook for most of the time and Cliff has told me recently in a personal conversation that he really didn't like cooking, but everybody thought he was such a wonderful cook that every time they needed a man they looked for Cliff to do the cooking in the camps. So, I think that you're going to hear a little bit about his adventures in cooking and how he learned to cook and what made him so special. Cliff has had a number of adventures in mining that were particularly interesting and exciting and we'll also get with that in just a few minutes.

Jim: Good afternoon, folks, and welcome to Alaska Gold Trails. And Cliff Haydon, welcome to the show, once again my friend.

Cliff: Thank you. As usual when I start out, I like to explain that I don't pretend to be an old pioneer, because there were pioneers when I came to Fairbanks that had been pioneering the town and the area—not only the area but the Interior of Alaska—for more than 35 years. All I like to say is that I am an old Alaskan.

Jim: An old Alaskan. Well, just to clear up the issue of how old you are, when were you born?

Cliff: Well they can tell from my voice, I was born June 19, 1910, in Spokane, Washington. That's what they tell me. Now I just don't quite remember.

Jim: Well, they could tell from your voice, Cliff, there's no problem with that. Not at all. Tell us something else, Cliff, what year did you come to Alaska?

Cliff: I first came to Alaska—I arrived in Petersburg—the first day of April in 1935.

Jim: How many years did it take you to get from Petersburg to Fairbanks?

Cliff: Oh, it took three years and two months.

Jim: It took three years and two months. You know, it's almost taken us three years on the radio, to get you here from Petersburg. You know how many shows we've had together? It's been wonderful, hasn't it. I think this is our fifth show together.

Cliff: It's been enjoyable, Jim. Well, all I wish to tell anyone, on the radio or anyplace, is the facts as I've seen them and still do look at them. It's through my own eyes, and perhaps I see and remember things a little more than a lot of people, inasmuch as I was always dreaming about Alaska and I was very interested in the country and the people. But these people have been here, so many of them, well they just accept it from day to day. But I can drift back and think of how unusually different it was when I first arrived here. I was one of these people that was fortunate enough to have a job when I decided, "I've got to go to Alaska and see what it's like." I gave up my job, sold my automobile, got enough money for a ticket one way, and so that's how I came to come up here, but I didn't have any idea that I was going to stop off along the way and take so long to get into Fairbanks. But many interesting things happened along the way, too. But I've told you all about that.

Jim: Tell us what you did when you first came to Fairbanks. What jobs did you have, Cliff?

Cliff: Well, to be honest with you, I was unemployed. But, one of the first things I noticed when I came to Fairbanks, was there were an awful lot, maybe 30 or 40 young men walking around looking for jobs, and it dawned on me right away quick that everything in the Interior of Alaska depended on mining, and mining alone. And there was just so many jobs and that was it. And everyone was trying to help anybody in need. Fortunately I still had enough money to take care of the bacon or things that I needed to get out of the bush, and I had some nice young men traveling along with me and we pitched in together. But already when I got here, I noticed that the delegate to Congress alerted Washington, DC that they were going to be overpopulated with young men with no jobs for these young men. So they had already started a C.C. camp. So they had trucks and a young forest ranger by the name of Virgil Heath, and he had an assistant (Verne Styce), and they were setting up to build a 40-man camp to take care of the men in the winter. They didn't think they might have that many, but they was just going to be on the safe side, which they did proceed to do. I came in from where I was living out on Badger Road— a little woodcutting setup out there, about what is six-mile Badger now. So, there was an old fellow by the name of Charlie Mortimer, (I may have mentioned that before); he was repairing houses. We worked for him, but then, if he'd seen where we could pick up a little extra money, he would put us in it. One of the things we did was go out and fight fires in the immediate area. In fact, my buddy and I came in to fight fires and also to work on setting up a little beam station out on Badger Road. Let's see, it would be off and around four-mile Badger Road, in the area where the Piledriver/Chena Slough runs into the Chena River. And that kind of work was what we did, primarily. But it amazed me that the forestry outfit got on the ball and got this camp set up to take care of the fellows, because all at once they could see there were going to be people in need, and they didn't want them to be out in the cold. Well, they ended up needing a cook. There was always somebody who would up and say that I was a good cook.

Jim: You loved to cook, didn't you, Cliff?

Cliff: Oh, I hated to cook. But somebody had to do it, and if I had to do it, well I cooked for the men. I ate the same food, there, so I did the best I could with it. Well, it goes back to one blond domestic science teacher. I got started in, what do you say, cook's training. We had a high school class. Then I met a couple of blond girls going to the University of Washington. Their father had a family bakery in West Seattle, and I told them, "Gee, I'd like to learn how to bake this way." And they said, "Well father doesn't like people to know the secrets." And I said, "That wouldn't make any difference. I'm leaving town, heading for Alaska. I don't know when I'll be back." They had me set up to talk with him, and for a week he had me come in about three or four in the morning and taught me and gave me all of his information. Of course, I scrubbed a lot of big pots and pans, but he taught me how to make good bread. Well, then word got around that I could do it, and sometimes I thought, "Well, the boys like my cooking and they run the other cooks off, or something, but then I hate to do it, but wherever I went I always got plenty of assistance, and it made it more of a pleasure, I guess. At the C.C. camp, I put myself on the night time detail, doing the baking, and then I wrote up the menus and ordered the groceries and found time to go as a special student out at the University of Alaska. I wasn't going actually for credit, but there was a small class. I tell you, it was wonderful the amount that you could learn. Anything from mining to the history of Alaska, or just anything you wished. They had special semesters set up that way.

Jim: Were they short courses during the semester, Cliff, or were they full semester?

Cliff: Oh they were a full course that you could take, if you wished to get credit. But for me, I never knew from one time to the next when I'd be taken off to do something around the camp, as the lead cook man, so I never tried to get credit. Although, there at the University they had a camp cook class, and I took that too, from Miss Tucker. I kid Lola Tilley and I tell her, "Gee, she heard I was coming into class, into the camp cookery, so she took off and got married to Greg Tilley, just to get away from there."

Jim: Cliff, I want to ask you a little bit about your first mining activity. I understand, also, you went to work for a logging company out on the other side of the old town of Chena.

Cliff: Well, that, sir, was after I came in from my mining venture over in Circle Hot Springs area.

Jim: Oh, OK, well we want to talk about that mining venture in Circle Hot Springs area, first.

Cliff: Now, I'm going over to Circle Hot Springs, up on the Portage Creek. But I have an interesting little side here, that it was a well known fact among people that I'd rather mine or do something besides cooking. So there was a lady downtown that gave me a call. In fact she sent a taxicab over to get me, 'cause she wished to talk with me about something she had in mind. Now, to those of you people who happen to have a fair memory, this lady was Colored Frankie, and she had her home down on Fifth Avenue, back behind Fourth Avenue, see. I think young Bob Oma was driving taxi—then, the son of Earl Oma, the shrimp king from Southeastern—he was up here for a few years. So he come pick me up and he says, "Now look. Frankie wishes to talk business with you." Well, I says, "All right. Okay." I go into her home and she says, "Now, Mr. Haydon, I've checked you out, and I understand that you know how to look for placer and evaluate it and hard rock and all this and that, and you know your way around and can take care of yourself. Now," she says, "I'm married to an old cuss over at Rampart, and most people like him. He's nice to everybody but me. But I don't hardly get any gold out of that. And so, now, I will pay you in advance to go over there and pretend that you're hard up and need a job. He's awful nice to anybody that's in need, so he'll pay you, but that's just extra money." So I said, "I'll think this over, ma'am." So then I walk over to the employment office. I don't know whether the federal or territorial, and Lowell Morgan, he was the man in charge, and I told him about this, and he laughed like everything. He said, "Well, I think that might be a good job for you. She came to me and she got a man lined out and he went over there looking for a job, and," he says, "you know something? He disappeared and has never been heard of again for a year and a half." So I passed that up and went out to Portage Creek, at Circle Hot Springs, around the first of April. That was the second year of their operation. They didn't even have a mess house there yet. But the owners of that project were Jack Boswell, his brother-in-law, Phil Shally, little Pete Stagger, and then they had a financial assistant too who was in there for a quarter of it. But what they wished of me, right at that time, was as cook and handyman. Because they were building the mess house and quarters at that time, most of the men would be living down at Circle Hot Springs and commuting back and forth and I would just be cooking for about half a dozen of us, and that wouldn't take up all of my time, and so I'd go out and cut wood or if Rafferty, one of the drag line operators, needed a helper, why I could go and help him and still cook. Most of the food I cooked in a little iron Dutch oven and I had just a small stove, but it was a lot of fun. So that went on until they got the mess house built, and then there was a fellow by the name of Brown, and I'm not kidding you, that man was one of the best camp cooks I've ever seen. His sister was Margaret, I think, ended up being Fergie, and she had a hotel and restaurant, I believe, downtown. But Brown, I'm not kidding, he outclassed me two to one, as far as getting the food ready and having it extra good for a larger crew. So once he finally got out there, he took over. Then I was a handyman at doing anything they needed. When we got to start sluicing, why I'd do anything from working on the boxes to assistant mechanic, and I also helped little Pete Stagger when he was wanting to do a little prospecting. If we needed extra wood, why I'd fill in. I could run a little Cat—we had one little Cat there, and then we had a practically brand new D-7.

Jim: Is this where you got your first real placer mining experience, Cliff?

Cliff: My first experience here, in Alaska, yes. So, of course, while I was helping them around these pieces of equipment I observed them and caught on to how to operate, and I guess I got to be a fair operator, but they only used me in case the other operators were under the weather. And the thing that put them under the weather was Old Uncle Glen Carrington's TD-40 bulldozer. She got them out in the doggone rock piles and they jumped up and around like a rabbit on a hot skillet. And it got to their kidneys and so forth. But they tried to keep the TD-40 just to pushing tailings and things like that. It was nice there, and there was many interesting things that happened along the way, like occasionally, and not very often, the cook would go down to the springs—oh yes, he was like me, he had a lot of friends, only in my case, I didn't drink anything stronger than soda pop. If I did it would make me sick. Brownie wasn't a drunkard or anything like that, but when he got to feeling a little good he didn't want to come up and cook. I coulda put in 10 hours—that's all we worked; we had two shifts, 10 hours, seven days a week, and I could put in 10 hours—and then somebody'd come up, normally the person who'd come up from the springs if they saw that Brown wasn't feeling well was Lois Shoddy, Jack Bob's little sister. And I just loved that gal, because she'd just run right in the kitchen and she'd say, "Haydon...." She came up, you know, about time to get breakfast. "You gotta come up. Brownie isn't feeling well." And she didn't come in to take the easy job. She put on a big white apron. I had these big aprons there and so did Brownie, and it was peeling spuds and washing pots, and she was a perfect person. I don't say helper; she was the perfect co-worker.

Jim: So the cook went on a toot once in a while, is that it?

Cliff: Yeah.

Jim: Cliff, you had some other experiences in some other mining camps. We want to get right back to them, the one on California Creek and some of the other creeks that you've worked at.

Cliff: Don't you want me to drop over on the loggin outfit for a little while?

Jim: Yes, I do. Let's do that next. But first, Cliff you wanted me to remind you to tell us about how you knew Bobby Ginther.

Cliff: Well, I tell you. In 1940, when I came in from the mines, I had decided to go stateside. I wanted to go back, and he's from Washington, and I'd been in Alaska off and on for five years then, and anyway, they were just getting started with Ladd Air Force Base, experimental station. The assistant forestry man that I told you about, that helped establish the C.C. camp, Verne Styce, he heard that I was getting into town and he dashed in to see me as he heard I was leaving, and I said, "Sure I am, Vernon, I want to go back and visit my mother and friends and go over around Mt. Tannan Pines and some of those hard rocks..." And "No, no, we need you for something," he said, "here." Anyway, he talked me into going to work the next day, out there for Ladd Air Force Base, and like everything else, it didn't take me long to get fed up with it—in 34 years I finally did. But now there was one thing though that I was missing out on. Bobby Ginther was a high school boy, quiet, still shy individual, not doing a lot of talking. So, I decided, "Well, if I'm going to stay another winter around here, another year, why I have a roll of money now," I've always been Scotch you know, so I was looking for an automobile. I had owned Chevrolets outside. In fact it was a Chevrolet I sold before coming up here, and it was always good and dependable. So I go down to Bobby's old service motor outfit—it was operated by Bobby's father and his uncle Percy and I said, "How long would it take you to get me a new pickup up here?" And one of them said, "Say, we have a man, an oldtimer, just wanted to come up for the summer from the states, and he had a relative along, and they wanted to take him around on what roads they have in the Interior. So ahead of time he ordered a Chevrolet 1/2-ton pickup, put everything you know—extra tires, tools, and you name it—onto it, so they could get around." And they said, "Now look, you could take that order even tonight if you wanted to, and we'll call the man." I said, "I came to buy a new one from you. What's the matter with you, as a salesman, you know." "This is a good guy and he's asking $1,000, that's exactly what he paid, delivered at Valdez for it, then he put an awful lot into it, and so we'd be helping him and we'll guarantee it as good as new." "Well," I said, "I can't beat that kind of a deal." And here's this quiet high school boy standing listening to us. So I made the deal, I just got out the checkbook, soon as they get the man over, and here I had myself a beautiful blue shiny 1/2-ton Chevrolet pickup. And so I noticed Bobby kind of edging over to me, and he said, "Mr. Haydon, my father and uncle said for this winter they'd let me get into business, so I'm on a payroll of my own. They take the cars and a lot of stuff, their own trucks and stuff, out of the garage at night, when the mechanics get through," and he said, "I could put in maybe a dozen vehicles to warm storage, and I'll do that all for 50 cents a night. Each evening you can park it out here and leave the keys in it and I'll put it in the garage, and then in the morning I'll get up and come down and check the oil and gas and get them warmed up and get them out of the garage in time for you to hop in and go to work out at Ladd Air Force Base." So then he said, "I'll see there's plenty of oil and gas, everything taken care of." And I said, "Boy, this kid's got something on the ball. Gee, getting out there like that all winter." Why I had my doubts, but I tell you I was wrong. It was always exactly what he'd agreed with me, so he always impressed me. So from him and his family and down through the years, Bobby—naw, I shouldn't call him Bobby because that sounds too much like Robby. But anyway, Robby's a good guy, you know, but I'm speaking of Bob, and I don't want them to be confused. He's a super salesman, but I tell you, in his quiet way, that's it.

Jim: A great story about one of our fine Fairbanks business people. Thank you Cliff. Unfortunately, once again, we have run out of time. I want to thank you for joining us on Alaska Gold Trails. It's been a true pleasure, my friend.

Cliff: Thank You, Jim.

Orea Haydon
with
Jim Madonna
December 29, 1988

Jim: This afternoon our guest is Orea Haydon. Welcome to Alaska Gold Trails, Orea. How are you today?

Orea: Fine, Thank you.

Jim: Orea, sometimes I ask the ladies this question and they're not so eager to give me the answer. When were you born, Orea? Well, you can also tell us where you were born.

Orea: I was born in the old St. Joe's Hospital in downtown Fairbanks, before it was remodeled and added onto during the spring of 1922. There was a flu epidemic at the time, and many people were dying.

Jim: Is that right? The old St. Joseph's Hospital. Is that located next to the Catholic Church off of Illinois?

Orea: Yes, where the Denali Bank building is now, behind the Catholic Church.

Jim: Right. OK. Go ahead with the story of the flu epidemic and what effect it had on you, during that period of time.

Orea: Well, according to what the doctors tell me, my mother had the flu and her body's resistance didn't cover me, so I've always had trouble with the flu; usually end up in the hospital with this disease, whenever it comes around.

Jim: You really have a hard time with the flu then?

Orea: Yes. It can be very serious.

Jim: By the, way how long did that flu epidemic last?

Orea: Oh, I would say it lasted about a year.

Jim: You were born in Fairbanks, Alaska, and have you lived here all your life? Or did you leave for a time, Orea?

Orea: No. I went with my mother when I was 18 months old to Seattle. She was expecting my sister at that time, and my sister was born in Seattle.

Jim: When you went to Seattle, did your mother just stay for a short period, until your sister was born?

Orea: No. She stayed. My father and mother were separated.

Jim: I see. And how long did you live Outside?

Orea: We lived in Seattle until I was around ten. We moved to Bothell, Washington at that time, and then at the age of 13 my sister and I left Bothell and came back to Fairbanks by ourselves on the Alaska Steamship *Alaska* in August 1935. We landed in Fairbanks on August the 22nd or 23rd.

Jim: You know, I've had a number of guests that have spoken about traveling the Alaska Steamship route, and is it correct that it ended up in Valdez?

Orea: Valdez, yes.

Jim: Was there another spur that went on to some other port? It seemed to me that sometimes you could go on to Seward or something like that.

Orea: Well, that could be. I'm not familiar with that.

Jim: Perhaps the line went to Seward as soon as the railroad was built. What kind of ride was that? Seems to me when I think about these old time ships I think it's kind of crude and perhaps not very hospitable.

Orea: Well, the *Alaska* was a small ship, a small cruise ship. It was really decked out as a cruise ship. We had a beautiful dining room with white linen table cloths and flowers on the table, and we were appointed bus-boys to take care of us. They would have dancing and a cocktail lounge. In fact, I think they were very similar to the first ferries in the marine system, before they made the changeover.

Jim: Actually then, it was almost a pleasure cruise.

Orea: Except that I was seasick most of the time.

Jim: You know, it's interesting to note that my other guests have also indicated that they became seasick. One of them said, "Oh we fed the fishes." That's terrible, isn't it. Well, when you got to Valdez how did you get to Fairbanks? Was the road open?

Orea: Our bus driver Roley met us. He looked for us at the dock and told us that he was to take care of us on the road to Fairbanks. He took care of all of our meals and our lodging. We stayed over one night in the road-house and stopped for all of our meals on both days.

Jim: What roadhouse did you stay at?

Orea: The one outside of Valdez.

Jim: Oh. The one at Thompson Pass.

Orea: Thompson Pass, right.

Jim: OK. Now, the total length of time to travel from Valdez to Fairbanks, was what, two days?

Orea: Two days, yes.

Jim: And was there anything exciting that occurred?

Orea: Well, it was a beautiful trip for my sister and me. We didn't know what to expect. Everybody was so nice and friendly, and explained everything to us. And we kept watching for wild animals. I must say that when my mother first came to Alaska, with my father—and that was five years before I was born—it took them a week to come up over the trail. He had one of Bobby Sheldon's Fords and it kept breaking down. The road was muddy and he would have to get out and cut logs and corral the road and do a lot of little things, so mother would take her sack of oatmeal out and cook it while he was busy working on the car or the road.

Jim: Perhaps we should explain that. The year was 1917, and the road was not paved.

Orea: That's right. It was a trail in those days.

Jim: We want to build the atmosphere for the listening audience so that they'll understand that what was coming up that trail was a little old perhaps Model-T type vehicle—one of the original vehicles that gained popularity in the early part of this century—and that the road was probably filled with mud ruts that approached very close to the bottom of the chassis of the vehicle. Tires in those days weren't as durable as they are today, either, were they?

Orea: That's true. They certainly weren't.

Jim: We were talking about the trip that you took in the bus. Did you have any flat tires or any inconveniences?

Orea: No, I don't remember any inconveniences. Everything went really smooth.

Jim: When you arrived in Fairbanks what was your first impression?

Orea: I thought it was the best town in all of Alaska.

Jim: Do you still feel that way?

Orea: Oh yes.

Jim: And you've lived here ever since that time, have you?

Orea: Yes.

Jim: You've probably had a lot experiences and can tell us a lot about what went on through those years. You arrived in August, 1935. What made it the greatest town in Alaska? What was it like? Did it have pavement on the streets?

Orea: A little. A little bit around Second Avenue and Cushman. Just a very little bit. Mostly there were wooden sidewalks.

Jim: You know, when I first came Second Avenue was paved and Cushman was paved up to Gaffney. That was the only pavement in town, if I recall correctly. We see all kinds of modern structures and homes here in

Fairbanks today. You know when I envision Fairbanks back in say the 1930s, I envision the older type frontier town with a lot of log structures. In the days when you came to Fairbanks, what was it like? What kind of structures were there?

Orea: Like you imagined, many log structures. But there were some frame buildings too. And of course, there was the courthouse, which is called the Courthouse Square now, which was a cement building. Cement block, evidently.

Jim: There on Cushman and Second?

Orea: Cushman and Second Avenue and Third, between Second and Third.

Jim: When I was a young lad a lot of the people in Fairbanks gathered in that building. If I'm not mistaken, the post office was in that building along with the courts. Had a neat elevator in it too. I guess it still does.

Orea: Yes.

Jim: In terms of areas in the Fairbanks district, were there little residential areas? It seems to me that off of Minnie Street was called, what did they call that area off Minnie Street?

Orea: That was called Graehl. I lived on Second and Noble.

Jim: Graehl. Yeah, that's it. And were those for the most part log structures in that area?

Orea: I would say so. There was a big nightclub over there that was all logs, and the ballroom floor was filled with mirrors.

Jim: Oh it was. Oh my goodness. What was the tone of the town? What were the people like?

Orea: The people were extremely friendly. And if you went downtown on an errand, to buy groceries, get your mail, or whatever, it took you hours just to go a few blocks, because you knew everyone and everybody had to talk to you, find out what was going on in your family and how you felt and just carry on a wonderful conversation.

Jim: And of course they had to bring you up to date on what they'd been doing too.

Orea: So, friendly. I just couldn't get over that.

Jim: We still have some of that here, and it's fun to recall walking out of a store into a parking lot to get in the car and have somebody that I know stop me and then seem like a few minutes went by, but in reality an hour and a half went by, as we sat there in the parking lot talking about everything that was going on. And that's the kind of thing that happened consistently here in the Fairbanks area in the early years around 1935.

Orea: Right. And also, the telephone operator knew where you were and where everyone else was that you were calling. So you got all this information.

Jim: I imagine the telephone operator knew quite a lot about what was going on in town as well.

Orea: She used to tell me that I had a nice voice.

Jim: I agree with her. Orea, there were a lot of activities going on in Fairbanks during the 1930s. There was a lot of mining. There was a lot of hunting. There was a lot of trapping. It was really a frontier community wasn't it?

Orea: Yes.

Jim: And I wonder, I'm not really clear about the ice carnival. When I was a young boy, I participated in the ice carnival, but it didn't really strike home as it might have for someone who was a little older than I was. Could you run through it for us?

Orea: Well, to begin with, the winters were so long in Fairbanks, Alaska, that the people got together and decided that they wanted something to break the monotony. So in March they would have a three or four-day ice carnival. They would have games and concessions and booths and so forth, and they would have dances, and different races, such as the dog races, and there would be a king and queen chosen. And my father decided to do the decorating, and he purchased different colored lights and Chinese lanterns and strung them up all over the streets of Fairbanks and on the bridge—the old bridge that was here, that's in Nome, Alaska today. He worked really hard and it was very cold. I can remember him recruiting the natives from the different villages to help him and then they would get free meals at the Model Cafe. But generally he supported the whole bill himself. It was just a real fun time. My stepmother used to burn little pennants and put green and yellow ribbons—that was the color—and the song was "Develop," with Don Adler, (I believe is the one that wrote the song) and everybody would sing it during these days, and in the schools as well. It was just a real fun time.

Jim: Now, specifically, the dog races ran different distances and they ran them up and down the Chena River, wasn't that right?

Orea: Yes.

Jim: And didn't they have incremental races that were like a mile, five miles, twenty miles, and so forth? I do remember from time to time that the lads would come in after one of the longer races and some of the dogs would be riding in the sled because they had succumbed to the effects of the journey. And of course they got the free ride back home. At any rate it was quite a festive occasion and I remember a couple of people commenting, just take a little bottle of brandy to keep the inside warm and keep the chill off. But we want to keep in mind, too, that the temperatures in March are starting to warm up.

Orea: Right.

Jim: Orea, we have a call. Hi. Welcome to Alaska Gold Trails. You're on the air with Orea Haydon.

Caller: Yes. I wanted to know if they had property taxes back then.

Orea: No. I don't believe so.

Jim: Did you have another question for Orea?

Caller: Yes. About the bridge that went to Nome, how was it transported?

Orea: I'm sorry, I can't tell you how it was transported.

Jim: We want to keep in mind, I don't know if everybody is familiar with the bridge that crossed the Chena, but it wasn't quite like the bridge is today. It was a suspension bridge with an overhanging structure for support. According to Orea, it now resides in Nome. But we don't know how it got there. We just know that it was taken down here in Fairbanks.

Orea: It was taken apart, that's for sure.

Jim: Maybe somebody else has the answer to the question of how it was transported to Nome and wouldn't mind phoning in and sharing that information with us. Thank you for your call. Good question. We were talking about the winter carnival.

Orea: Oh, another thing, every year there was some type of structure built out of ice and Dad would light that—put all of his different colored lights on it. It really was a beautiful sight.

Jim: This past year they built the ice sculptures down by the Catholic church. Was that kind of ice carving going on, and was there any competition involved, or was it just strictly for the pleasure of constructing?

Orea: No, it was just one structure, generally, such as a log cabin one year and an igloo another year and a palace another year, and a throne another year. You know, just different ones. It was just the one structure that was built each year.

Jim: Orea, we have another call. Hello, you're on the air with Orea Haydon.

Caller: Yeah. I just wondered, was that when they were curling on the ice and everything down in front of the N.C. Company?

Orea: Yes, I believe that's where they were curling. Everything was pretty much done down on the river in those days—ice rinks and the curling rink and everything.

Caller: The river was a lot more solidly frozen then, wasn't it?

Orea: I think at that time the power plant was behind where the Nordstrom building is now, and it didn't have all that steam going down into the slough. Therefore, it didn't thaw the ice, so we could use that ice. It was a lot safer in those days.

Caller: Then the power plant was over where the N.C. or Nordstroms is now.

Orea: In back of where Nordstroms is.

Caller: Where the parking lot is.

Orea: Yeah.

Jim: Thank you for the call. Orea give us some more history. Let's go back to the time when you first arrived here—not the first years you arrived, not 1935, but the next year—the spring of 1936. We want to know what you did for the spring and the summer of 1936. Where did you go, what did you do, and how did you do it?

Orea: Well, our father put us in an old Model-T that belonged to Blanche Cascadin, my aunt, and drove over what was beginning of the road to Livengood. And we got so far, and then we had to be dragged through the mud with a Cat that came out from the Livengood side. They had a road finished for 20 miles out, and the Cat came and pulled us through, and we went up to her mining camp, up the creek in Livengood, and spent our summer rocking.

Jim: Is that a dance?

Orea: No. Using an old rocker.

Jim: An old rocker? That must be some kind of gold retrieval device, is that right?

Orea: Right. That's what it is. She borrowed one from one of her neighbors and put it all together for us, showed us how to do it, and each day we would go through the old pile. We had a pond of water and we had an old can on a stick. We would shovel in dirt and rocks, and wash the dirt and the rocks, and it would go down through the sluice box, and each day we had a clean-up. We never left it in the boxes. And that's what we would do. And then on other days, when she was doing her open cut work, we would go out and help her with her sluicing—wash the rocks and throw the rocks out of the way and that sort of thing, and dig.

Jim: Now this wasn't rocking when she was doing her open cut.

Orea: No, that wasn't rocking. She was just doing open cut and then we would be washing the water through the dirt and go down through the sluice boxes and we would get the big boulders out of the way and you know wash them in the water and so forth.

Jim: How did they get the gravels into the sluice box entry chute? Did they have some kind of Cat or a dragline.

Orea: Yes. She had a Cat to push them in.

Jim: This was at Livengood.

Orea: Yes, Livengood.

Jim: Now, if I'm not mistaken, Livengood is just about 70 miles from Fairbanks, is that correct?

Orea: I think at that time it was 80 some miles. They have shortened it with the road.

Jim: I think the question that is burning in everybody's mind right at the moment is, after rocking all summer, how much gold did we get?

Orea: You know, I can't remember. I know that Blanche put it into bonds for us.

Jim: U.S. Savings Bonds.

Orea: U.S. Savings Bonds, right. But I couldn't even remember how many bonds now, isn't that sad?

Jim: But you did get a little summer earnings out of that.

Orea: Oh yes. We got summer earnings.

Jim: Do you think today that people could go out and get a little earnings?

Orea: Oh, definitely, because at that time gold was only $35 an ounce.

Jim: OK, and so today at four hundred and some dollars an ounce, you think a person could make a few dollars "rocking"?

Orea: I should say. They ought to be able to.

Jim: They ought to be able to buy a few U.S. Savings Bonds.

Orea: Would you like to know a little history about Livengood?

Jim: I'd love to.

Orea: OK. Livengood is named after a fellow by the name of Jay Livengood. And Jay Livengood had a partner, and his partner's name was Hudson. And my aunt, Josie Shattuck cooked for them. And she finally became a partner with them. But the two men didn't get along too well. One day, when they were mining, one of the fellows decided to make some coffee. So he left the mining site and went to make coffee, and Jay went ahead and did some panning. He discovered some very good colors. And so he ran to tell his partner. And his partner was so mad that Jay had made the discovery that he threw his hand out and knocked the gold out all over the ground. And that's how Livengood became named after Jay Livengood, because of his discovery.

Jim: I see. Did they split up as partners, or did they continue on?

Orea: No, they continued on. They disagreed a lot, but they did continue on.

Jim: After your experience rocking in Livengood, did you return to Fairbanks then to go to school that fall?

Orea: Yes.

Jim: And did you ever go back to Livengood?

Orea: Oh yes. In the summertime. And in those days the road commission had many of the high school boys working for them, and they would even be out there in the different camps. They had set one camp up the creek near where we lived, and on Saturday night they'd go down to the inn and dance.

Jim: They didn't have a band, did they?

Orea: No, they didn't have a band. They had a nickelodeon.

Jim: Oh, a nickelodeon.

Orea: Right. Take a lot of nickels. And that's what they would do on Saturday night. Everybody loved to dance. Even the cooks. Blanche had ground leased to Charlie Anderson and Charlie Peterson. They had put in a drift mine, and their cook, Mrs. Walker, would go down to the inn every Saturday night. Sometimes she'd even walk, and that was several miles, into Livengood to dance.

Jim: She was just getting warmed up.

Orea: To dance all night, and then she would walk right back and have breakfast on the table for everybody in the camp the next day.

Jim: What a chore. I'll say. When you came back into town, you went to school. You went to the one school that was in Fairbanks at that time, Main School, wasn't it? You know when I came to Fairbanks I went to Main School. It housed all the students didn't it?

Orea: From kindergarten through high school.

Jim: That's right. It still did back in the days that I first came here, a couple years ago.

Orea: There were just a little over 100 students in high school when I was there.

Jim: And you went then from 1935 and completed high school?

Orea: 1941.

Jim: In 1941. Did you ever venture out into the University system?

Orea: Yes. In 1942 I went to school for one semester and then I married my husband.

Jim: I'll bet that was an adventure in itself. Tell us something. What happened? You went to college, and you did what?

Orea: We eloped.

Jim: You eloped, really?

Orea: My husband and I.

Jim: What's your husband's name?

Orea: Clifford Lloyd Haydon.

Jim: Clifford Lloyd Haydon. And where did you meet this dazzling young man. Was he going to college?

Orea: No. My father brought him home one day. Dad worked in the power plant at Ladd Field and he used to invite a number of different people to our home for coffee, and one day Cliff appeared.

Jim: For coffee.

Orea: For coffee. That's how I met him. And then I went to work. It was right after my first semester of University. I was working at Ladd Field in the main hangar and I used to go right past the power plant each day with my paperwork, and Cliff would come out and talk to me. So, he started taking me home because we were both working the night shift. Then he proposed to me.

Jim: Now wait a minute here. I think the listening audience should know something. That over in the corner sits Cliff Haydon, here in the studio, and he's making some funny motions here. But I have to clarify one thing. Now, he was taking you home from time to time.

Orea: Yes, right.

Jim: And so, one day he was taking you home and he subtly proposed to you?

Orea: Right. Well, actually he proposed to me on our very first date. The night of the midnight sun. It was after the Midnight Sun Dance, June 21st.

Jim: He was an aggressive little guy, wasn't he? And tell me, what happened? You got married. Tell me about it.

Orea: OK. Well, we were engaged for a couple of weeks, and Cliff kept saying, "We better get married pretty soon." And he didn't tell me why, but he was going to be shipped out, and I had no idea. So I told my stepmother, "Cliff and I really want to get married. We don't want to wait 'til next year." And she said, "No, you can't. You've got to promise me not to." So, one day I just couldn't take it any longer. We went down and got our license and we went out and got his trunk and we rushed back to town and took his trunk to Herb Koske's home and Herb was a stutterer. So, Herb was to take me up to the house to get my clothes. He took me up to the house, and while I was getting my clothes, first of all I wrote a note out saying what I was going to do. And in the meantime my stepmother drove into the yard, and I knew she'd find the note. Poor Herb was sitting there, stuttering with all he could think about. He was so scared he didn't know what to do. So he drove out of the yard. So I went out the back door, running with an armload of clothes, down the street. Cliff came up First Avenue and he saw me running with all these clothes, and he said, "What happened to Herb?" And I said, "I don't know. He left me." So then he said, "Well come on, we'll go over to his house." So we went over to his house and put my things in the trunk, and we were getting ready to leave. And Herb had come back in the meantime, and he was shaking our hands, and here comes my stepmother down the street. She spotted us, and Cliff spotted her, but Herb didn't see it and I was trying to get rid of Herb and I said, "Herb, here she comes. Here she comes." And he grabbed his hand away and off we went. Well, the light was in our favor. So we got across the bridge safely and she had to wait for the light. We got way away from her, because our pickup was newer than hers. So she never knew whether we went to Livengood or Circle Hot Springs. And so since she didn't know, she couldn't find us to stop it.

Jim: Fascinating story, Orea. Thanks so much for joining us on Alaska Gold Trails today. It's been a pleasure having you.

Orea: You're always welcome, Jim.

Juanita Helms
with
Jim Madonna
August 3, 1989

Jim: This afternoon, our guest is Juanita Helms. Welcome to Alaska Gold Trails, Juanita.

Juanita: Well, good afternoon, and thank you for inviting me, Jim.

Jim: Oh, I've been looking forward to it. Juanita, could you give us a little information regarding where you were born, and maybe generalize the year, somewhere, plus or minus three or four?

Juanita: Certainly. I was born in Chicago, Illinois. That was around 48 years ago. We only lived there three years, then we moved to Michigan, and when I was nine, we came to Alaska.

Jim: Where in Michigan did you live?

Juanita: We lived on a little island outside of Detroit, called Grosse Ile, on the Detroit River.

Jim: Was it in the middle of the river?

Juanita: Right in the middle of the river.

Jim: I see. And how many people were there? Was it a town?

Juanita: It was more a residential area, not technically a town. It was like a bedroom community to Detroit and Wyandotte and Trenton, the big towns across the river. We lived there about six years, and then moved to Alaska

Jim: Where did you go first in Alaska, Juanita?

Juanita: We came to Elmendorf. My father had seen an ad in the National Geographic saying that they needed engineers in Alaska, and he answered an ad and came up to Alaska in 1950, to Elmendorf, just outside of Anchorage.

Jim: As an engineer. What did he do there?

Juanita: He worked for the Corps of Engineers.

Jim: I see. And what kind of activities did you participate in there?

Juanita: Mainly, since I was pretty young, the things I was interested in were the more athletic kinds of things. The buildings had ice rinks in between each building, so we did a lot of ice skating. That was in the wintertime. And there were square dances every Friday night. School consumed quite a bit of our time, and during the summer, Dad would take the whole family and we would travel around the state, on the weekends.

Jim: I'll bet that was fun. Did you visit the roadhouses along the roadways around the state?

Juanita: Yes.

Jim: How long were you at Elmendorf and where did you go from there?

Juanita: We were there a year and a half. Then my father got the concession to manage Mt. McKinley National Park Hotel. And at that time the old hotel was still standing—a very charming building. The road was not open between Fairbanks and the hotel. You still had to get there by way of either the railroad, or by small plane. And for a year and a half we lived there. As I understand it, it was the only winter that hotel had ever been open to the public.

Jim: Tell us some of the things that you remember most, about Mt. McKinley and the park.

Juanita: Well, that was one of the best periods of my life. We did a lot of outdoor things. Dad had built an ice rink, because we liked ice skating. We had a toboggan hill. There were two ski runs that he put in, one with a rope tow, so we could go up the mountain behind the hotel. In the summer we did a lot of traveling out into the park. At that time Celia Hunter and Ginny Wood ran Camp Denali, on the other side of the park, right across from Wonder Lake, and we used to go out there, and we knew a miner, in Kantishna, that we used to visit. Our time was always occupied with something.

Jim: Did you see quite a lot of wildlife there? Would you maybe explain some of the wildlife that you saw in the park and how easy it was to see them, to our listeners?

Juanita: Oh, it was beautiful in the park. The animals seemed to sense that they were safe, in the park, so they didn't run and hide, unless you got too close to them. You got a good view of animals. We were out in the park one time and my brother and I were walking up a small hill, and at that time we didn't know it, but a bear was coming up the other side, and we all met at the top. Well, the bear ran down one side and my brother ran down the other, and I stood up there screaming and waving my arms, and my father was a little upset because we'd scared the bear away and he wasn't able to get a good picture of him.

Jim: At that moment I'll bet you didn't care a whole lot about that picture.

Juanita: Right. I was glad he took off.

Jim: Tell us about the dump.

Juanita: Well, just outside the park, in the hotel area, was where they had the dump, and that was really the only place that you had to be careful of the animals; the bears would attack if you came near the dump. So people were real cautious if they went around there, and I didn't. But the bears would come up to the hotel, around the kitchen area, because there was always the smell of food. They'd sometimes raid the garbage cans or something like that, but I don't remember anybody ever being hurt inside the park, by an animal.

Jim: I recall—speaking of the beauty of the park—when I was a graduate student at the University, I was fortunate enough to participate as the field assistant in the mapping program there, and we had the opportunity to map the Polychrome Pass area, which was, of course, one of the more colorful areas within the park, in terms of variable shades of maroon and brown and so forth.

Juanita: Beautiful country.

Jim: It was an interesting area, and we got well acquainted with the park, in that respect, and the wildlife. I did have the thrill of running into a sow and two cubs one day. That memory will stay with me for quite some time. Sometimes, in the valley adjacent to Polychrome Pass, we saw caribou running along, and they were simply majestic. I'll never forget the picture they made. One day there were two caribou with great racks upon them, and they were running across that tundra. It was quite a picturesque thing to see.

Juanita: That is beautiful country. I believe that is where they traveled when they migrated, was through Polychrome. It's a wonderful opportunity for people, if they get a chance, to go down there and visit. It's not the same, in some ways, and in some ways it is.

Jim: Well, sometimes I think that maybe Alaskans don't take advantage of those things. They say, "Well, the park is here, and we'll see it some day." But they don't realize that it's really a wonder and is breathtaking to see.

Juanita: It is. And that mountain. I went out in the park, stayed at Camp Denali one night, and the window was just above the bed. I woke about three in the morning and looked out the window, and there was that beautiful mountain, bright pink. And then reflected in Wonder Lake—a double. And that is breathtaking.

Jim: You know, they had a picture like that on one of the calendars recently - the reflection of Mt. McKinley in Wonder Lake. I have met a lot of tourists who have waited weeks in the park and never gotten a picture of Mt. McKinley, because it was always veiled in clouds one way or the other, so it prevented a good photo. I better get back on the trail here.

Juanita, we were talking just briefly about your activity during your year and a half at Mt. McKinley Park. Did you have anything else to add to that?

Juanita: Yes. That was the first time I'd ever ridden in a small plane. The only way we got to Fairbanks, unless you wanted to take the train, was by plane, and Bob Rice and Holly Evans used to fly between Fairbanks and Mt. McKinley. That was exciting, because they were always willing to show you a view of the ground, by dipping the plane and showing it to you. So it was exciting to me.

Jim: What year was it, then, that you came to Fairbanks?

Juanita: Let's see. I must have been about 12 years old by the time we got to Fairbanks. We actually moved to North Pole. I finished up grade school there, and then, when I got into high school, came into Fairbanks.

Jim: What school did you attend?

Juanita: We started out in Main my freshman year and moved into Lathrop. That was the year Lathrop opened up. It was that fall. I remember all of the students walking from Main, carrying a load of library books and moving the library over to Lathrop.

Jim: You actually participated in the move, then?

Juanita: Yes, that's right.

Jim: I bet you were really proud of that school when you moved into it.

Juanita: Oh, we were. It was a brand new school. It was our school. And we took good care of it. We were very proud.

Jim: Well, it is a beautiful school. I remember when I was a young lad here in Fairbanks. Of course, everything was at Main. And it was interesting to have everybody concentrated into the one school. And I remember also that we were going to half day sessions at that time because there really wasn't enough room.

Juanita: Double shifting?

Jim: Yes. Some students would go to school in the morning, others in the afternoon. I think that was very close to the time of the move, early 50s. Do you remember the year?

Juanita: '54 would have been the move.

Jim: Was it? Tell us what kind of activities you participated in during your school years at Fairbanks. Did you graduate in 1959, I believe.

Juanita: Right. Thirty years ago.

Jim: I saw you on the float in the parade. The banner read, Lathrop High School Class of 1959. What did you do at Lathrop High School, besides get good grades, Juanita?

Juanita: I didn't do a lot of extra-curricular activities. We had a lot of interest in basketball, and I watched the games a lot. We had to compete with Anchorage when we wanted to compete with anybody, so everybody was real enthusiastic about that. There used to be a talent show, called Arctic Capers, that was put on once a year, and I participated in that—myself and a friend of mine, Nelda Larson, did the hula.

Jim: Is this an Alaskan version of the hula?

Juanita: Right. We had Liberty Hellany, he was our hula teacher. I don't know how many people remember Lib, but he is still around.

Jim: Well, you actually got professional help, then.

Juanita: Oh yes.

Jim: And other than participating in that entertainment. Have you ever done any other kind of entertainment in your life?

Juanita: No, unless you count being on the Assembly and being mayor entertainment.

Jim: I wouldn't have said that, but OK.

Juanita: No. I was always very bashful, very shy.

Jim: Have you found that you're not bashful any more?

Juanita: No. I've just found that I can control it better than I used to.

Jim: Is that right? What kind of work did you do in the summertime, while you were in high school?

Juanita: Oh, well, in high school, I used to work for Bill's Drive-In—Bill Sexton, that had the drive-in on College Road. At that time it was right across from Miller and Bentley Salvage Yard.

Jim: Oh yes. I remember it well.

Juanita: Right.

Jim: Kind of a little building where the front glass was hung over at an angle from the roof to the ground.

Juanita: Yeah, it used to be an A&W, then it was Bill's Drive-In. And it was a good job to have.

Jim: Were you a carhop?

Juanita: I was a carhop, right. And then, of course, anybody that worked there filled any job that had to be done. So, it was good experience.

Jim: It was? You mean you came out with a little tray and you hung it on the window.

Juanita: Yeah. Usually. Sometimes it would tip.

Jim: Did you ever have any disasters?

Juanita: Yes. I remember one especially. A big truck came in and I had to take the tray overhead to get it on their window. And he helped. And we had a chocolate milkshake and several other things that landed on me.

Jim: I was having visions of that one. Embarrassing moment wasn't it?

Juanita: Oh, it was. And very sticky.

Jim: I'm not going to ask any more questions about that moment? How long did you work for Bill's Drive-In?

Juanita: I worked two summers.

Jim: Two summers. And what did you do following high school?

Juanita: Three of my friends and I went to Hawaii, after we graduated from high school. Took a plane to Seattle, a train to San Francisco, and then a boat over to Hawaii. And stayed there about five weeks. So that was a big adventure for us. Then I went to work for an insurance company, got married, and went to work for Superior Court, and worked there for four years, and have gone on to various jobs, and here I am.

Jim: Well, along the road, through all these jobs, you said you got married.

Juanita: Yes.

Jim: Expand on the romance of how you met your husband. A lot of people like to know about the romance part of lives. Tell us, Juanita, how did you meet your husband?

Juanita: Well, my husband and I—my husband is Sam Helms—I'm not sure exactly where we met. I do remember that when I worked for Bill's Drive-In, Sam used to come in there, and he and Bill Sexton used to enjoy embarrassing me. So they'd get together and do a real good job of it.

Jim: They must've really enjoyed it when that milkshake hit you.

Juanita: Yes. Sam and I knew each other for several years and we were friends, and when I needed anything or needed someone to depend on, Sam was the one I would think of, because he was an honest person and you could trust him, and a nice guy. I don't know where along the line we all of a sudden discovered that it was more than just friendship. I do remember the time that Sam gave me my engagement ring. We were in the Co-op and he slipped it to me under the counter, rather than formally presenting it to me.

Jim: You mean he didn't get down on his knee and go through all that?

Juanita: No. I wanted him to, but he wouldn't do that.

Jim: In Co-op? You know, that sounds like a place where a person would make a proposal, though, the Co-op Drug Store.

Juanita: At that time the Co-op was where everyone met everybody.

Jim: What a way to present an engagement ring.

Juanita: Right. But I took it.

Jim: You took it? And what did he say, just as he presented it to you?

Juanita: Actually, he didn't say anything. He flushed a little, but he didn't say anything.

Jim: What did you say?

Juanita: I said, "What is this?"

Jim: You didn't know what an engagement ring was?

Juanita: Oh, I knew what it was.

Jim: Did you know it was on its way?

Juanita: Yes, I was pretty sure.

Jim: You were pretty sure. But you didn't know it was going to happen in the Co-op.

Juanita: No, I didn't expect it to happen in the Co-op.

Jim: Now, this'll go down in history, you know. I hope Sam's listening. So, you accepted. How did you accept? You say, "OK, Sam, I'll do it?"

Juanita: It was more like I accepted by wearing the ring.

Jim: Did it fit?

Juanita: Yes, it did.

Jim: And then tell us what happened. How long was the courtship, following the engagement?

Juanita: We got married about six months later.

Jim: What year was that?

Juanita: 1962.

Jim: You have been married a while. What does Sam do?

Juanita: Sam at that time, and for 32 years, was an active member of the Laborers Union, Local 942, here. When he retired from the Laborers Union he went into contracting for himself. He sold his share of the company last year, and is now retired. He takes care of the rental units that we have and is generally retired right now.

Jim: Tell us what happened after getting married.

Juanita: Besides having four children, we, over the years, accumulated several smaller houses that we use as rental units, and up until my fourth child I worked, and then retired for a while when I had the fourth child, and actually became a full-time parent, which was a totally different experience.

Jim: Juanita, full-time parent, you like that change?

Juanita: I enjoyed it. It took a little getting used to, because when you've got children and you work full time, you forget that sometimes sitting down on the front step with your child and staring at nothing and just being a companion is part of the job of being a parent. It took me a while to get to the point where I didn't feel like I constantly had to be doing something.

Jim: Now, tell us a little about your four children. Start with ages.

Juanita: 27, 24, 22, 20.

Jim: These aren't children. These are full-grown adults.

Juanita: That's right. That's right. And I haven't got one of them at home right now.

Jim: How many boys and girls?

Juanita: One boy and three girls.

Jim: Oh, my goodness. That poor guy.

Juanita: Yes, I know.

Jim: It happened, didn't it.

Juanita: He survived it.

Jim: He did it, didn't he. I can't believe it. Yes. Tell us, how old's the boy?

Juanita: He's 22.

Jim: 22. Right in the middle there, trouble from both sides.

Juanita: Yes. Yes. One of the two middle children.

Jim: Do they live in Fairbanks?

Juanita: Yes. Actually, I've got one daughter that just left, that's going to be living in Idaho, to complete her med-tech education, for a couple of years. And my other daughter went with her to go to school for one semester. And my two grandkids, of course, went with her.

Jim: I see. It's quite a family and growing.

Juanita: Yeah.

Jim: How old are your grandchildren?

Juanita: three and seven months.

Jim: And what are they?

Juanita: A girl and a boy.

Jim: Oh, you got 'em divided.

Juanita: Yeah. It's perfect.

Jim: I want to again let the audience know that they're welcome to call in about two minutes. But we should first talk a little bit about Bud. I know Bud, or I knew Bud, and he's your father (I should explain that to the listening audience). And where did Bud go after McKinley? I know he went to North Pole, apparently. What did he do there?

Juanita: Right. Dad went to work at Eielson, and eventually, after several years of working at Eielson, became the chief Civil Engineer. We also, during that time, my mother had a couple of restaurants, one in North Pole, one at 16-mile.

Jim: How long did your family live in North Pole?

Juanita: Well, Mom and Dad lived there until they bought Sourdough Roadhouse in about 1967, just about flood time.

Jim: Just about the time to move. We've got a call, Juanita. Hi, you're on the air with Juanita Helms.

Caller: What's Juanita's maiden name?

Juanita: Lauesen

Caller: Lauesen. OK, I was just wondering. I've lived up here so many years, but I never did know your maiden name.

Juanita: Yes. It's spelled Lauesen. So it's the Scandinavian Lauesen.

Caller: Oh, yes. I was trying to think. I knew somebody that was connected with a restaurant. My husband was the business agent for the Culinary union, here in Fairbanks, for 11 years. And of course that name Lauesen rings a bell. But that's all I wanted to know. Keep up the good work, Juanita.

Juanita: Thank you.

Jim: That was a nice call, Juanita. Tell us about the restaurant.

Juanita: Oh, the restaurant. Well, my mother had one restaurant in North Pole, and then one at 16-mile. The one at 16-mile she was running for Jack Parks. I don't know how many people remember Jack. He was a partner, I believe, with Pete, that had the junkyard at 6-mile. He and Jack were partners for many years. And Jack had Mom run his restaurant for him. It was an interesting time, and Jack was an interesting person.

Jim: What was the name of the restaurant?

Juanita: 16-mile Cafe was what it was called.

Jim: We have a call, Juanita. Hi, welcome to Alaska Gold Trails, You're on the air with Juanita Helms.

Caller: Hi. What a delightful show. Hello Mrs. Helms. This is one of your fans. Believe it or not, I'm ashamed to say it, this is the one time that you've kept my attention. I really have enjoyed it. And don't forget, now, you've given out the kids. Now next in line is that worried little dog of yours.

Juanita: Oh, that's right.

Caller: We've got to mention that fella.

Juanita: That's right. I forgot a member of the family.

Caller: This is a great show and I've enjoyed it.

Juanita: Thanks.

Jim: We've got a couple of minutes left here and we have a call. Hi, welcome to Alaska Gold Trails, you're on the air with Juanita Helms.

Caller: Ask her if she knows the name of the miner that she knew in Kantishna, when she was in the park, as a child.

Juanita: Yes. That was Johnny Bouchet.

Caller: Yes, that's who I thought. There wasn't another miner in there at that time, was there?

Juanita: Not anybody that I remember visiting. I think Johnny was the last of them at that time.

Caller: Yeah, my Dad went in there, but I couldn't remember just what year he went in.

Juanita: Oh, OK.

Caller: Yeah, I was just curious.

Juanita: OK.

Jim: Thank you for the call. And we were there with Mom, she was running the restaurant, and again, when did Bud move down to Sourdough.

Juanita: Sourdough was 1967. Actually, Dad was still working at Eielson for several years after that. My mother and my older brother Raymond ran the lodge, and then Dad would drive down every weekend and work during the weekend, then come back.

Jim: As I understood it, from many of the people that I talked to along the roadway, the lodge got quite a reputation for having excellent pies. I used to teach mining courses in Glenellen and Valdez, and I would make weekly trips back and forth from Fairbanks, as an extension instructor out of the University of Alaska. I would teach a month at each town. And so, I'd make four or five trips, or up to eight trips a year through there, and I'd always stop there with Bud and we'd chat about rocks and mining and whatever else he wanted to talk about. He had, of course, a big lapidary and rock shop where he worked on a lot of slabbing material and polishing material and so forth, and of course, we had a lot in common in that respect. I'll never forget the time that I'd been running back and forth there for a couple of years, you know, and one day I was sitting in there having a piece of pie and a cup of coffee with him, and he said, "You know, Jim," he says, "We sell gas here too." So from then on I tried to gauge myself so that I'd be sure and fill up with gas at Bud's Sourdough Lodge.

Juanita: Quite a salesman.

Jim: Yeah, that's all he had to say to me, and I made it a point. It just didn't dawn on me that I should be stopping there for gas. I was always looking forward to the pie and coffee.

Juanita: That's great.

Jim: Well, Juanita, he moved down there, and he stayed there right up until the time he died, didn't he.

Juanita: Right. He had sold the lodge a couple of years before. He just died last October. But he still had his Rocks and Relics Shop, and he was still, as he called it, the Chief Relic.

Jim: Juanita, you've had an interesting life here, and I hope someday that we can get together again, maybe recap some of the same thoughts that we've had here, and perhaps talk in detail about Bud and his activities in Alaska.

Juanita: I'd like that.

Jim: When were you voted mayor of the North Star Borough?

Juanita: 1985.

Jim: You ran again and you were successful a second time.

Juanita: Last year. Right.

Jim: And are you pretty well satisfied with the way things are going?

Juanita: Well, I think it's like any big company. Things could go better in some areas, and in some ways I think we're doing very well.

Jim: You always have an open door policy, don't you.

Juanita: Right.

Jim: Juanita, thank you very much for sharing this time with us today.

Juanita: Thank you, Jim.

Duke Kilbury

With

Jim Madonna

Special Interview at Ketchikan, Alaska
February 16, 1988

Jim: We're here today, in Ketchikan, Alaska, conducting a private Alaska Gold Trails interview with Duke Kilbury. Duke, tell us the year and where you were born. Also give us a little background regarding the attraction that drew you to Alaska.

Duke: I was born in Spokane, Washington, on the 24th of October, nineteen hundred and eleven. My family moved to Bellingham in 1919. I went through high school there, got out of high school and had a chance to come to Alaska on a trolling boat in 1929.

Jim: You summed that up very clearly and precisely. Did you work on the trolling boat?

Duke: No, I just hitchhiked a ride on it because I wanted to come to Alaska. That first year I worked in a sawmill for awhile, then I shipped out on the Lighthouse Tender "*Cedar*".

Jim: Was that here in Ketchikan?

Duke: In Ketchikan, yes, and I went out to Westford on the tender for the summer, serviced the lighthouses, came back that fall, and Alaska appealed to me to the point where I made it my home, although in the winter time, when there was no work, I would go south and sail in maritime. Then I would come back every spring and work. Ya know, one winter I got off a ship in San Francisco and I went up into Virginia City, Nevada, and went to work in a mine, and that was the beginning of my experience in mining.

Jim: Was that the Comstock Lode country?

Duke: Yeah, that's correct. I was in the Overman Shaft, and I got hurt up there and went back down to San Francisco, and it was time to come back to Alaska anyway, so I headed back north again. In 1936 I bought a little trolling boat and I never left again until the war. And then I was gone for four years in the service. Got back and worked a couple of years and finally went up into the Unuk country and started my mining career.

Jim: The Unuk country, now where's that located?

Duke: The Unuk River is on the mainland in back of Revilla [Revillagigedo] Island, comes down out of Canada.

Jim: This must be very close to the border then.

Duke: It is. Yes, I staked 10 claims just below the border on the American side, and I worked in there for three years. And Kenny Ikener of Temsco Helicopters was bringing me out, the fall of '69, and suggested that I should look at the Sulphurets country up in Canada. And so he flew me up there that fall with Bruce Johnstone, who had mined up there in the early '30s and was familiar with that country. So Bruce flew up with me, and I looked it over, done some sampling, and immediately staked a claim. In 1970 I built my cabin up there and I have been there ever since.

Jim: Did you let the 10 claims that you had on the Unuk go?

Duke: Yes, I dropped them, because there's lots of fine gold there but it's very difficult to recover.

Jim: Are all these placer deposits?

Duke: Yes, placer deposits. I prospected the Unuk from Burroughs Bay to the Canadian border, and there's no place along that river that you don't get some sign of values, although some are better than the others. The area I staked was just below the border and had pretty good showing, ya know. The assay on it was very good. But up where I was, it was all fine gold. Where I am now you get coarse gold, so you know it's near the hard rock source.

Jim: If you were going to relate some prospecting techniques to people, and the method that you used to make your discovery, what step-by-step procedure would you suggest for people prospecting in an alpine area such as yours with very steep slopes?

Duke: The Sulphurets and Mitchell Creeks where I'm located are glacier streams. In the summertime, it gets real hot up there just like it does in the Interior, and the runoff is terrific, and there is a lot of fast water. But right at the U.S.-Canada border, it opens up into a valley, and that's where I am located. The river slows down there and drops out the gold and other heavy minerals.

Jim: That's one of the key points, then, where the mechanical energy of the river decreases, it's going to drop the load, and that's a good place to check.

Duke: That's correct. Above there, in past years, the glaciers off of Mitchell Creek and McTagg Creek have expanded and come clear down into that valley, and when they receded, they left five alluvial benches up on a mountain, and I have prospected the first two benches, and got some real good results from them, and have gold, although it's awful hard to work, because of the big boulders deposited by the ice. In 1930 to '35 there was a syndicate on this property, and one of the fellows that was associated with it was Stan Bishop. And Stan, in his spare time, would snipe up on these benches under big boulders, and he had some real nice results. I worked over some of the ground that Stan had opened up, and I still get good results out of it. Under one big boulder, I took out 57 ounces.

Jim: That is amazing. Your suggestion to prospectors then would be to look around the big boulders because they are a good accumulation point for the gold?

Duke: That's correct. Around the base of those big boulders is where fast water has been in time past and it drops the gold off on the eddy (down stream) side of those boulders, and a lot of it will hang up under the front side because its jammed right into the pocket, you know. If you can move those boulders why you're going get some results out of it.

Jim: How did you move those boulders, Duke?

Duke: Well, the big ones, why you drill them and shoot them and/or if the ground is right, you undermine one side of them, and you can use a jack and roll them over in some cases. You can't do it all the time, but if the ground is just right you can do that. Any stream with large boulders, work the eddy side of them, or down along the sides where the eddies would occur. That's where you'll find your gold.

Jim: Good information. Is there any other little tips you might give us, Duke?

Duke: Well, where there are natural rock dikes, you know, depending just how they're sloped. You get on the downstream side of them where you get an eddy. Any time you can find an area where there's a slowing of the water, in a fast stream, it is a likely spot for gold to be deposited.

Jim: I see. So look for the slowing of the water.

Duke: That's correct.

Jim: Let's get back to some of the experiences that you had when you came to Alaska. When did you get married, Duke?

Duke: Well, I got married right after I got out of the service in 1945. I had my discharge on the 26th of October, right after my birthday, and I was married on the 7th of November.

Jim: You didn't waste much time did you? Was your wife an Alaskan lady or was she from Outside?

Duke: No, she was from Outside. I met her when I was back on leave in '44. I was introduced to her. I just met her twice, and then we corresponded the rest of the time I was in the service. When I got out of the service we got married. We've been married 43 years, this fall.

Jim: What's your age today, Duke?

Duke: I'm 76.

Jim: You're 76 years old, and it sounds like you love Alaska.

Duke: I wouldn't be any place else.

Jim: Have you spent most of your time here at Ketchikan?

Duke: Yes, other than going to Westford, and then I went up and worked on the Trans Alaska Pipeline too. Yeah, I was up at Valdez. I worked on the Pipeline up there as a carpenter boss.

Jim: And, how long did you work there, Duke?

Duke: I just worked one session, 13 weeks. Then I come back on my break, they were putting in this Loran station down below here, and I went to work down there for the same money I was getting up there, and I was home every night. So, I stayed right here.

Jim: You've also done a lot of carpentry work around here, and you've got quite a reputation for your masonry work.

Duke: Well, cement finisher, I've done lots of cement work, and I've built a lot of houses too. And I worked for a construction outfit that was a local one here for 19 years, McGillery Brothers. In 1966, why, I broke off and went contracting on my own. And in the wintertime, why I'd do that, and in the summertime, why, I'd go mining.

Jim: Duke, when did you start your mining activity here around the Ketchikan area?

Duke: Actually, I started prospecting the river in 1966.

Jim: Well, you're very close to the molybdenite deposit owned by U.S. Borax. Did you have any knowledge of that molybdenite deposit prior to their coming in and working it over?

Duke: A little bit. Bill Huff, who was a professional prospector here, was doing some work down in the Behm Canal area. And there's a creek down there, I don't know what the name of it is, but Bill found molybdenum there. He knew the area had molybdenum in it, ya know, but the Quartz Hill Deposit I think was known about a long time ago. Nigger Watson, who was an old, old timer here, covered this whole country. I mean you can find his sign just about anywhere from the Graham Duke area in Canada to down there in the Quartz Hill area and clear up around Annette. This man was all over this country, and he would find something and keep going.

Jim: Can you give us some details about this fellow. He seems to be quite an adventurous prospector.

Duke: Oh, he is a legend, that man. What I have learned about him has been primarily hearsay from people that knew him personally. There's a few people that really knew him. Tom McQuillan, who is a Canadian and was very active in this area for over 60 years, knew Nigger Watson personally. He told me about him, merely saying that there's very little of this country Watson hadn't covered, but he was the kind of a man that would find something and then just move on and look for something else. He never really cared whether he mined or not, he was just interested in finding the stuff.

Jim: So prospecting was an end in itself for Nigger Watson, is that right?

Duke: That's right.

Jim: Did you ever hear of any significant finds that he made?

Duke: Well, to my knowledge, he was the first person to discover the big copper deposit at Frank Mackay Glacier in Canada. There's was also some gold and silver mixed in it. That country back there is just fantastic as far as minerals. Tom McQuillan told me a lot about Nigger Watson.

Jim: Is Tom still around?

Duke: Oh, Tom is 87 now. He was partners with me in the Daly property which is a silver deposit up there. And Tom has properties up around Mackay Lakes and down on Gracey Creek and different areas. Plus, the fact he and I had the Daly property for awhile, which we've let go because it is a low-grade silver deposit and too expensive to operate.

Jim: Can you give us a little more detail about Tom McQuillan's life?

Duke: Well, Tommy was head of the syndicate that had property that I'm on up there in Sulphurets and Mitchell Creek in 1930. The group that was affiliated with him was Stan Bishop and Ken Sampson and Ray Rhody and there was one other one; I can't remember what his name was. But anyway, they mined that area for five years. But, in those days, the only way they could get any supplies or anything else in was by backpack. And it was a tough, tough trip, and they'd get in there, and by the time they got in there in June, and then they'd have June and July, and by the latter part of August, they'd have to get out of there because if they got snowed in, they'd be trapped.

Jim: It seems that McQuillan was a prospector and miner. Where'd he come from?

Duke: Well McQuillan came from Vancouver. But he was well-known around Ketchikan too, because he did a lot of prospecting around here. Juan Manoza and him were affiliated in some properties out here, and Juan Manoza's here now. He's living over on Prince of Wales Island. And, I think on the Harris River—he's got some properties over there he's messing around with. Juan Manoza would be an interesting man for you to talk to because he's prospected all the way from Alaska to South

America, down through Mexico—spent lots of time in Mexico. Very interesting man. And one of the other people that you should meet is Kenny Ikner.

Jim: Tell us about Bill Huff. I met him, oh, must have been ten years ago.

Duke: Well, Bill, Angus Lily, and Hawkin were professional prospectors, and Kenny would move them around to different grounds with his helicopter, and they would do the prospecting and Kenny'd supply 'em.

Jim: He was in charge of the transportation?

Duke: That's right, and Kenny liked to do a little rock busting himself, ya know. They have a property up on what they call the Whistlepig, which is up in back of Virginia Lake in the Wrangell Mountains there. That's a very good one. That's a silver deposit, and up on the Bradfield. They did a lot of work up in the Bradfield country. Angus Lily will be going in any time now. He's the only one left; Hawkin died and so did Bill.

Jim: Where was Bill from, do you know?

Duke: Well, Bill was a retired Army major. He was a Army engineer.

Jim: When did he come to Ketchikan?

Duke: Well, I think right after the war. I didn't meet Bill until sometime later. I met Bill about, oh around about 1960.

Jim: Was he a prospector at that time?

Duke: Yeah. He's been working with Kenny and them, and they have covered a lot of ground. Now the big companies—Union Carbide for instance—were interested in nickel at one time, and Bill prospected the Lake Creek country, up the Unuk and then he went up into Thomas Bay above Petersburg. Then, he went from Cape Spencer to Yakutat, and he did find quite a big nickel deposit up along that coast there. And Bill covered an awful lot of country, but Kenny would spot him and then he would work from the base camp.

Jim: So he did make some significant discoveries.

Duke: Yes, he did. Bill was also the one who pointed me to certain areas of the Unuk. Because he prospected a lot of the Unuk himself. So, Bill pointed me that way too. Well, the only way that you can make any progress here is talk to people who've been there. Until I could break free after raising my family, I had to depend on somebody else to point me in the right direction you see. And I had a lot of friends who helped me out.

Jim: Well Duke, you said that you had not only this gold property you're working currently, but you also had a silver discovery. Have you had any other discoveries that were promising?

Duke: I don't know how extensive it is, but on the lower canyon of the Unuk, there's a ridge, and on the back side of that ridge there's a pretty good copper deposit. How extensive it is, I don't know. All I know is, it's there. And, up around Blue Lake, I spent a few days up there. There's a creek up there that has a little color. I didn't go clear up on the ridges to find out where it's coming from, but it's breaking loose from somewhere up there.

Jim: So, that's an area that you still want to look into?

Duke: Well, the one I would really like to go up into is the Porcupine, in the Upper Stikine country, but I don't think that I'll make it. I'm getting too far along to take on such a large project.

Jim: The area you are speaking about should not be confused with the Porcupine out of Haines?

Duke: That's right.

Jim: Duke, one of the questions that I commonly ask my friends is, have you had some exciting experiences or a memorable moment that you might like to tell us about?

Duke: Yes. Yes. I had a dandy about four years ago. My ground where I am working, or my pit, is about 400 feet from my cabin, and I was coming from the pit; just about dusk. I have a stack of empty gas drums along the trail there, and I was right down by them and I heard a snort, and I knew what it was right away—a big grizzly—and I was less than 30 feet from him. Well, I had my rifle with me, but he was close enough I'd maybe have one shot. However, he went away from me, so I shot over him to speed him up. I didn't want to kill him. And he went down, crossed the river and stopped on the other side and spun around. I thought if he was coming back, I could beat him to the cabin. But I shot over him again, and he went off into the brush.

Jim: Those big fellows always put the adrenaline into your system, don't they?

Duke: And he was a big fellow. In all the years I'd been up in that valley, about five years ago is when I first saw him; he's moved in there. Oh, he's a beautiful bear. I wouldn't kill him unless I had to. He is a big fellow, yeah he's a big-un, but I leave him alone. They don't bother nothing. I burn all my garbage; there's nothing for them to forage in, so they don't bother me.

Jim: Tell us about getting slung in by helicopter.

Duke: That was for the Daly property. A Vancouver Island Helicopter boy, Usta was his name, was working with an exploration drill crew working up above me, and they used to come down to my camp and take showers. I've got over a thousand paperbacks up there in my library, and they'd borrow books from me. But, Usta flew me down to the river. I wanted to put up a helicopter pad up by the portal on this Daly property, which is over 700 feet up on a side of the cliff there, and in order to get tools up there, I'd have to pack about three miles over some tough country. So, I talked to Usta about it, and he brought a net, and we sat down on a river bar and got everything ready. I got all of my tools and my chainsaw in there, and the morning he was changing the drill crews, he got them moved, and he flew me down there along with their cook from the camp. She took the pictures. They loaded me in the net, with my tools, and he picked me up over a thousand feet and then dropped me down through the trees, and I told him I'd have the pad ready that night, and I did. He come down, landed up there and picked me up.

Jim: Riding in the net must have been an exciting experience.

Duke: Oh, it was kind of fun, ya know. I got pictures of it from the time he picked me up in the net 'til I'm way up there.

Jim: Are there any other experiences that might have been particularly exciting or memorable to you?

Duke: Yeah, down on the Lower River, the oldest boy was with me in late fall. I had an A-frame with my donkey on it and my drag-line outfit, and they had about four or five inches of wet snow, and then it turned off and rained. That Unuk River is a treacherous son-of-a-gun anyway, and that river rose over seven feet there, in just a few hours. I mean, it just come right up to the point where it was clear up around my drag line and A-frame. It came up and covered the logs on the skids, then it slacked off. But, for a while I was pretty worried. I sat up all night long watching. It was a wild river and that's a big bottom in there, and she was water, mountain to mountain.

Jim: Thought you were just about to go downstream did you?

Duke: Well, we would've been, alright, but I was close to losing all my equipment, and that wasn't fun.

Jim: That is something people should be aware of. For a variety of reasons, rivers in Alaska can rise very fast.

Duke: That's right.

Jim: And you should build your structure high enough to be safe

Duke: Be safe, yeah. That's why the cabin on the lower river is up on pilings. The floor of the cabin is a good eight feet up, and that was for bear, because there's lots of bear walking up and down the river there. I had built that cabin up on pilings, and I got a ladder up onto the porch, which we pull up every night. Because I wouldn't like to wake up with a bear's bad breath in my nose.

Jim: What a frightening experience that would be. Duke, is there anything else that you can think of that your friends might like to know about or that might be interesting to the public?

Duke: Well, my friends could tell you a lot of stories. Bruce Johnstone could tell a lot of stories. Bruce is a good friend of mine, but he's prone to elaborate his stories to a point where he stretches a little bit.

Jim: You think so? I thought that was standard for all the old-timers, to stretch their stories a little bit.

Duke: Well, yeah, that's true. The things that I've told here are just basic things which have happened. I've had an incident up there. To get power, ya know, diesel fuel, I got a hundred gallons of fuel flown in from Stewart. Cost me $1,088, so it's expensive fuel. Well, I got to thinking, I got a good stream there, so I spent a month, and I stuck a couple of logs out over the river and built a deck on it, and I built a ten-foot water wheel to power a generator. Well, the day I put her in the water, the whole drill camp come down and took pictures, and I have pictures of it there. It's quite a deal.

Jim: Still operating?

Duke: No, it was a stationary wheel, and when that river's high, big boulders roll down it and keep knocking the blades off.

Jim: Oh, I see.

Duke: So I designed a float wheel on a counterbalance, so that as the river rises, it rises, and when the river goes down, it goes down see? And then the fins only draw the water. I bought a 20-kilowatt generator to take in, and then I'll have electricity for powering my pumps, ya know. I have a generator up there for lights for the cabin. I have a big cabin—I mean a big one. There's over 1,100 feet of floor space there, hot and cold running water, gas range for cooking, electric lights, the whole works.

Jim: All the conveniences.

Duke: Way back in the bush.

Jim: An unbelievable bush camp.

Duke: I like my comfort.

Jim: I guess you do. Do you use a drag line to mine with?

Duke: Yeah, I have a little 5/8-yard bucket, and a two-drum donkey. On good days I can move oh, maybe up to 30 or 40 yards in a day. I have a grizzly to screen out big rock, and about 100 feet of sluice.

Jim: And what kind of recovery do you get out of that?

Duke: Well, I have a set of good riffles in there, of angle iron. Then, I have this expanded metal with a corduroy blanket under it to catch the fine stuff. The recovery is good on it, real good. Not too much gets by that.

Jim: Is it a single-channel sluice?

Duke: Yeah, it's single channel sluice.

Jim: And what do you think the ground runs per yard?

Duke: Well, down on the bottom now, it'll run probably oh, anywhere from about 15 to 18, 20 dollars a yard.

Jim: Oh, that high? That's good ground.

Duke: Yeah, it is. After I got down to it. But I had to go through over 20 feet of overburden to get there. A lot of hard digging.

Jim: Do you work it alone, Duke?

Duke: Yeah, I work it alone.

Jim: You don't have anybody up there with you? Could that be a little bit dangerous? If you got hurt or something, you wouldn't have anybody around.

Duke: Well, that's true enough, but I have a radio. If I can get to it, why, they'll come check me out. But, when I'm up there alone I check into Temsco everyday, and if they don't hear from me for a day or two, they'll come looking. So they kind of keep an eye on me.

Jim: That's good. You have a safety system worked out.

Duke: And the Vancouver Island Helicopter boys are at Stewart [Island]. They also stop in there if they're back in that country. They always stop and have a cup of coffee and a little conversation.

Jim: Well, tell us. You haven't been in for a couple of years because you've been building a house. Do you plan to go in next summer?

Duke: Oh, I'll be going in about the end of April or the first week in May.

Jim: How long will you stay in there, Duke?

Duke: Well, this year I'll be staying until the snow flies, and that can happen anywhere from oh, late September 'till November.

Jim: That's a long five months in there all alone.

Duke: Oh, I've done it before.

Jim: Yeah, it's a good life, isn't it?

Duke: Oh sure, and when you're busy all the time, I don't pay any attention to the time.

Jim: Well good. It has all been very interesting Duke. Thank you for the very enjoyable interview.

Duke: You're welcome, Jim.

Don May
with
Jim Madonna
November 20, 1987

Jim: Welcome to Alaska Gold Trails, Don. I understand we are going to talk about mining and frontier adventure, is that right?

Don: Yes, Jim, that's right. But first, I want to make a comment to the audience. Jim takes us young fellas and he instructs us up at the University, and then he sends us out in the field to go prospecting and mining. And then we gotta come in and buy things, and then we go to his wife's store. And now I see him on the radio station here. He's sitting over there and he's cheering us on. So Jim, I'll tell ya, you're a man of many talents, and it's an honor to be here today. I didn't know just what was in store, but I appreciate being here today. It's enjoyable to sit up here and maybe put in a little plug for our industry.

Jim: Well, Don, I think we grew up together in this industry, beginning back in probably 1973, if I'm not mistaken. You took a class from me at the University of Alaska Mining Extension. But before getting into that, Don, let's talk for just a moment about what brought you to Alaska and some of the activities that you took part in when you first came to the state. Where were you from originally, Don?

Don: Well, Jim, I came up from North Carolina in 1950. I had wanted to come to Alaska for a long time. It was the frontier glamour that attracted a lot of young fellows I grew up with. I had an Alaska bug and still had it when I went into the service in 1948. I just turned 18, when I left home and went in the service, and it was kind of interesting because you know how it is after basic training. You have three choices, and I put all three of them as Alaska, and of course, the way the Army does things, they kept me in South Carolina, and that just intensified my desire to come here. So as soon as I got out of the service I left for Alaska. I arrived here in July of 1950. The Korean War had just begun and Fairbanks was a beehive of activity, except on the particular day we got here the whole town seemed to be on strike and men were standing around looking for work. And so we decided to go on to Circle, and our adventures really began from that point. This was pretty much my idea of coming to a country that was new, had a lot of opportunities, a lot of adventures. And I'll tell you, Jim, it has not disappointed me, as far as adventure is concerned. I've had it to the full ever since I've been here.

Jim: When you came your primary objective was to take advantage of the frontier activities that were available here in Alaska, including trapping, fishing and mining, is that correct?

Don: That's correct Jim, and like I said, you know we talk about it being a frontier, of course that's well overdone. We're all well aware of that, and there were old timers around who had been right here from the very beginning, and you'd see em around town and these were men who had been here 40 and 50 years, and they were just living out their last days. We would sit around and listen to some of them talk. It was very very interesting. I think of some of the old timers—Mr. Nordale, Fred Parker (father of Carl Parker), and the list just goes on and on, of old timers. And I could sit down and talk to them and they were very congenial people and they would tell you some of the stories and things that happened when this country first opened up, right at the turn of the century, and the hardships they had to face. And, of course, a lot of the records are in the archives, where they should be. History that shouldn't be lost, because these are the people that helped blaze this country, and the reason Fairbanks is here is because it was a mining town. And Fairbanks, of course, has always been a mining town, but times are changing.

Jim: What was the first activity that you launched into when you arrived here in Fairbanks and the Interior of Alaska, Don?

Don: Well, of course we came to Fairbanks looking for adventure and we were willing to accept things as they worked out day by day. We got up to Circle and we—I say "we", because there was another fellow I grew up with who had accompanied me—we were both 20 at the time. And we put in a little collapsible canoe, a Kalamazoo Canoe. And we floated down the Yukon, and our thoughts were, "well, we can certainly paddle back up." But boy we found out otherwise; it takes a mighty strong arm to be able to paddle against that current. So we wound up in Fort Yukon, and there was a forest fire going on at the time, and they pressed all the available young fellows into work, and next thing we knew we were out there on the fire lines. Now, of course, it was considered an emergency, and nobody got paid for that. It was just expected for you to get out there and work. Well, we ran across a fellow there by the name of Jerry Revard, and he had an old boat, and he said he was going to go back up to Circle and he was looking for a couple of deckhands. If we'd be interested in caulking the boat we could get passage. So, it took us five days to go 90 miles, coming back up the river. It was so slow going, it was unbelievable. But he had a trapline over on Birch Creek, and next thing we knew we were over there in August of 1950, and our adventures were really beginning from that point on.

Jim: And that's where you really started the Alaskan experience, right there on Birch Creek?

Don: That's correct, Jim.

Jim: Give us a rundown on just what you did out there on Birch Creek, Don.

Don: Well, Jim, we tried to live off the country, and that's a pretty rough way to try and do it, I'll tell you. We had taken in provisions with us, what we could afford. I think, if I remember, we had about $8 in our pocket when we went in that fall. 'Course you have $8 when you come out in the spring, and we were pretty lean and mean by the time we got out of there in the spring. Now we did have access to Circle Hot Springs there. I don't remember what the mileage was. It would take a full day of breaking trail. There was no snow machines. We couldn't afford a dog team. So everything had to be snowshoed to wherever we were going, with a pack on our back. So we would get down to the hot springs once a month, first for a bath, a shower, a dip in the nice pleasant waters there, and pick up our mail. And Mrs. Leach was the postmistress. I'll always remember. She was the old Alaskan style. She and her husband had pioneered that hot springs up there right after the turn of the century. And very congenial nice folks, you know. "Come on in, boys, have a cup of coffee or a cup of cocoa and some cookies," you know, and after what we'd been facing for the previous month it was always so much of a relief to come in and spend time there. But I would never advise anybody to go out and try to live off the country, Jim. It's a hard thing to do. We ate all the squirrels that were in the trees. We ate all the porcupines that were around, and we had some moose there. We ate three moose that we had, and we were just continually hungry.

Jim: What were the experiences that you had on Birch Creek in terms of living off the land? What did you do to generate money when the wintertime was over?

Don: Well, we had a trapline, and of course everybody thinks, well, you go out in the hills and there's a lot of fur out there. But boy, it sure wasn't. I remember we had about 12-1500 miles of snowshoeing under our feet and we wound up with about 14 marten and several weasel, and that was about it. We weren't set up for beaver trapping. You had to have a special setup for that, and so that was the extent of seven months out there. And like I say, it's a very hungry country. Before we went in though in the fall, we'd run across some ground up on Ketchum Creek. We'd gone on over there. There was no need to set up any claims as such. Some of the other old timers said, "Just go on up there." There was a fork up there. That's ground that Joe Vogler has had now for a number of years. This was before Joe had it. So we set up a box and we started producing there, and this was hand shoveling now, mind you, and at $35 gold, or gold that was anywhere from about $28 to $31 an ounce in value. We started shoveling the yards through by hand and after you get eight or ten yards through a box like that in a day's time, your hands start getting those old blisters and you start thinking there's gotta be an easier way to make a living. I remember my partner, Joe, came back to town and worked for about three weeks on construction that fall, and I continued to hold the area out there, and he did right well on construction. A guy would make a buck and a half to two bucks an hour here in Fairbanks, and that was a good wage, so we were able to keep going, but again it was the experiences that we picked up that winter that I have held with me to this day, because if things start getting easy for me, all I gotta do is start remembering the harder times like that and it shakes me right out of it, out of that lethargy. And I think it's good for everybody to have to experience severe hardships in their life somewhere, so that they can always go back and say, "I don't want to go back to that. It might have been a good experience at the time, but there's better things out ahead."

Jim: Just how well did you prosper from that full winter's worth of work. Just how much revenue did you gather from your trapping and mining experiences that first year here in Alaska?

Don: Jim, it was very poor. I remember, it was in the spring, and we knew that F.E. Company would be hiring young fellas. This was up in March. The mail plane would come by Circle Hot Springs every week, and we finally decided we'd close the trapline down and head to Fairbanks. Wien had the weekly mail run up there. And it was a big old Norseman. So we came in and of course we had no money to pay for our airfare in, so they asked us to leave all our stuff there while we took our furs uptown to John Swagler. He was the fur buyer at the Nordale Hotel. So we spread out our whole winter supply of fur on the bed there and he made an offer to us, and of course it wasn't enough, and we had to haggle a little bit, and he finally met our price. It was about $200 for these marten, and we took it back out, and we had a few dollars after we'd paid off our airfare to get to Fairbanks. So that's about the extent of it. We had enough to stay in town for a few days and to look for a job, and I remember we had gone to Al Seeliger. He was the man that was in charge at F.E. Co., on Illinois Street there, and Al was very congenial and he said, "Yes, they would be looking for some young fellows like us," but it would be awhile before they could hire us. Meantime, we picked up a job with P.K. up at Murphy Dome. Murphy Dome was just in the building stages and we went to work up there and we were actually getting 25 cents an hour more. I remember that. And all the food you could eat. And you never seen a couple of chow hounds like us. We really put the weight on. From there we went into another adventure, after we had saved $1,000. We went down along the coast to

Cordova. And that was another long story. We wound up on a salvage ship and went out to Cape Newenham, and a whole long list of adventures happened during that trip. But, then again, it was all part of the overall frontier experience. Good things for young fellas to go through, but I would never care to go through them again.

Jim: When you came back to Fairbanks, did you go into business for yourself, prior to launching into the gold mining business full time?

Don: Oh yes, Jim. I came back to town, and just like a lot of fellows in Fairbanks, you're not really sure what you want to do, or what you want to get into. I started to work for Standard Oil over there, about 1954, I believe it was. I'd been in the ice cream business, too, before then, and worked for Mrs. Hill and Mort Cass. I can't hardly remember their names now. They used to have the old Alaska Market about where the Woolworth building is now on Cushman Street there. And they had a warehouse down on 219 1/2 Wendell Street, called the Broken Arms Apartment, 'cause you fall down the steps you were sure to break your arm. But it was very interesting, because these were a lot of old time pioneers and they owned a lot of the ground around town. It was most interesting dealing with these fine people.

Jim: What type of sluice box do you have in your gold mining operation today?

Don: We have three of them, three plants. I purchased those from Hector's Welding, out at North Pole. We had some boxes that we'd gotten from him, and they were nice, but then, just like everybody, you get different ideas, so we went back to Hector's with our ideas and he said, "Sure, we'll custom make them for you," and that's just exactly what he did. He went ahead and he built two of these. We called them flush boxes because they were high volume. There was a good price tag tacked to them, but I'll tell you, they sure paid for themselves fast.

Jim: When you first entered the mining industry full scale, it was about 1972, wasn't it?

Don: Yeah, Jim, I had always been interested in mining, of course, from those first days up here, and never was able to get my weight into it because of raising a good sized family—three sons and three daughters here. Kept my nose pretty much to the grindstone just to put food on the table each month. Finally there came a day when we were willing to take a risk, and I went in with another fellow on some claims right up here at Ester Dome. We worked the arm for about four years. And I would compare that experience to a college education any day. I learned a great deal up there on that hill, digging holes and working underground. Again, it was something that we did not come out on, and many times I was ready to give up, but again it was just hanging in there, day-by-day, year-by-year sort of thing. About 1978 I gave up on that and we picked up a lay on some ground down in the Richardson area. We got a lease from a gentleman by the name of Gil Monroe. From that point things started turning around for us. We actually started getting some gold for a change, and that was a big encouragement to us after all those years.

Jim: Now this was placer mining, was it Don?

Don: This was placer mining, but it was high up on a ridge, and other people had tried down in the creeks over the years, and there had been a long succession of failures. We had our chance at it, and we were either going to succeed or fail, plain and simple.

Jim: This particular type of placer deposit that we are speaking about wasn't the kind that you would find directly in the stream then. It was up on the hill and probably associated with the original ore deposit or the lode veins.

Don: That's correct Jim.

Jim: What was the character of your gold there? Was it coarse, reflecting the source area?

Don: Some of it was very coarse. Some of it was residual gold of course, and then others had been hammered and fairly flat. But, consistently, it was chunky porous gold. A lot of it, of course, was formed right in place. It would be formed right in the schist. So we'd have all sorts of contortions and beautiful designs in the gold, and when we were selling that gold here in Fairbanks years ago, the jewelers liked it because it was a nice unique type of gold. It was low-grade as far as gold was concerned. It was running anywhere from 640 to about 690 on the fineness. You could call it almost 14 carat gold, because there's so much silver in it.

Jim: That's called electrum then, isn't it.

Don: That's right. So people would ask are we gold miners, and if we wanted to get technical, no, we were electrum miners.

Jim: Don, there were some stories early on that led up to the discovery of that area and there were some successful mining ventures that took place in the streams that drained that particular mountain system. Could you give us some information on those?

Don: Well, of course that was called the Tenderfoot Mining District, and that started in 1904. It was very interesting. How it ever got its name, we're not really sure. Of course, Fairbanks came into being in 1902—1903, and a stampede started here, and a lot of miners would be coming through from Valdez. They would come right through the Richardson area there, and a lot of these were tenderfeet, tenderfoot, and that may have possibly lent emphasis to the name because a lot of these guys were getting their first taste of mining, and they were tenderfeet when they arrived in the area, and they would mine there, and then they'd realize that there had to be an easier way to mine, and they would go on to Fairbanks.

Jim: Did they make any big cleanups out of those streams at all?

Don: Yes, on Tenderfoot there. That was always considered the Million Dollar Mile, and that was on $20 gold. There was some very rich claims there. It was deep, and of course, that gold was mined out years ago. And now the highway runs right over the top of those tailing piles as you come down off the ridge. It's about 82-83 miles from Fairbanks on the Richardson Highway.

Jim: How long did you work in the Tenderfoot area, Don?

Don: We were there about three to four years. I can't remember now, Jim, 'cause we started pulling out of there just like we started phasing in. We had a number of claims that were on up Banner Creek and then on up into Democrat, where we took a lease from another party and worked one summer. It became a whole episode of different events. After we'd worked the ground out we had to decide one of two things. We were going to give up and get rid of all our machinery, or we were going to locate new ground. We decided to find new ground.

Jim: In mining the Tenderfoot area, you were up on a hill. How did you get the water to wash the gravel, or how did you process the gravel, Don?

Don: Well, it took us a couple of years to figure out the best way, Jim. We finally wound up with a pipeline that was 5,000 feet long, to get that water up on that ridgetop. This is, of course, where others had tried and were unable to come up with a successful plan. We needed about three quarters of a million gallons of water a day up there, so we relocated through the oldtimers ditches that were still there from the turn of the century. We brought water around from Banner Creek, and into Buckeye Creek, and ultimately to four large holding ponds, where our primary pump station was installed. We had a secondary pump station part way up the draw, in Hankley Gulch. From there, we piped the water clear to the ridgetop. One of my sons had an excellent idea for a flapper, using a piece of the Alaska pipeline. It worked out just beautiful. After every day's operation we'd let the water flow. The pumps would run all night to fill the upper ponds with water. We had a good system going. Mining engineers from the University would visit and appreciate what they would see. I just wish the thing could've gone on forever Jim, but that's not the nature of mining.

Jim: That's right. Sooner or later the ore reserves run out, don't they? Don, following your experience out there in the Tenderfoot area, you went into mining up in the Central Mining District of Alaska, off the Steese Highway, didn't you?

Don: Yeah, it was almost like going back home again, Jim. Ground that we had walked over and trapped over years before, now all those areas were claimed up, and it was just like we had missed a golden opportunity by not staking up a lot of that ground, but that's mining for you, so now if we were going to do any mining back in our old home turf there, we had to lease the ground from other people.

Jim: You then leased the ground and put in some pretty large equipment and mined efficiently and effectively.

Don: Well I guess so, Jim. We had about 22 people working for us there on Crooked Creek. We were going around the clock, seven days a week. We had five D-9s going and about three or four loaders going. We were producing and were real pleased to see the way things were going. Could never seem to quite get enough material moved, and then a D-10 became available, and we thought well, let's take a chance on that piece of machinery. And I'll tell you Jim, I have been a good fan of Caterpillar, but even more so when I saw what a D-10 is able to do.

Jim: On a couple of occasions when I visited your mines, Don, you have said that every placer miner in Alaska ought to have a good D-10. You seemed well satisfied with that piece of machinery. How long did you mine on Crooked Creek?

Don: We were there about two years, on Crooked Creek. Actually, production-wise, about five months. The gentleman that we leased the ground from thought we would be there eight to ten years, and of course it just wasn't that way at all, because we got into high gear and were able to go through it a lot faster. Also, we did not go all the way up the creek, because of the fault that went across the creek at an angle. It really changed things for us. And of course, people wonder why gold is where it is, and all these different factors, and you know Jim, after you get through mining an area you understand it so much better than you do before you go in.

Jim: I don't want to be too inquisitive, Don, but when you're mining with that much equipment, and we're talking now a D-10, and a couple of D-9s, and large sluicing equipment. This is no small endeavor. What are we talking about in terms of required gold recovery, just to pay for the equipment on site.

Don: Boy, Jim, that's a hard question to answer. These have always been things that we've struggled with over the years. You, of course, have a good cleanup, you look at all the bills you've got, you look at your payday. You know, most people say "Oh boy, I can hardly wait 'til payday comes around." But, when you get to be the employer, you dread payday, because if you're not producing enough, and it's a struggle, it seems like no matter what you do, you can't quite get enough to handle the bills. I guess this is just part of the curse that the miners are all under. You have to keep it in the family by staying mighty small, or you have to be large enough to cope with all the problems that are out there. And when you come down to a dollar and cents point on this thing, that is the real tickler. I know that you teach the economics of placer mining in classes up there at the University. It all comes down to one thing. If you're not making it, why waste your time out there.

Jim: Absolutely. Don, as the size of the equipment increases and the volume of gravels that you can process increases, what is perhaps the lower limit of values that a large mining operation can expect to retrieve out of say a cubic yard of gravel, dollars-and-cents-wise?

Don: All right, can I just go back a little bit and say what F.E. used to have to figure? What they'd figure, on $20 gold, they'd figure 10 cents a yard. Now this was on a large volume. Now that confuses a lot of people, but remember that the price of gold has gone up around 20 times. So we're looking at maybe $2.00 to $2.50 a yard material. I can't quite make it at $2.25 per yard. The F.E. Co. was extremely efficient, with the bucket dredges. We had a breakoff point figured at about $3.65 a yard on Crooked Creek. The ground wasn't too deep, running 12 to 14 feet to bedrock, and then we would take a foot or so of bedrock, depending on where the particular cut was. It became a high volume situation to see whether we could survive or not.

Jim: Since the Crooked Creek experience you have opened up several more mining operations. How many operations did you have last year?

Don: We had three operations going last year. We had two of the large boxes from Hector, and then a medium-sized box.

Jim: Next summer, you think that you'll probably be looking at two or more operations?

Don: Yeah, we may shrink it back down to two. It just gets to be too much for me to handle, and of course, my sons are excellently trained. They're the project managers on these creeks, and they hire and they fire their own men, and by now we've got all excellent personnel. We're still working right now, even this late in the winter (November).

Jim: I want to thank you for joining us on Alaska Gold Trails today, Don. We appreciate your willingness to share experiences with us. We have all learned a great deal and wish you the best of luck in future years.

Don: Thank you for inviting me, Jim.

Don Nelson
with
Jim Madonna
January 12, 1989

Jim: Welcome to Alaska Gold Trails ladies and gentlemen. Today, our guest is Don Nelson. Hello, Don, thank you for joining us.

Don: Good to join you here on the program today, Jim. We appreciate the opportunity to be with you and to participate in your program, and see what you've got to say.

Jim: Well, actually it's not what I have to say, Don, so much as what you have to say. We are interested in what happened to you before you came to Alaska—where you were born and what kind of environment you were raised in, and then we're going to take it a step farther, what brought you to Alaska, what was the magnetism that drew you up here to the cold frozen north country, and what are the activities that you have participated in since you came to Alaska? How's that for a start?

Don: I was born and raised in Minneapolis, Minnesota. Big city, really. Most of my younger life was spent right in the middle of the city, 1636 Hillside Ave. North, Minneapolis. And of course I went to the schools in that area. Then of course, during my training, or vocational training, I worked for the National Youth Administration, training for maintenance and rebuilding of aircraft. It was during that period of time that Northwest Airlines hired me to work up on the construction of the Alaskan Highway in 1942. So I took the job with Northwest, servicing aircraft. They were hauling supplies in to the construction camps along the Alaskan highway. I was stationed in Edmonton at first, and then because my deferment ran out, and they wouldn't renew it because I was in Edmonton, they suggested I move further north. So I went to Fort Nelson, 300 miles up on the Alaskan Highway, where I was eligible for a new deferment, and there I serviced the aircraft that were hauling supplies in the lend-lease aircraft going to Russia. The temperature started going down, in the fall of the year, you know—10, 15, 20, 30, 40, 50 below zero. And being in those days I wasn't in the Christian realm as it were, I was just a plain old heathen up there having a time, I told them to take that job and do something with it that I won't repeat. And so I quit my job up there, lost my deferment, but I was a pretty good mechanic, so when I got back to Minneapolis, because I was a good mechanic, I had an opportunity to take another job with another deferment, that was over in California. I went to the Richmond shipyard, worked there for about three months, and I was inside working on the steam turbines and all that and it was too noisy down there with all those riveters and chippers and welders and everything, and I told them to do with the job the same as I did up north. I didn't like the cold; I didn't like the inside of the ship either. And so I went back home. Of course, there was no more deferments. That's how I got in the military. But it was that occasion, of working up on the Alaskan highway back in 1950, that put a hook in my jaw for the ministry. In the meantime, I'd had an experience with the Lord, in a church in Minneapolis, where a sinner was turned to a saint, believe me. I want you to know, it was that great a transition situation. And in that church, there was a strong emphasis placed on ministry and missions. So I began to wonder about the north, and so on one occasion back in 1951, I drove to Alaska as far as Northway. And the only reason we stopped at Northway was we ran out of money. And so we went back, and I said, "Well, boy, that was tough. It's still as rough up there as it ever was. So back in 1955 I'd been attending Bible college and so forth, and it was during that time I believe God spoke to my heart to come back up. In '55 I came back up and got as far as Central, Alaska. The road was washed out, so I couldn't get to Circle, so we visited Central, Fairbanks, and went back home, and decided then to come back to Alaska, and of course came back in '56 as a missionary. The call of God brought me back to Alaska, not the cold weather or anything else. Because if I'd a went by the cold weather, I'd a went to Florida or Phoenix, or someplace like that.

Jim: Don, what did you think of the towns that you came into contact with—places like North Pole, Fairbanks, Central, Fox?

Don: When I went through North Pole the first time, there was no gravel, there was no pavement at all. In fact there was very little gravel anywhere. The first night I spent at North Pole in 1956, when we moved up, I spent on the only gravel driveway in North Pole. They'd just started putting them in that spring, and that was the first one they put in. Can you imagine that? The Alaskan Highway was gravel. But no other roads or driveways were. They were just dirt roads. And so I pulled up on the road, and this fellow had just put his driveway in and I was stuck, and he said, "Come on over and use my driveway." So I used the first gravel driveway in the city of North Pole in 1956. And stayed there for a whole week. And by the way, backing my trailer into that guy's driveway, I tore it all up. You know how it would be, fresh gravel. But I finally got backed in it there, and was out of the mud, and thanked God for that gravel driveway. That was back when it was rough.

Jim: That was a great experience for you. I lived in Fairbanks about that same period of time and recall some of the same characteristics that you're describing here.

Don: Well you remember downtown Fairbanks. There was only one big street.

Jim: That's right, one paved street. No, actually it was, the paved street was Second Avenue, and then Cushman was paved when I was here, clear up to fifth.

Don: Oh yeah.

Jim: All those ruts. When you came here, did you have a church, were you a minister, did you pound the pulpit? What did you do?

Don: No, I was just a plain old worker. I was ordained at the time, but I didn't pound the pulpit, because I had no pulpit. So I actually went to work for two different churches. I went to work for the Pentecostal Holiness Church and for the Assemblies of God. I was a member of neither one of those groups or congregations; it just was a place to serve the Lord. I was a custodian for the Pentecostal Holiness and a carpenter for the Assemblies of God, and that's how I got to Stevens Village in 1956 'cause a presbyter, B.P. Wilson, knew I was a carpenter. I had gained a reputation, in the short time I was here, as a pretty good carpenter. So he said, would I go to Stevens Village and work on a building over there—a cabin that they'd just purchased and they wanted to prepare it so he could go in there in the wintertime and hold services and have a comfortable place. So I went over there with my wife and daughter, and there we got hold of that cabin and refurbished it (and it was a mess, believe me—it hadn't been used, the windows were out, it was a hopeless mess). I never knew a thing about log cabins, but the Indians over there, the native folks, really helped me and taught me, and so I refurbished that cabin, never dreaming that I would spend the first winter there. I didn't know the plan of B.P. Wilson. He knew that if I got into that village, that God would put a hook in my jaw and bring me back, and that's just exactly what happened. And I spent almost eight years in that village, as a missionary. Then I was in the ministry.

Jim: He threw you out there, did he?

Don: He threw us out there, in a little old Piper Pacer, that was just a little tail dragger that had patches all over it, that when you looked at it you wondered whether you should junk it or use it, you know. It was just unreal.

Jim: That was quite an adventure for you, wasn't it Don?

Don: Well, that was back in those days when airplanes weren't as sophisticated as they are today, and they were true bush airplanes back then. We kept them flying by gum and wire and patches and tape and so forth, and that's basically what that plane was. I've got a picture of it. People who see it say, "You mean you actually got in that thing to fly?" Well, yeah, we did. I don't think there was a dime's worth of insurance. We didn't worry about it.

Jim: Would you do that again?

Don: Oh, sure.

Jim: Don, you were out at Steven's Village, where you repaired the cabin. Following that adventure you came back to Fairbanks and then what?

Don: We decided to move into the village. You know, there was an old trader back there that was involved in mining. He ran the trading post, mining and trapping, and he used to tell some of those stories about those miners that trudged the hills near Rampart and Dall Mountain. We got some interesting stories from the people, about the mining industry in the area, and of course there is a lot of mining going on over in Manley Hot Springs and the Rampart area, back of Rampart. So there was a lot of interesting information that we used to sit and listen to, on those cold winter nights, in the small little trading post on the banks of the Yukon. We used to have an old gas lamp hanging from the ceiling. We had a kind of a strange little stove that he used to chuck wood into, and he had a glass eye. Sometimes that glass eye wasn't put in right, so you'd just see all white, you know, and I'd come in and I'd tell him, "Hugh McGuire, you got your eye on backwards," and he'd had it that way all day, you know. He'd go and adjust it and then he'd sit down and, "Oh, let me tell you some stories," you know, and away he'd go. Late at night he'd finally close the trading post and I'd go home. Maybe a little cold, at 60 or 70 below, and he'd chunk a few pieces of wood in there to warm it up in the trading post, and then on he'd go with the stories of the Interior of Alaska, particularly trapping and mining. He used to love to tell stories about that, and so we are familiar with the mining industry and trapping, because of the involvement we had with a number of the miners and folks that lived back there. Hiney Carson, for example, up at 101 on the Steese Highway, and others that we know, that are back there even yet today, mining. And we enjoy being with them and enjoy visiting their mines and involving ourselves with them. And of course some are our personal friends up there in the Circle-Central area. Even today, I was with them last weekend up there, so we have been quite close to the mining industry.

Jim: I had the enjoyment of introducing Peggy Carston as the Mining Woman of the Year, here a couple of years ago, at the Alaska Women in Mining's Chatauqua festivities, and Peggy and I got acquainted at that time. She has had quite a life here in Alaska.

Don: First time I mined for gold and panned for gold was up at Hiney and Peggy's there, at 101 mile Steese Highway, and I just enjoyed that. Still got that ounce of gold—I gave it to my brother and he made some kind of a piece of jewelry out of it. I think he put it in a ring. The whole ounce.

Jim: The whole ounce in a ring.

Don: It made a big ring, but it was beautiful. I got some, they were nice little nuggets, you know. Got it from Hiney Carston.

Jim: Have you ever mined gold anyplace else?

Don: Well, just fooled around, you know. I didn't try any of that mining up at Fort Yukon. Remember the great Fort Yukon gold rush.

Jim: The fish wheel event. Yeah, I heard about it.

Don: I was around then.

Jim: You've traveled and worked at a lot of the villages around the state of Alaska. Name a few of the villages you've visited and lived in during your period of time in Alaska.

Don: Well we visited or lived in Rampart, Stevens Village, Beaver, Chalkitsik, Fort Yukon, Venetie, Arctic Village. Then, of course, Circle and Central area, and then of course we've been over in the Northwest Territory, in Canada. We've been in Old Crow in the Yukon Territory, then in Aklavik and Inuvik in the Northwest Territory, in Inuvik. Then we've been up to Tuktoyaktuk in the Northwest Territory. Then of course northern Alaska—Barter Island, Kaktovik and Barrow, and we've been places like that. We've been a lot of places in Alaska. Then heading south, you know, down in the Glenellen area, we've been down in that part of the country. Northway and Tanacross and places like that, and of course then down in the Dot Lake area, we've been in that part of the country, with services and worship missions. We give away toys at Christmas time. So our involvement has been quite an extensive involvement in the Interior, and then to the east and north of Fairbanks.

Jim: You have told us one of your stories about talking to some of the old timers that you ran into, about their activities. These were really the old timers.

Don: These were old timers 25 to 30 years ago. And so, they were old then. They were 35, 40, 50 years in Alaska when I was with them 30 years ago. So that's 70, 75 years ago, when they came, or 80 years ago. And some of them were very active in mining. I remember one time at Cantwell. I was there at Cantwell looking at a mission. The missionary had gone to another denomination, and they were considering selling it, and we were considering taking it over and operating it as a mission again. So my wife and I boarded the train, which was the only way to get to Cantwell at that time, and we went down there and stayed in the building overnight, and we were going to come back on the train the next day. We were going to spend about 24 hours in the village, looking it over, but something happened. That train had an accident and blocked the tracks. Almost four days we were stuck in the village. But we didn't mind, 'cause there was a trading post there. And, by the way a miner ran that trading post. So we would go down and talk with the people of the village at night. It was one of those occasions that I went down to Westney's, who was a miner and a very old man at the time. If I was ever tested to find out if I was a real Christian, that was the test, because he brought out fruit jars full of gold. I'm not talking about little bottles, I'm talking about fruit jars. And they weren't just a little bit in the bottom, of various kinds of gold; they were fines in some jars and coarse nuggets in other jars but full jars of it, you know, and they were heavy. You can imagine what a fruit jar full of gold weighs. And he was showing it to us and he was handling one and he handed it over to me and I looked at it, and he said, "You know something? I'm a very very old man. You can see I'm kind of crippled up, and I have difficulty defending myself. And nobody knows I got this gold. You could either hit me on the head and take it or you could just walk off with it. How could I stop you? Here you have all this gold." And I can't remember the exact words that he said, because I must confess it kind of shocked me, you know. I thought, "I wonder what made him think I would be tempted," is what kept crossing my mind. What'd I say or do that would make him think I would even want to do that. I believe he was trying to find out if this creature, this missionary was real. And so he said, "There it is. It's yours, if you want to pick it up and walk off. How could I prove you did it. Nobody even really knows I've got it." And so I thought that was a test of faith. And I looked at it and saw that it was beautiful. You know how fruit jars of gold nuggets might look. I didn't know much about mining back in those days, so I was just pondering what this was all about, you know? But I put 'er back down again and left him. I don't know who ever got that gold. You know, it's an interesting thought. I've never heard of any great amount of gold in that area, that came as a result of someone passing away. I wonder if somebody did take that gold.

Jim: Well, Don, you know, it might have been interesting to you to see all those fruit jars full of gold, but I don't think it was close to a test of your faith. Not at all.

Don: No, I had another one, similar to that, right here in town.

Jim: Did you?

Don: Oh yeah, yeah, I saw gold by the jars full that time too.

Jim: Was that a test, or was it just a study?

Don: No, no, that was just a person who knew me and showed me. They had one of the new machines that turns, you know, and sorts it.

Jim: A concentrating wheel?

Don: Yeah, whatever it is. I don't really understand all that, but it was turning and making the little nuggets come out the other end, you know, and man there was a lot of them.

Jim: Isn't that impressive to see that gold just draw right up into that chute?

Don: Oh, I've seen a lot of that take place. I remember one time up in the Central area, I was with Warren, and he was separating gold.

Jim: Jack Warren, on Crooked Creek?

Don: Yeah. He was taking it out of the sluice. it comes out in a concentrate, and he was separating the gold from the concentrate, and I watched. And boy, I tell you, that can really be a beautiful sight when it shows up. Particularly when all of a sudden you spot a couple of big nuggets. That's really nice. Well anyway, we appreciated the opportunity of being with those miners, and we've done some programming. In fact, we're putting together a video tape of the Steese Highway, and it's going to incorporate some of the mines up there. The travel video will take you up the highway from the Fairbanks area, by the big dredge out there at Chatanika, then visit some of the mines at 101, down there in the valley, and then go into a mine and show a whole mining operation, then up to Central and through the museum. By the way, if you want to see the early mining, the Cats, and the steam engines, and all those mining machines from the past, they have a museum up there, in Central, that the folks in that area put together. And if you want to see the mining in its really old historic type setting, they put a road back next to the creek there and they set some of the old pieces of equipment back in there. It's really something to see. Then inside, you see a lot of the personal effects—the smaller items, in a little cabin of a miner, you know? And all the things that were in there, and the maps and so forth. And then of course you can see some of the early day maps of the mapping of the claims around the country. And so it's a very informative place. I'm putting a plug in for them, if you don't mind. They don't make any money on it, it's just a public service. You go in there free of charge, you sign your name. They have a little curio shop in there, they sell some books and that, but other than that it's free, and you can just go in and enjoy. You can spend a half a day in that museum looking at all the different things that they've accumulated there from the various mines in the area. Some of the miners have been very gracious in giving some interesting museum pieces that give you, like I said, a real insight into how difficult it must've been in those days of mining back there.

Jim: The people who run the museum up there can also tell you some colorful stories about the history of the Central and Circle mining district.

Don: Well, that's going to be on our video too. Then we are going to go on up to Circle Hot Springs for a visit and then on up to Circle City. So it'll incorporate more things than the mining, but that'll be one of the prime targets of the video.

Jim: You mentioned a little earlier that you met Hugh up there at Stevens Village?

Don: Yes. Hugh McGuire.

Jim: Yeah, Hugh McGuire. And that he would sit down at nighttime and tell you some stories that were particularly fascinating to you. Don, do you have any that you'd like to relate to us? Or any other stories? I recall you telling me a story about a fellow who had collected some gold on some stream near the Colville River area, not too long ago. What was that story all about? Kind of the hidden treasure story.

Don: There are a lot of so-called hidden treasures up there. A lot of stories about gold that hasn't been retrieved, that was discovered by someone, and I don't know which particular story you're making reference to. But Purgatory is probably the best story. The two gentlemen that were trappers and miners there, that ran that, were brothers. And they pulled a trick one time on the folks that were on the steamer. You know they used to have the old sternwheel come through there. And so back in the woods (now this is a true story, old Hugh McGuire told me this one) and back in the woods it looked like they'd dug a grave, you know? And they had it mounded up like a grave, with a cross on the end of it, with a headstone. The headstone was made out of wood. It said, "Here lies the thief and the robber. He's learnt his lesson. His dues have been paid. His grave is here to identify his thievery." And so the tourists got off the boat, you know, and were walking around, and some of them wandered back on that trail and saw that grave back there and said, "He-he-he-he murdered somebody and buried him here. It was a regular size grave, see? And so they went up to Fort Yukon and they got the marshal up there, or whoever was up there, and back down the river they came, you know, and come in there and they're investigating this so-called murder that the tourists had reported. And so, they went back there and they dug up that crazy grave, and what was in there was the bird—the camp robber. You can imagine the embarrassment when they dug it up. And there he was. He was a robber and a thief. You know how a camp robber is. But those are stories that old Hugh McGuire would tell us, you know, and some of them were true too. Some of them were very true.

Jim: We have a call, Don. Welcome to Alaska Gold Trails. You're on the air with Don Nelson.

Caller: Good afternoon, Jim. I've got a question here for the good reverend.

Jim: OK. Let's hear it.

Caller: I wonder if perchance he would have known, about 30 years ago, a fellow by the name of John W. Holland. He was about six foot four, redheaded, feet about a yard long, and he was a cook and mess sergeant on the Alcan, in the building of it, went from day one to the last day of the highway.

Don: No. Most of the Alcan sites where I was were operated by the military. In fact, we ate with the military mess.

Caller: That's what John was.

Don: He was? Then I probably could have met him.

Caller: He was a military mess sergeant.

Don: OK.

Caller: Big ornery dude. You talk about those ornery dudes, you should've met him.

Don: In our travels on the highway, we could've bumped into him. My problem back in those days was that I loved to eat. So I was in the line and stayed long.

Caller: You had to know him then.

Don: Yeah. That was an interesting crowd up there.

Caller: I'll bet it was.

Don: It was a rough crowd too, you know. The fellows had to be, to endure the cold and the conditions that prevailed there. We lived in tents, you know. That was tough, man, that was rough.

Caller: That was doing it the easy way. Before you fellows did that I spent a winter up in Northern Wisconsin in tents.

Don: Oh boy, that's tough.

Caller: C.C. boy.

Don: The coldest I've ever been, in a tent, is 50 below. And that was over in the Northwest Territory, at the reindeer herd station. You know those reindeer herders they live right out with the herd. And their tent city, as we would call it (they don't call it a tent city) moves right along with the herds. When the herd moves, they pick up the tents and go to the next area and set up their tents again. And I was in one of those tents and lived there for a while. It got down to 50 below zero, and that's really cold.

Caller: Right. Underneath the stove, eh?

Don: Well, I was in my sleeping bag right next to the stove. It was cold.

Caller: OK. Well, I wish you'd'a known that dude. I'd like to talk to you about him.

Don: Well, I wish I would've too. Sorry for that.

Caller: Talk to you later then.

Don: Yeah. Bless you.

Jim: Thank you for the call sir.

Caller: You betcha.

Jim: Hi, you're on the air with Don Nelson.

Caller: Yeah, Don. I was wondering, the other guy was asking you about people you may have met. Have you ever met a guy up around Livengood, Manley or Rampart area by the name of Red Anderson?

Don: Red Anderson. I've known several fellows by the name of Red. Two or three of them up in that country, but I don't remember the last names. You know you meet a fellow and call him by his first name mostly, but no, not to identify Red Anderson. What did he do?

Caller: Well, he was a miner up there. He come up in the country around 1902, I believe, and was mining up around, mostly around the Livengood area, and he'd get into Rampart.

Don: Some of those fellows in Rampart I got to know because I was there giving services. But to identify them individually, I don't know, that's tough. But we were up there and we did get involved with some of those fellows. Some of the traders mostly, in that area. Sorry for that.

Caller: OK. Thanks a lot.

Jim: Thank you for the call. Don, you've talked about precious metals and things. We've got some folks here in town called the Precious Metals People, Oxford Assaying and Refining. Are you familiar with them at all?

Don: Oh, I'm familiar with them, because I've been doing business with them. What happened is, Don May gave me 100 ounces of silver. Placer gold in Alaska contains quite a bit of silver, and so when they refine it they get a little silver bar with the gold bar. Don was on television with me one night and handed me, as a gift, a hundred ounce silver bar. But he asked me to keep it until the price of silver went up. Well, I don't want 100 ounces of silver hanging around so I said, "Don, can I do something with that silver that would be the equivalent of getting more money for it?" So I got all inspired to go down to Oxford, and traded it in for ingots and coins.

Jim: Some of the Oxford ingots?

Don: Yeah. So I got a bunch of them and I sold them for $15 apiece in the states down there, and I got $15 an ounce.

Jim: That's almost capitalistic, isn't it?

Don: Well, you can call it what you want to, it made money for the mission and that's what I was after.

Jim: Bought more bibles.

Don: Buy more bibles. That's exactly what I did it for. And so I actually got up to $15 an ounce. No, I've got to correct that, because some people that got some of those ingots in coins, gave me a check as an offering, so I remember one time I got $100 and all they took was one ounce of silver. So that particular occasion, I got $100 for an ounce of silver. So that's how I worked around that. And Oxford's been very gracious to give me those little sealed units and all those things, and so I've been going on. Now I'm using the profit made (I've paid back the money for the price of the silver) now I'm using that profit that I made to go on with that, because I found that there in the states people like that little ingot that's got "Alaska" on it in big letters. One ounce of silver, for $10 they go just "click."

Jim: They're beautiful, aren't they?

Don: I have trouble keeping them because people look at them and say, "Oh, isn't that beautiful. That's real silver?" And I say, "All I want is $10." You know, what did I pay for it? The price of silver. So I still make a couple dollars for the mission and it leaves behind something to remind them of us.

Jim: It has the state of Alaska on one side. What's on the other, the flag?

Don: Nothing. You can engrave it on the back.

Jim: I thought it had the stars. They have several styles, one of them might have stars.

Don: Yeah, I think it does. One of them has, the smaller one just says "Oxford" on it. That's got a flag on it. I think the other one's blank so you can engrave someone's name. I'm going to try to figure out how I could imprint KJNP on it, then leave them as souvenirs, you know? I haven't figured that one out yet. But they go real good with that "Alaska" on them.

Jim: Besides that, they make beautiful gifts. Don, let's get back to another one of those experiences that you've had and some of the stories that've fallen out from those experiences. You got another one for us? Just a short one, Don.

Don: We invent all kinds of experiences flying, and of course, in the ministry you involve yourself with people, and when you involve yourself with people you have a lot of stories to tell.

Jim: Saved by the bell, we have a call, Don. Hi, you're on the air with Don Nelson.

Caller: Reverend Don Nelson.

Don: Yes sir.

Caller: Can I ask him a question that he doesn't have to answer?

Don: Go ahead.

Caller: How many times does a person have to go to jail before they decide to become a reverend?

Don: Well, I didn't get throwed in jail, but I was a prisoner of war. But that isn't what caused me to turn to the Lord. That was the strange part. You know, a lot of people thought my deep religious experience came through my experience of being shot down. I must confess, that almost turned me into an atheist, because I looked at it from the wrong standpoint. I said, "Well, how come God would let that happen to people?" you understand? So it kind of turned me off to the church and to things of God. So I had a real problem overcoming that, in order to get back to the Lord. So my experience came after years of drinking and carousing, and then finally, one day, I went to a church and the preacher preached, and I got saved. Praise God.

Jim: Thank you for the call. Looks like our time is up, Don.

Don: Nice to have been with you, Jim.

Jim: Don, it's been nice to have you here on Alaska Gold Trails. Thank so much for joining us.

Jeannette Therriault
with
Jim Madonna
February 19, 1988

Jim: Good afternoon, ladies and gentlemen. Welcome to Alaska Gold Trails. Our guest today is Jeannette Therriault. How are you today, Jeannette?

Jeannette: Just fine, thank you, Jim.

Jim: Give us a little background, Jeannette. Where were you born?

Jeannette: In Alberta, Canada. Actually, Alberta is a province, so I should say Pincher Creek, Alberta, Canada.

Jim: Pincher Creek. That sounds like a little town. What is the size of Pincher Creek?

Jeannette: About 1,000 people.

Jim: About 1,000 people. Did you go to high school there?

Jeannette: Yes.

Jim: And what kind of town was Pincher Creek?

Jeannette: Oh, a cattle ranching area town. Actually, my folks owned a farm 10 miles out of town. I went to a little one-room country school 'til I was in the fourth grade, then I went to the town school.

Jim: Explain the high school situation.

Jeannette: At the time I started school, my sister, who's ten years older than I am, was in ninth grade, and we used to ride horses to school. Well, I was involved in music. My mother wanted me to take music, so I went to the town school, so I could take music lessons, you see. And then, before I got to high school, they had closed the country schools and put on school buses, and they would bus all the children into the town schools. So, actually, my high school days were in the town school.

Jim: But you were a country farm girl, is that right?

Jeannette: Right.

Jim: What kind of history did you have prior to coming to Alaska? What kind of activities, other than music, did you get into?

Jeannette: Work. During the war years there were no hired hands for the farm, so it was the kids that did the farm work.

Jim: What was that magnetic attraction that brought you off to Alaska in the early days?

Jeannette: Well, it was a matrimony ceremony.

Jim: Oh, it was one of those kind of things. What happened, did you land a husband, is that it?

Jeannette: Right. I caught one of those Yankees that was passing through.

Jim: A Yankee. Was he an Alaskan Yank, or was he a lower-48 Yank?

Jeannette: Oh, he was an Alaskan Yank.

Jim: I see. And what was his name?

Jeannette: Hector.

Jim: Hector. Well, how did Hector happen to mosey into a little town like Pincher?

Jeannette: Actually, he was born and raised there also, and he had relatives who were still there. And he had come to visit his relatives.

Jim: I'll be darned. So you snagged him and he drug you off to Alaska.

Jeannette: Right.

Jim: What year was that?

Jeannette: We came in May of 1951.

Jim: How did you get here?

Jeannette: We drove the Alcan Highway.

Jim: What was the Alcan like in those days?

Jeannette: Actually, that May it was mud, I think, and water, all the way from Dawson Creek to the border. It was breakup season and it had been raining quite a bit. I just remember there was water flying from the car all the way, it seemed like.

Jim: Did you ever get stuck in all that muck?

Jeannette: No, we never got stuck. There were days when we just made it. The next day the road washed out. So had we been a day later, we would have been delayed. But we made it through OK.

Jim: And were others stuck along the road, or was everybody making it?

Jeannette: Yes. I remember three young fellows who were driving pickup trucks for Lonnie Hall, who owned the Ford agency at that time. Actually, some people made a business of driving vehicles, new vehicles, up—they got their transportation paid up and their airplane ticket back. So they would make a tour, to experience the Alcan Highway and life in Alaska. But I remember, in one section, between Pouce Coupe and Dawson Creek, it seemed like they were just in and out of the ditches, from one side into the other side.

Jim: My goodness. Was that rather typical of that time of year and the type of environment the traveler might see?

Jeannette: Right. Highway conditions at that time. I'm sure they're not like that any more. It's been probably 10-12 years since we've driven the highway.

Jim: It was all gravel.

Jeannette: Right.

Jim: Was it gravel all the way into Fairbanks?

Jeannette: No. There was pavement at Delta. In 1950 the road was paved from Fairbanks to Delta. Actually, Hector worked on that project for Lyle, Green and Birch.

Jim: Jeannette, when you came up the Alcan, what did you think, when you first arrived in Fairbanks? What did you think about Fairbanks?

Jeannette: Well, it wasn't the town it is now, that's for certain. I think the pavement was Second Avenue and about from Fifth Street down Cushman. The Post Office was there at the intersection of Cushman and Second Avenue. That was the only traffic light in town. I remember walking to the bus depot on Noble Street, in the old Greiman Building I believe it was, and it was wood sidewalks. The Northward Building was a brand new building in 1950. I think it was built in 1950, so when I came in 1951 there was a grocery store. One of the bigger grocery stores was Big Ray's Grocery, in the Northward Building. And Piggly Wiggly, I believe, had a store on Cushman. Then they moved from there to Second Avenue. The Lathrop Building had a grocery store in it. There was also a grocery store in the N.C. Company, which is the Nordstroms building now. It was a department store, a grocery store, a hardware store and a clothing store, all in the one building. And the power house was where the parking lot is now. The planes used to land in Weeks Field, which is behind Main School, which was the only school in Fairbanks at that time. The little float planes landed on the Chena near the bridge.

Jim: Were there frame houses for the most part, or were there a lot of log cabins?

Jeannette: Yes, a lot of log cabins.

Jim: In and around the frame houses?

Jeannette: Right.

Jim: And the wood walkways. What other kind of characteristics did Fairbanks have that were particularly interesting to you.

Jeannette: You mean the Fourth Avenue line?

Jim: What was the Fourth Avenue Line? Explain that to us.

Jeannette: It used to be the red light district of Fairbanks.

Jim: Oh, is that right. And that was how long?

Jeannette: Oh, I don't remember. I only remember parking there once.

Jim: Only once.

Jeannette: Right. I made the mistake.

Jim: Jeannette, other than your one stop off on Fourth Avenue, what other experiences did you have in Fairbanks that were interesting?

Jeannette: Of course, at that time, there was no TV, plus the fact that the first year, we spent in a little 16-foot trailer house, parked at the north end of the Eielson Base runway. Mr. Casperson, Bob Casperson, had a homestead there and he allowed us to park our trailer there, because that was where Hector and his brother were working—at Eielson on some of the construction that was going on there at that time. They were working for O.B. Felid Construction, and I know one of the jobs they worked on was the big hangar that's out there at Eielson. I think it was built in about the early '50s.

Jim: Jeannette, I think you have a phone call. Hello, welcome to Alaska Gold Trails you're on the air with Jeannette Therriault.

Caller: Yeah, this is Bob Turnbull, here. I wondered if Jeannette...perhaps I'm bringing up a subject she'd care less to talk about, but she did mention Fourth Avenue. You can still see when you go walking around town, they tell me, local gossip of course, one of those old houses still remains there. It's kind of a ramshackle house. It's obviously very old. I came up here in '48, but I did not come to stay 'til 1955. Over the years, of course, you hear all the talk of this old Fourth Avenue Line. But a friend pointed out to me that it was actually one of those houses, that still remains there. Summers, during these guided walking tours, it is pointed out. I don't know who operates those guided walking tours. There's never a "for sale" sign on it or anything, of course, and boy, it looks like something out of the Old West—one of those ghost towns. When you run across it, it kind of stands out from the other houses in the neighborhood.

Jeannette: I think some of those houses ended up at Alaskaland, if I'm not mistaken.

Caller: Oh, this is true. In Gold Rush Town. That's quite true, Jeannette. It would be interesting to know who owns that house today?

Jeannette: We don't live in the city limits, so I wouldn't know.

Caller: It's mostly boarded up, of course, but there are a couple of windows that are heavily hung with curtains. You never see any smoke coming out of the chimney. Nobody lives there I guess. Well, just plain curiosity.

Jim: Thank you for your call.

Caller: Thank you, Jim.

Jim: Jeannette, I think you have another call. Hello, you're on the air. Do you have a question for Jeannette?

Caller: Yeah, I sure do. Jeannette, this is Raymond number one. I remember you from Six-mile Village, and I remember you too from Sig Wold and the Hideaway. Do you remember Peter Billings, at the Hideaway?

Jeannette: No.

Caller: You don't?

Jeannette: No. Sure you have the right person?

Caller: Yep, I do. It was at the Hideaway, and Sig Wold was right there on the corner of Wickersham and Second. And my sister worked there for a long long time, and Obie Sieland had a plant out at Six-mile.

Jeannette: That was a concrete batch plant that he had. That was much later than when he had the construction business out at Eielson.

Caller: Yep, that's right. I came up in 1948. I was flying airplanes up here, but I came back in '52, and I put a Laundromat down in the bottom of the Ice Palace.

Jeannette: OK. I washed a lot of clothes there.

Caller: Do you remember where the Ice Palace was?

Jeannette: Yes. Vaguely. Yeah, we used to come in to do our laundry. I remember it when you said in the basement.

Caller: It's the Northward Building. But then we built the White Swan Laundry - the neighborette laundry and the Numastic Cleaners on Wendell Avenue. And that's been a couple of years ago.

Jeannette: It sure was. Thank you for calling.

Jim: Well, thank you, Raymond. And it sounds like a lot of people out there want to talk about old times, Jeannette. We have another call. You're real popular today. Hello, you're on the air. Do you have a question for Jeannette?

Caller: Not a question, but I was just going to make a comment. She probably remembers it too, but back in the '50s, until they moved the old bench from in front of the post office. I used to pass there and see little older men, dressed in black, sitting. And finally I asked someone, a native, what those little men sat there on that bench and waited for, and they said it was for a pioneer's funeral. They always sat there and waited for a ride. And when a pioneer would die, the little men would sit and wait there until someone came by and picked them up to take them to the funeral.

Jeannette: Well, that's interesting.

Caller: Do you remember that?

Jeannette: No, I don't remember because I didn't spend that much time in town. I didn't drive when I first came here, so my trips to town were sometimes once a month.

Caller: Oh. And you were mentioning the N.C. store. It was a credit store too. I remember people went in and you saw a lot of the old miners there.

Jeannette: Right. I think they could bring in their poke of gold and buy groceries on their gold, couldn't they? They could also get groceries on their grubstake there.

Caller: Yes. And I think the first long-haired man I ever saw was some young fellow used to come in from the mines. Well, quite a few of the miners had real long hair, but this one fellow wore it in a ponytail.

Jeannette: Who's this that's calling?

Caller: This is Marge Clark.

Jeannette: I see.

Caller: And the friendliness of the town. I only came here for a vacation, but I never left it until about seven years after I got here, because it was just the friendliest nicest town in the world. It still is a good town.

Jeannette: Right.

Caller: OK, thank you.

Jeannette: Thank you for calling.

Jim: Thank you, Marge. Well, that was a fascinating bit of information, wasn't it?

Jeannette: Yes.

Jim: Well, Jeannette, as I recall you saying you lived off the end of the runway, off Eielson there. Pretty noisy place,? How long did you live there before you moved out.

Jeannette: Oh, we arrived in May, and we were there until that Fall. About the first of October, I think, we went outside for the winter. Hector and his brother Frank used to work for the rock-crushing plants making concrete mix. So after the water would freeze, why then their jobs were done for the season, and that was standard living conditions in those years. You worked until freeze-up, and then you were out of work 'til the next spring, when the water started to run in the streets again, and then you went back to work.

Jim: They worked a lot of hours in the "Land of the Midnight Sun," didn't they?

Jeannette: Right. Because I was from the Interior, where there were very few planes, the experience of having planes flying over was something unusual for me. What I remember the most about living at the end of the runway was that one day this big plane was coming in and the dishes were rattling and the whole trailer shook and everything, and finally I thought, "My Lord, can't that plane land out there? What's the matter with it?" So that night when Hector came home he said it wasn't one plane, it was six B-36's.

Jim: I'll bet you were happy to move. When did you move to North Pole, and the area you're in now.

Jeannette: In September of 1952.

Jim: When did you start Hector's Welding?

Jeannette: I think the first business license we bought was in 1956. And like I say, you were unemployed through the winter months. We had a family, and somehow you had to buy groceries through the winter too, so he started doing odd jobs in the back yard.

Jim: You then experienced quite a few boom-and-bust cycles in Fairbanks, didn't you?

Jeannette: Yes. I remember going to watch the big dragline and the dredges out here at Ester and Fox. They were all in operation when I first came here. In fact, they were still hydraulicking the soils.

Jim: Was that your weekend fun?

Jeannette: More or less.

Jim: Kind of like going to the drive-in movie in the lower states?

Jeannette: Right. At that time there was only one movie a day and a matinee on Saturday, and probably, I don't remember if they even had movies on Sundays. It was at the Empress Theater on Lacey at that time, of course.

Jim: Well, the big dredges worked up until what, 1960? And then there was still some construction going on around. But even that was starting to dry up, wasn't it.

Jeannette: Right.

Jim: And did you start feeling an economic crunch coming into the Interior of Alaska at that time?

Jeannette: Well, Hector started thinking more seriously about a full-time year-round job. So he went to work at the power house at Eielson for about a year and a half, two years, and then went to work at Gilmore Creek, at the NASA site, for a couple of years. He quit there in 1969, and that's when we went into business full time.

Jim: Jeannette, you indicated that there was a bit of a decline in the economy after 1960. Following that, when did you see a big boom in the economy occur?

Jeannette: During the pipeline. At the height of the pipeline.

Jim: That was what, about 1974?

Jeannette: '74, '75, possibly '76, I don't remember exactly when.

Jim: That was probably the biggest boom that we've had. Things were amazing in Fairbanks at that time. Did you get a feeling for the change that occurred in Fairbanks? What was the change in the atmosphere?

Jeannette: Busy and lots of lines. Every place you went you had to stand in line. I remember that was when they started building the drive-up windows for the banks, so you didn't have to stand in line at the bank.

Jim: I recall in the beginning that we went into the grocery stores and the shelves were almost bare, at one point. Did you see that happen?

Jeannette: Yes.

Jim: The grocers weren't quick enough to catch up with the flood of people that came into Alaska. That was quite a boom for Fairbanks. Then about 1976, was it, that we began to experience a decline in the economy?

Jeannette: Right.

Jim: And what was the next boom?

Jeannette: Gold mining.

Jim: The gold rush. Let's see, would that be about three years later, 1979?

Jeannette: Yes. First part of the '80s.

Jim: And that's when Hector started producing gold mining equipment. The large-scale processing equipment.

Jeannette: Right.

Jim: Let's see, that took about four years for that gold rush to reach its peak.

Jeannette: Right. We were very busy, and we tried to convince the miners that our slow period was during the winter time. If they wanted equipment the next spring, not to wait 'til March and ask us to have it completed so they could haul it out on the frost, but to let us do it during the wintertime, when there was no other work to be done.

Jim: About 1983 that dropped off, and we began experiencing a lull at that time. We don't know what's next, but something's bound to happen. In summarizing it, we've seen three periods of more or less boom and bust. First of all, we saw, up to 1960, a lot of construction associated with the Air Force bases.

Jeannette: Right. Military bases.

Jim: And the gold mining, which was a major contributor to the wealth of the Interior. Then we saw a decline, then the pipeline was another mining-related activity, and we saw a boom then, in which people came in from all over the world to take part and gain their fortunes, and then that declined. Then gold mining came in, when gold reached, what, $850 an ounce?

Jeannette: Right.

Jim: So. Those are the cycles that we've had. I wonder what's next. That's a question that needs to be answered. I'm certain a lot of people have an idea. So you have some other activities that you participate in, and that's square dancing. We've got about a minute, Jeannette. Tell us about square dancing.

Jeannette: Well, every fall, in September, they start classes. Most of the square dancing here in the Fairbanks area is done at Alaskaland, and there's always advertisements in the paper in the fall. One of our most rewarding experiences was to attend the international square dance convention that was held in Saalfelden, Austria, last September. It was quite an eye-opener to be able to intermingle with people from Austria, Netherlands, Germany, West Germany, Japan and China. I think the attendance was in the neighborhood of 1,150 people. Almost 700 were Americans who had come from various areas. We didn't go with a group. We went on our own, but joined a group in Munich. We flew over the pole.

Jim: What a wonderful and exciting experience that must have been. Sorry to say that our time has come to an end, Jeannette. Thank you for joining us on Alaska Gold Trails, today. We've learned a lot from it. It's been refreshing.

Jeannette: Thank you for inviting me, Jim.

Hector Therriault
with
Jim Madonna
April 27, 1989

Jim: Today's guest is Hector Therriault. Hector and I have known each other for years. Hector, welcome to Alaska Gold Trails.

Hector: Thank you, Jim. How are you?

Jim: I'm doing real well. How are you?

Hector: Very good today.

Jim: Better than yesterday, is that it?

Hector: Yes.

Jim: Give us a little of your background. Where were you born and what year Hector?

Hector: I was born in 1920, back in Pincher Creek, Alberta, Canada, and my folks were American citizens, so I didn't have to take out any papers when I came across the line. I crossed the line when I was 22 years old and went to California. I worked in the aircraft factories there for about five years. Took up welding there. I was a certified aircraft welder for about four years. After the war, in 1947, I came to Alaska.

Jim: You were a welder there during the war period.

Hector: Well, I started out on the assembly line for North American Aviation, and then I was working 10 hours at night and going to school in the daytime, taking up welding.

Jim: Did you have any extra time?

Hector: Not much.

Jim: Did you finish that welding class in 1947?

Hector: No. I finished in '43. Then I began welding on aircraft until 1947.

Jim: Where was that?

Hector: In Los Angeles.

Jim: How long did you work at that job?

Hector: I stayed there 'til 1947, and then I came to Alaska from there.

Jim: In '47 what drew you to Alaska? Was it because it was a frontier, or what?

Hector: Well, I don't really know. I didn't want to go back to the plant where I was working, because there didn't seem to be much future there, and I came up to visit my folks in Montana—they lived in Missoula, Montana, at the time—when I got laid off there in the plant. And their neighbor had been to Alaska, and he said, "Well, if you're a welder you should go to Alaska. You shouldn't have any problem." So, while I was there visiting my folks I got a call to go back to work at the plant in Los Angeles, but I thought, "Oh, I'm going north, instead." So, I'm still here.

Jim: And did you drive up?

Hector: No, I flew up. It was a DC-4 or DC-6. It took eight hours to come from Seattle.

Jim: That was a long flight. I flew up on one of those back in 1948.

Hector: Yeah?

Jim: What airline was that? I don't even remember.

Hector: Pan American.

Jim: PanAm, right. So you flew up here. What did you expect to find?

Hector: Well, I don't really know. I landed here about mid-April, and there was a lot of snow, but the weather had turned nice. However, it had been a horrible winter. I think that all of part of Second Avenue had burned down, and the streets were level with ice from one sidewalk to the other, when I landed here.

Jim: I see. From what? Putting out the fires?

Hector: Fighting the fires, yeah.

Jim: Did you expect to see what you saw, in Fairbanks?

Hector: I think so. Of course, I was raised in Canada, so I knew what cold weather was like. But one of the things, of course, was that the days started getting longer, and that was quite a surprise, you know?

Jim: You were getting what, 14-16-hour days about that time. What did you do when you landed here? Explain the frontier type atmosphere.

Hector: Well, it was very much a frontier. I don't know, it seemed like everybody knew everybody, but you knew they didn't, you know? Myself, I came in here, there wasn't a hotel room to be had, so I was walking down the street and I asked where I could find a hotel room and they said, "Well, you should contact Eva McGown." So I went to the old Nordale Hotel, and there was Eva McGown sitting there behind the desk, and she found me a bed under a church, let's see on Noble, the church was on Noble, and the pastor had some beds under the church there, and he'd rent them out for $2 a night. Very nice beds. They were clean and everything, but that's what it was. I was lucky to get a bed.

Jim: When I think back, there were a couple of areas like that, where you could just rent beds by the day, or by the week or month. Just stalls, and all they had in them was a bed and a bureau. And I used to run and hawk the Daily News-Miner up and down these rows in these big long buildings I'd say, "Daily News-Miner," and all these hands would go up and over the stall, you know, and there was the dime, and I'd hand them the paper. And there was quite a lot of that around Fairbanks at that time. I think that a lot of the miners in the mining camps at the time took up residence in some of those places, especially during the winter.

Hector: I imagine they did, yeah.

Jim: What kind of activity was going on here at that time, Hector?

Hector: Well, what I was looking for, of course, was a welding job, and being as I came from aircraft welding I didn't know if I could handle what was coming up, but I had worked for a farmer there in Montana for a couple days on the farm. He said, "My boy is driving a bus in Fairbanks. Maybe you could find him and he could steer you around." So I knew this fellow was a tall kid. I went down to the bus station and I said, "Is your name Tommy?" And he looked at me kind of funny, you know, and he said, "Yes, it is. Who are you?" He thought I was the sheriff or something, that was the way he acted. Anyway, it turned out that he was a real nice guy, and we got along very good. He said, "Well, if you're looking for a welding job, you should go out to Ladd Field," he said, "that's where you might get a job, out there. Get on the bus," he said, "I'll take you right by there." So he took me out there. Let's see, I got into town on a Thursday, I went out there on a Friday, and they wanted me to go to work on Saturday. I thought, "Well, I was broke, but not that broke."

Jim: They were in a hurry.

Hector: Anyway, I had to come downtown and join the Operating Engineers, and there was no problem there. I had been welding long enough to join the Operators. And then I went to work out there the following Monday. And I fell right in, and it worked out real good for me.

Jim: How long did you work there, Hector?

Hector: Well, I worked there 'til that fall, then got laid off for a few months. I went back to my folks in Montana. And then the following year, I came up and I worked in Delta for a little while on the base there.

Jim: Was that Fort Greely?

Hector: Yes. Fort Greely. And then I came back to work for B.J.L., which is the contractor I was working for at Ladd Field.

Jim: What were you doing at Ladd Field?

Hector: Just about anything. Repairing. At that time they'd brought in a whole bunch of old equipment from the Aleutian Islands, and we'd repair it. And they were starting to build a base at that time.

Jim: Do you recall why they changed the name from Ladd to Wainwright?

Hector: Well, they went from an Air base to an Army base. I think that's primarily the reason for the change in name.

Jim: Tell us about some of the activities you participated in at a social level in Fairbanks, when you first came.

Hector: Well, when I first came here, I kind of behaved myself.

Jim: That's hard to believe. I mean, we're lucky we're not on television, my friend, because you'd be red-faced.

Hector: No, I behaved myself pretty much, because I had plans. I thought I'd stay here a couple years and make a few dollars, then go outside. But it didn't work out that way. I tried to save money to buy myself a new car, and that kind of stuff. Which, in the fall, I did go back to Missoula and buy a new car. But I got to going to ball games.

Jim: Well, you didn't bet on them, did you?

Hector: No.

Jim: You just got interested in the baseball games.

Hector: I didn't play, I just went to watch the ball games

Jim: Were you married when you came up here?

Hector: No.

Jim: Was the ball team the Goldpanners then?

Hector: I don't think so, no. That was before the Goldpanners started.

Jim: I see. Was that your only social outlet? Didn't you do any square dancing or anything?

Hector: Well, we were working seven days a week, and 10-12 hours a day. Well, let me tell you about a couple little deals.

Jim: I thought I'd drag one out of you.

Hector: Right out there on Cushman, say about where the Drop-Inn is right now, or along in there, that was all brush at that time. And we used to go out there and snare rabbits. There were four of us. Let's see, one of the guy's father's name was Fry, and one was Al Latondris, and John Betruva. Two of those fellows have passed away, so far. And we'd go down to one of the guy's houses—two of the fellows had houses in town—we'd cook these rabbits up, and we'd have a feed. And I might as well tell you the rest of it. I was the bartender.

Jim: Did you pour pretty stiff?

Hector: And then a time or two, I was the only one awake.

Jim: You did pour it stiff, didn't you. Get these guys drunk and feed 'em rabbit. Is that what you're trying to tell me?

Hector: No, we had some good feeds. We really had some good feeds.

Jim: I guess you did. You know how to make the taste buds liven up a little bit. What kind of beverages did you serve.

Hector: Mixed drinks or whatever you wanted. Or whatever we had.

Jim: Hector, tell us some more stories that you might have regarding the early days here in Alaska.

Hector: Well, that's a long time ago, and I really had to scratch my head to come up with that kind of stuff. You know, you gotta think about it, cause it's almost 40 years. After we got settled down a little bit and found my way around, we used to go down to the old time dances down in the Eagles Hall, and Johnny Carlson was calling square dances and that kind of stuff, and that was our social life, pretty much.

Jim: You got involved with square dancing pretty heavily, didn't you? Didn't you like to call a few yourself, in your time?

Hector: I still do. I still do. I call every first and third Saturday down at Alaskaland, for Polar Promenaders.

Jim: Is that right? Well, tell us a little bit about that. We're kind of jumping ahead of things here, maybe. We'll get back to this square dance calling in just a few minutes. Let's bring you up to this time. We're back there, around the 50's right now, aren't we?

Hector: Around the '50s.

Jim: Yeah. You've been here a couple of years, you have done some welding work out at Ladd Air Force Base, and then you went to Fort Greely, you roasted some rabbits. And what took place after that?

Hector: Well, of course, I worked for the contractors, and I worked for B.J.L. and I worked for, let's see, it was Birch, Ladd and Green. I worked out at Eielson Air Force Base, for a long time. And then I went to work for M.K. [Morrison-Knudson]. Oh, I worked for O.B. Sielett. O.B. Sielett had a concrete plant. Well he had a plant at both bases, and I worked at the one at Eielson for a couple years. Then I got to working for M.K., and I worked for M.K. for about 12 years in a row, right here in Fairbanks. I would get laid off in about October or thereabouts, and go to work in about February or March, first thing in the spring. I guess I was the one that worked for Morrison-Knudsen the most and the longest, at that time.

Jim: Strictly welding?

Hector: Well, repair work.

Jim: My father worked for Morrison-Knudsen, back in the late '40s and early '50s, welding.

Hector: It was a good outfit.

Jim: Yeah. They were involved in some of the bridge building around here, as well, weren't they?

Hector: Oh, they did about anything. I think in 1951 they were the ones that built the first concrete section of the old hospital, in downtown Fairbanks.

Jim: I see. And when did you meet Jeannette?

Hector: Oh, one of them trips that I took through Canada. Of course I'd known, her folks and my folks had been friends for many many years. But, one of those trips when I went through Canada, why, we got acquainted, and we'd done a lot of dancing and things like that. We had a lot of things in common.

Jim: Did she like rabbit?

Hector: I don't know. But I haven't been a bartender since, either.

Jim: She likes square dancing though.

Hector: Oh yes.

Jim: Where you came from and where you met Jeannette, did they do a lot of square dancing?

Hector: Oh yes. I hate to admit this, but I can truthfully say I've been square dancing for 57 years. I remember square dancing when I was 11. My Dad was a caller at that time, where you stand up on a chair in a corner, you know, and had the fiddle and the banjo, and just go to it. But my Dad was a caller. He quit calling a long time before I started calling.

Jim: When you met Jeannette, did you meet her at a square dance.

Hector: We were going to some dances, yeah.

Jim: And that was in Canada.

Hector: Yeah.

Jim: And what year was that? I don't want to pry into your private life too far, but just tell me everything you know.

Hector: About 1951.

Jim: And did you fly up here with Jeannette, after you got married in 1951?

Hector: No, we drove up.

Jim: I see. Well, tell us about the drive up. You drove up the Alcan.

Hector: Yes, we did.

Jim: Tough road in those days.

Hector: Well, it was tough because we ran into about 1,200 miles of rain. It just rained all the time, for about 1,200 miles. And I was driving a Buick car and I'll never forget one afternoon, about 3 O'clock, I pulled into a service station and that Buick had been wet for so long, splashing water all over, up in the engine, it just stopped right there, in the service station. But after a few minutes, it got going again, and we come on ahead.

Jim: And was there any other adventures other than that momentary setback?

Hector: Oh, I remember there was three fellows driving Ford pickups, and now and then, those three guys, well, I wouldn't say they'd all end up in the ditch at the same time, but quite often they'd run in the ditch and somebody'd pull them out, and we'd see them up the road again. They were always passing us. But we were plugging along a little slower than they were. But they were driving those pickups up here for, I'm not sure, but I think it was Lonnie Hall, owned the Ford agency at that time.

Jim: And, I wonder who bought those Ford pickups.

Hector: I don't know.

Jim: Would you buy one of those?

Hector: No, I sure didn't.

Jim: That was a hard way up. In fact, I remember people would order those cars and it would take months before they arrived.

Hector: Oh, yes. I don't think those young fellows really hurt those pickups. They'd just slide in the ditch, you know. I don't think they dented them too much or anything like that, but they were getting stuck all the time.

Jim: Was that because of the rain and the mud?

Hector: Yeah, and their driving, of course.

Jim: Anything else about the trip? What was the road like? Did it have a lot of bogs in it, because of the rain?

Hector: Oh yes. A lot of times we could only go 25-30 miles an hour. And like I said, it just rained continuously for about 1,200 miles.

Jim: How about the Buick, did it ever get stuck?

Hector: Nope. We never got the Buick stuck.

Jim: What did Jeannette think when you brought her up? What did she say when she saw Fairbanks and the condition it was in? Was she happy to see it?

Hector: She fit in very well, really. The worst part of it that she had to put up with, was I had a little trailer house parked at Casperson's Trailer

Park out at Eielson Air Force Base, just this side of the gate there, and she had to stay there all day alone without any electricity or water or any other conveniences. And, of course, I was gone 10, 12, 14 hours a day, you know.

Jim: It's a wonder she didn't get cabin fever.

Hector: Well, it was in the summertime, and she'd visit Mrs. Casperson. It wasn't too pleasant when we first got here, but we were determined that we were going to save and get ahead a little bit, and it finally paid off.

Jim: We have a call, Hector. Hi, welcome to Alaska Gold Trails. You're on the air with Hector Therriault.

Caller: I've known Hector for quite a while and I just want to say, this is the most I've ever heard him talk at one time.

Jim: Is that right?

Caller: But I want to suggest something else. Sometime along the line, somebody ought to interview Jim Madonna.

Jim: Yeah. Well, I appreciate that. Thank you for the call. Well, Hector, we were talking about sitting in that little trailer and all. Tell me a little bit more about when you came up to Fairbanks, how long was it before you began Hector's Welding, out there at North Pole?

Hector: Well, when we first got here, we stayed in that little trailer, the first year. And then the second year, we decided to buy a bigger trailer and moved it on a lot there at 13 mile Richardson Highway. And I was working for the big contractors, and smaller contractors were always asking me to do welding for them. So, I bought myself an old welder and got a cutting torch, and I started doing some of that work at home. I didn't have any shop, or anything like that. All I had was that old welder and that cutting torch. I'd pick up pieces of iron if I could here and there for different things. But most of the time, they would furnish the iron. But I used to do fish plate, frames, and stuff like that, on weekends at home. Finally I got myself an old piece of a building that came off the base, an old wooden building, and I started in that. But even then it wasn't Hector's Welding. It was just someplace where you could get work done, if I was home. But then it went along like that for a year or so, then I finally bought that property on the Old Rich, and moved that old building over there—took it along with me and I operated out of that for a while. And then I finally got a little steel quonset hut from Clear—after they built the facilities at Clear, the building became available, and I hauled that steel building home with my pickup. I'd go down and tear down a load every day and haul it home, and go back the next day and get another load, and finally got everything except one load—the stuff was too long for my pickup, so I got a bigger truck and made it in one load. That was quite a job, right in the wintertime, you know. And that's where Hector's Welding, you might say, started. But after I got done working for Morrison-Knudsen, I went to work at Gilmore for about two and a half years. And while I was up there, they had several people stop by the house and say, "Well, why don't you open up a shop?" The pipeline is wanting some work done. I thought, "Hey, this is too good a job to quit. But then, I was gone away from home 12 hours a day and didn't have much time to do any work when I was at home. So, come the next summer, I finally quit Gilmore and opened up Hector's Welding for good. That's when it started. I don't remember what year that was.

Jim: Now, was that at the present location or was that the shop next to your home?

Hector: That was at the little shop next to my home.

Jim: When did you move over to 13-mile Rich?

Hector: Well, in the meantime, 1969, we bought 60 acres there, where the shop is located now, from Mrs. Pennell. The lady had moved to San Francisco by then. And that's the third time that I had bought property from her. So, we bought that property, and there was absolutely nothing on it, just trees. There was not even any rabbit trails or moose trails. But anyway, we started clearing some of the land over there, and let's see, the first building I got over there was another quonset that I got from S.S. Mullens, when they got done with a job at Eielson. There again, I went out there and tore it down in the wintertime to move it, and the next summer we started putting it up. We didn't get much of it done that summer, but the following year we put enough of the building up to move into it. Of course, by that time, I was working for the pipeline pretty strong.

Jim: What year did you finalize the 13-mile Richardson shop?

Hector: Well, let's see. It must've been about 1974. It grew very slowly at first, and when the pipeline got about halfway over is when Hector's Welding started to really come alive.

Jim: Hector, how did you get involved in preparing sluice boxes and mining equipment for the placer mining industry of Alaska?

Hector: Well, I'd been working for Morrison-Knudsen, running the crusher for many many years. I was the repairman out there and I knew how to handle gravel pretty well, and then when the miners came along, they wanted sluice boxes. That's where we started. The one that of course was quite popular was what's been known as Hector's Welding. I didn't name that, the miners did themselves. They named it "Hector's Box." And a fellow by the name of Bill Carl helped me design it, and we went on from there. Now we do anything the miner wants us to do—we build trommels or feeders or conveyors, or put the whole plant together. Some places we've done the entire plant, for miners—not in one piece, but I mean in different parts—and they seem very satisfied.

Jim: Time has run out on us today, Hector. I want to thank you for joining us here on Alaska Gold Trails. I want to also thank the folks out there in listening land for joining us today. Thank you, Hector.

Hector: Thank you, Jim.

Rudy Vetter
with
Jim Madonna
November 13, 1987

Jim: Our guest today is Rudy Vetter, a well known Alaskan prospector and miner. Welcome to Alaska Gold Trails, Rudy. I understand we're going to talk about prospecting and mining in Alaska.

Rudy: That's right. That's the subject.

Jim: First Rudy, why don't you give us some background information on some of the activities you were involved in prior to coming to Alaska.

Rudy: Well, I was born June 6, 1917, in Roof, Washington, which is in the Southeastern part of the state. I was a twin. My twin brother Adolph also lived here in Fairbanks for a number of years. He took part, with me and my wife, in our mining operations. I came to Alaska in 1951 with the purpose of going into mining and prospecting. Adolph spent several years here before I did. My background prior to coming to Alaska was primarily in ranching—cattle ranching, wheat raising, and fruit production in the Quincy-Alfreda area. After my tour of duty in the Air Force, overseas in the South Pacific during World War II, I went to Wallis, Idaho, and worked for Sunshine Mining Co., underground. We worked at the 3,600-foot level there, that is 3,600 feet underground, in the old Jewel Shaft. Sunshine is still in operation. I worked on a number of construction jobs and in the woods in Washington and Idaho, and in May of 1951 I came to Fairbanks for the first time.

Jim: What caused you to come to Fairbanks, Rudy? What was the magnet that drew you up to the cold north?

Rudy: I was always interested in Alaska because I knew a number of the people who worked here in fishing and primarily in mining. I don't remember how many, but a large number of them made some fortunes and moved into Washington state, and invested in various enterprises. I think some of the really old timers here in Fairbanks may remember the E.J. McKenna family. Their stories about the gold and gold mining in Alaska intrigued me and this is, as I said before, why I came here to do prospecting and mining.

Jim: In their stories did they tell you about the big gold discoveries in Fairbanks?

Rudy: Oh yes, those people were enthusiastic. A large number of them made some substantial fortunes and took their money and invested it in a little milder climate as they were becoming older.

Jim: How did they mine in those early days, Rudy?

Rudy: Most of it was drift mining, or underground mining of placer ground.

Jim: And was Fairbanks a big drift mining area in the early days?

Rudy: Yes, and I knew many of the people that were drift mining here from 1902 'til about 1930.

Jim: And it was because of these people that came down and visited you and perhaps made their new homes in Washington, that you got struck with gold fever?

Rudy: Yes, that's right, Jim. That was a primary factor. That's why I came to Alaska.

Jim: When did you get married, Rudy?

Rudy: Grace and I were married the second of February, 1944, in Brisbane, Australia. She was born and raised in Sydney, Australia. She was a big city gal. Sydney had a population of about 600,000 at that time.

Jim: You mean you drug her off to the frozen north.

Rudy: Oh, yes.

Jim: You and your brother Adolph were twins, and Adolph came to Alaska a couple of years before you did, is that right?

Rudy: Yes, 1949. He worked for the old F.E. Co. in placer mining and on the dredges.

Jim: And then you came about two years later?

Rudy: That's right, two years later.

Jim: Once you came to Alaska, Rudy, what was the first job that you entered into?

Rudy: I went to Healy and went to work at the Cap Lathrop mine building a new power plant. And from there I came back to town and did some work constructing sidewalks, streets, and roads in the Fairbanks area, in general construction.

Jim: At that time did you do any prospecting or mining in the Fairbanks area?

Rudy: We prospected generally in the Fairbanks area, although we did look at some other areas within the Interior. As many people will remember, I was head custodian in the school system for about 17 years. During that period we had a lot of free time to do a lot of prospecting. And of course I want to thank my wife Grace because there were some times when we spent a lot of time prospecting where I should've perhaps spent more time with my wife. I really appreciate her forbearance there.

Jim: These "prospectors' widows" have to put up with a lot don't they Rudy? Prospectors lead a rough life away from home in many cases. Tell us about some of the areas that you looked into during your prospecting adventures.

Rudy: We prospected the Nation River country north of Eagle, the southern slopes of the Brooks Range, and the Wood River country. We finally settled down and concentrated our prospecting effort northeast of Fairbanks, in the Cleary Hill area.

Jim: What was the result of your hard work over in the Cleary Hill area Rudy? Did you make some valuable discoveries?

Rudy: Yes we did. We made a significant discovery over there on what's known as the Christina group. We did some production on that. I think we produced about 5,000 ounces of gold. We mined and milled that at the old Cleary Hill and the High-U mill.

Jim: What kind of mill was that High-U mill?

Rudy: It was on old five-battery stamp mill. It's a mortar and pestle principle with amalgamation for recovering the gold.

Jim: You recovered about 5,000 ounces of gold using that five-stamp mill then?

Rudy: That's right. That was prior to about 1962. We didn't do much mining after that. All we did was the assessment work, and then we optioned our ground to a large company for seven years. They did a substantial amount of work, including running some drifts. One drift on the Christina claim is 1,700 feet long. Perhaps the best way for the general public to understand what I'm talking about when I say "drift" would be a tunnel. However the word tunnel is not proper mining terminology. They also did a lot of core drilling which is now valuable information. It would cost about three million dollars to do that today. It's now being reviewed by another company, and it looks like maybe eventually we will get a mine up there on the hill.

Jim: Rudy, could you run through the method that you used in discovering the Christina claims and how you went step-by-step through the prospecting adventure that brought you to the discovery.

Rudy: I want to stress access. That's the one thing a prospector should keep in mind. We finally decided after several years that we would move into the Fairbanks area, and we attended several Mining Extension courses out at the University. One of them was the Total Heavy Minerals method, which is a calorimetric method of mineral determination, and we used that, along with certain other geological evidence that we had acquired. Most of our prospecting methods we have used was by experimentation and a self-learning process. After we started prospecting with the geochemical method, we found an anomoly, or a target area, and from there we decided that the geochemical prospecting results were such that we had to go in and attempt to explore and make a mine out of it. We took a Cat tractor in there, a D-8, and made several cuts, and in the first cut that we made we found mineralization from which the geochemical target was derived. And the first year we took out about 100 tons and recovered about 300 ounces of gold. For the next four successive years we mined and recovered, as I said, about 5,000 ounces. Then we had a small problem regarding the leases and we let it lie idle for about nine or ten years. During that interim my brother stayed here and worked in the school, and I worked on the North Slope as a service oiler for eight years. 1978 is the year I believe that we leased to the first large company, and as I said they explored it for about seven years. Approximately a year ago, we leased the property to a new company.

Jim: Rudy, a few years ago you permitted some of my students and me to come down and visit the mine where you were working—actually it was a decade ago if I remember right—and you provided us with a few small samples of ore taken from the claim. In the samples there was visible gold, along with stibnite, the ore of antimony, in a beautiful white quartz matrix. Can you tell us about that ore vein and the tenor of the ground.

Rudy: Well that was the main vein system we found with our geochemical prospecting methods. It was in what we assume to be a shear zone, a large fractured area where the ore was deposited, and it had broken sections of very high grade gold, visible gold in quartz. Some of it assayed at 100 ounces to the ton. The vein averaged about 18 inches wide, and the average grade, by careful selective mining of the ore, ran an average of about three ounces to the ton of recoverable gold. However, we sold all of our production at a base price of $35 an ounce and with the dross, or the sulphide minerals that were associated with the gold product, decreased the total net value to us to an average of $30 an ounce. One of the peculiarities about that vein is that it had a blue aluminum silicate gouge. A gouge is a product that's derived from these types of veins, that looks like a clay, and it is an aluminum silicate. Wherever you run into these clays in the placer mining areas, it would behoove you to make a good check of those areas.

Jim: From your experience it appears that the blue clay is a pathfinder to a lode gold deposit then?

Rudy: Yes, it is a pathfinder to lode deposits. Iron and iron pyrite are also good pathfinders to lode deposits, especially the very fine-grained pyrites that are an eighth of an inch or smaller. Antimony, of course, is another pathfinder. I rely very strongly on a field check of the Total Heavy Minerals geochemical method of prospecting, using dithizone dye and gasoline for an oxidizer. It will lead you into the area and provide a target to investigate further.

Jim: So this dye, then, indicates the presence of valuable heavy metals in some cases.

Rudy: That's right. Primarily zinc, copper and lead. It's a calorimetric method. Each mineral of the three I cited will produce a different color.

Jim: It's the association of gold with these minerals then that give you an indirect prospecting technique.

Rudy: That's right. It's especially true in the Fairbanks area I think, but worldwide it's becoming very evident that antimony, iron pyrite, lead and silver almost always are good pathfinders for gold. You can either locate the high grade gold vein systems or you may find a halo of highly disseminated gold that is perhaps not as rich. But with new prospecting methods and new methods of extraction and mineral development it makes it very lucrative to investigate these areas thoroughly.

Jim: Rudy, in your experiences as you've prospected around the country, have you recognized that the ore veins and ore deposits are distinguished by a much higher and brighter coloration than the surrounding country rock? Is color a possible indicator of ore deposits?

Rudy: Oh yes, and there are several factors there. Color is a very definite factor and color varies with the degree of moisture that you have in the soil or in the earth. Sometimes some of the minerals show better when they're dry. Always when prospecting, you should use your rock hammer to break rocks, especially when you think you're in a mineralized zone. Don't hesitate to break the rocks and look at a fresh surface. Once you've broken your rocks, if there's any show of pyrite or mineralization, get it sawed on a diamond saw. Your minerals show up with greater strength if you have a flat sawed surface than they do on a broken surface. Carry a hand lens at all times so that you can look at the rocks. One of the primary attributes, I believe, of a prospector is to be curious. Don't let me or anyone else tell you that a mineral deposit will not occur, because about the first time you make a statement like that someone proves you're mistaken.

Jim: I did that in one of my classes once. I told some students that gold wouldn't occur in a particular locality. They wouldn't take my word for it and went to take a look, and sure enough there was the gold. Guess you can't win 'em all, can you? Well Rudy, what about that antimony that was associated with your gold. Do you ever make any money off the antimony?

Rudy: Well, antimony is rather a sporadic occurrence and the price fluctuates very widely. I would say don't anticipate making any money on antimony, at least in the Fairbanks area. If these low-grade high-volume, large-tonnage deposits are ever developed, undoubtedly there will be some money made from it, but for the small prospector.... if you find some antimony, see if you can find a market for it and attempt to sell it, but I certainly wouldn't say that antimony in itself is going to be a profitable thing. But it is a good highlight or target area to work in, because where you find antimony you usually find the gold.

Jim: Would you suggest that miners collecting antimony stick it in a barrel for a later rise in prices?

Rudy: Yes, that would be a very good thing to do. Had we done that I could've made a considerable amount of money. Antimony was so cheap that when we first prospected in the area and did our mining in the area it really didn't pay. You would not have made 50 cents an hour putting it in barrels and saving it. But that definitely, Jim, would be a very good thing to do. Don't throw it away.

Jim: Well, it's kind of a long-range plan isn't it?

Rudy: That's right. It has been up to approximately $2 a pound at times. One of the things, you asked me Jim, was in regard to prospecting and what I would do or how I would start prospecting. If I were new to the area, one of the first steps would be considerable research out to the college and find out where the mines have been in the past, going back as far as 1902. There are a lot of old U.S. Geological Survey bulletins around. They will get you target areas. Then the next thing, of course, is research the B.L.M. and the state records to find out where there are valid mineral claims, because you don't want to waste any time staking on valid mineral claims and it will cause a lot of trouble to other people. I would then learn the geochemical method of prospecting that I described. Are you still teaching that Jim?

Jim: Yes, we teach it once a year. By the way Rudy, one question that I have, regarding the U.S.G.S. publications. Are those available at the University of Alaska's library?

Rudy: Yes they are.

Jim: And where else might they be found?

Rudy: I think there are a few down at University and Geist, at the State Department of Natural Resources.

Jim: You also made reference to the Bureau of Land Management and if I'm not mistaken that's still out on Ft. Wainwright.

Rudy: Yes, and D.N.R. is at University and Geist Road in the bank building upstairs. Mildred Brown, Carol Stevenson, or Joy Zuke are in charge of the records division. Those ladies are very important and do a very good job. I want to compliment them and thank them for their efforts. They have a great deal of information that isn't even on file. They have a very good knowledge of how that system works, and if you check with them they can help you and assist you in locating the areas that are really heavily staked and show you how to use the process and determine where you might do your staking or filing of minerals rights. They've been very helpful.

Jim: You mean they've been there so long that they have items coming through that aren't necessarily written down?

Rudy: That's right, and they remember those things.

Jim: Well Rudy, we've hit on a couple of areas to gather information. One of the areas of course is the U.S. Geological Survey. One of the comments that has been made by you and a lot of other prospectors is that if you want to go prospecting, go prospecting in an area where valuable minerals have been discovered before. And that's probably one of the reasons for investigating these areas of high mineralization that the U.S.G.S. has defined early on in the century. The other is, and you pointed this out clearly to us, we don't want to go prospecting on land that is already set aside for another use or is otherwise taken up as mining claims. So we go to the Bureau of Land Management or the Division of Geological and Geophysical Surveys for that information. From there where would you go on your prospecting adventure, Rudy?

Rudy: Of course, the final step is field work. There is one other source at the university that you might check. And that's in the archives. There's a lot of old information there that might help in your field work. You should learn all you possibly can in regard to rules and regulations in mining. Spend a lot of your time in reading. I believe that you should be well informed when you go out into the field. There is one book I'd like to recommend, and that is Boyle's book, and the title is "The Geochemistry of Gold and its Deposits." That's available here in town. It's rather expensive but it will answer a lot of questions once you get into mining and are interested. The answers are there, and if people learn to interpret them and follow his information I'm sure that they can become very successful in mining and prospecting.

Jim: There's a footnote to that, Rudy. Boyle just recently came out with a new book simply entitled "Gold," and both of those books deal strictly with gold and its deposits—one from a chemical standpoint and the other more from a geological and depositional standpoint.

Rudy: I've heard of Boyle's new book on gold, and I've ordered one. The next step after being sure that I understand the rules and regulations and doing extensive reading concerning where you might want to prospect, and as you said, Jim, if you're going to prospect, prospect in areas where the minerals have been found before. That's becoming more apparent all the time. Prospect in the accessible areas. We have hundreds of miles of roads and streams that permit access from here south, all the way into Southeastern Alaska, and from here all the way north to the Arctic Ocean, that have not been checked at all, and access is of prime importance. The next thing I'd do, as I said before, get myself a good hand lens and learn how to use it and learn mineral identification. Classes are available every year out at the University of Alaska Mining Extension. Then I would enter the field, be inquisitive, break rocks, look for coloration, look for breaks in the formations and the general structure of the ridges and hills.

Jim: Rudy, thank you so much for sharing your experiences with us. We have all learned a great deal from the information you have so freely given. We hope some of our audience will use Rudy's suggestions to guide them in locating a valuable gold deposit.

Doris Vogler
with
Jim Madonna
October 19, 1989

Jim: Welcome to Alaska Gold Trails, ladies and gentlemen. Folks, we are going to do something real new here today. We are going to attempt to have the guest, who is having some trouble getting out of her driveway and down the road because she is snowed in, talk to us over the telephone. And I'm wondering if our guest Doris Vogler can hear us.

Doris: Yes, I can.

Jim: You can? OK, Doris, welcome to Alaska Gold Trails. I hope the listening audience can hear us all right. It amazes me, all these little buttons you can push and wonderful things happen. I don't know how they do this. But at any rate, Doris, welcome to Alaska Gold Trails, and why don't you start by giving us a little bit of background concerning where you were born and maybe even before that—how your parents met and what went on. I know they had quite a history and there was some interesting background that occurred prior to your coming to Alaska. Why don't you fill us in on that. You can even tell us your age, if you'd like.

Doris: Ooh, I'm getting pretty old. Let me start back in the run of Oklahoma. Of course, I didn't make the run, understand, but my grandparents did, and I'm an Okie from Oklahoma, born in 1919, but anyway they did make the run, and they set up saloons, right next door to each other, in competition.

Jim: Saloons?

Doris: Saloons. Yeah, that's where they made the run into Oklahoma, I believe into Guthrie. And then they set up saloons right next door to each other, in competition, and that's where my mother and father met. My grandparents came from the old country. My grandfather had set up saloons on that side, came from Germany, and his wife came from Poland. And they didn't speak much English. The grandparents on my mother's side, they came from oh, Kansas, really, they were farmers. But anyway, that's the way that my mother and father met, Their parents set up saloons next door to each other in Oklahoma.

Jim: Tell me about this land rush. What is that all about.

Doris: You know, Jim, I wasn't there. I really don't know. That's all I know, is that I just remember hearing stories my mother telling us that's how she and my dad met. It was long before my time.

Jim: When I was a young man, I used to watch movies, and it seemed like there was wagons and covered wagons and horses and everybody'd started in a line and somebody'd shoot off a gun and that was the start of the race to the area that was being opened up. Is that kind of what we're talking about here?

Doris: Yes. That's what I understand that it was. And I do have a brother that's 17 years older than I am, so you know that it was a long time ago before I came along, after they met and after they married and had my brother.

Jim: Tell us, did you grow up in this little town with the two saloons?

Doris: No, no. I grew up in Oklahoma City.

Jim: In Oklahoma City. You're a city girl. Tell us about how life was in Oklahoma City back in the days that you grew up there.

Doris: Well, it was an oil boom town, and we had oil wells—they were going all over the place, in south Oklahoma City, oil wells sprung up everywhere. In fact we had one in our back yard. Well that's true. There was some sitting right in front of the capitol in Oklahoma City.

Jim: This must be similar to what's happening in southern California, where you sometimes see these oil pumping stations in peoples back yards.

Doris: That's right, that's right. As I said, we had one in our back yard, so I pretty well know what an oil well looks like.

Jim: Tell us some about growing up there, in terms of what you did as a young person growing up in Oklahoma City, in the high school environment. Did Oklahoma City have a lot of students in the school or was it pretty small at that time?

Doris: No, Oklahoma City had competitive schools. There was Central School, Claxon School, and Capitol Hill. And then later, I believe, there became Britain, but not while I was going to school. But anyway, we had the three that were competitors, as far as football teams were concerned and basketball and, you know, the sports events.

Jim: Sure.

Doris: That's the way it was back there. And in my younger years, I grew up in a parochial school, a Catholic school, in Wichita, Kansas. I mean, that's where I went to school. And, of course, I was home in the summertime, but I did that until I was in the ninth grade in junior high school, then I went into public school.

Jim: How far in school did you go?

Doris: Well, I went into college. I mean, you know, I graduated from high school, and I was in college and also business college.

Jim: In Oklahoma City?

Doris: No, in Norman, Oklahoma, it was only 19 miles from Oklahoma City. Also I did go to Oklahoma City University, which is in Oklahoma City.

Jim: What did you major in, Doris?

Doris: Well, I majored in English, but did very poorly at it.

Jim: What caused you to stop college?

Doris: The war.

Jim: What did you do when the war came along?

Doris: Well, I went to school then I worked for IBM until the boys came home from the service, and when they came home from the service, you naturally gave up your jobs and they took over. But we did the payroll for Tinkers Field and for Douglass Aircraft, and some of the oil companies there in Oklahoma City, I remember also, and Anderson-Pritchards. So, I worked for IBM—International Business Machine. There wasn't many others in the office. Of course, those machines could do it all, you understand. There were only about 10 of us in the office.

Jim: You gave that job up when the boys came home?

Doris: Well, yes you did, because I had worked up into a tab operator, that's pretty close to the top there, and of course when they came home, they had IBM machines in the field there, at the latter part of the war. And when they came home they were qualified to step in, and besides that, I guess we took their jobs when they left, or some of them, when they left. During the war they didn't have much of a choice, 'cause I think we only had one man that worked for IBM, and the rest of us were all women.

Jim: Doris, what happened following your employment with IBM. What did you do then?

Doris: Well, after the war, I traveled to Anchorage, Alaska, for a while then returned home. Then I came back when Vince Monten, out of Oklahoma City, contracted to build the utilidors out here at Ladd Air Force Base, in '48. '49, '50, I believe. But anyway, I got a job, but I was only supposed to be here for a month. Two years later I went home and got the rest of my clothes and came back.

Jim: I understood that you came up here with just a little hand-carried bag.

Doris: I did. I carried one suitcase, 'cause I was only going to stay one month. I liked it so well in Fairbanks—I didn't think I'd like Fairbanks at all. I mean, Anchorage, you know, was more of a city.

Jim: More what you were used to.

Doris: Yes. But you know what? I loved Fairbanks. I just loved everybody in it and everything about it. I'm still here, and I'm going to die here, I suppose, and I'm going to be buried or something's going to happen to me here.

Jim: What was Fairbanks like when you first dropped in here? What did you think? I mean the first moment.

Doris: Well, when I first dropped in here, I landed at Ladd Air Force Base and rode Pan American. And I don't know, about four or five o'clock in the morning, and it was beautiful out there, and I got a cab to town. I didn't know anybody, didn't know anything in town, and I wandered around and there was a cafe down there. I passed it and I don't believe it was open. It was the Model Cafe that I ended up in and had breakfast— I mean a cup of coffee and what have you—'til somebody came and salvaged me. And they did. They finally found me and took me out to the base, where Vince Monten had a contractor's barracks out there, and I stayed in the barracks, and ate in the mess hall.

Jim: I see. And what was Fairbanks like? Did you see it as a frontier, rough tough frontier town?

Doris: Yes, but I loved it. Everybody was friendly. My gosh, people spoke to you whether they knew you or whether they didn't know you. You'd go into a store, and they'd welcome you with open arms. It was just wonderful.

Jim: Hi, Doris, are you back with me?

Doris: Yes, I am.

Jim: The phone fades your voice in and out, but we keep getting you back. This is marvelous.

Doris: You've got little gremlins up there in the studio, and they do all kinds of funny things. You know, Halloween's coming up.

Jim: I think that's the truth.

Doris: And I think Bill Walley probably planted some up there and they breed faster than he planned.

Jim: Doris, I don't know what's going on, but you want to try this again? We have another caller. They want to ask you a question.

Doris: Well, go ahead.

Jim: Hello.

Caller: Hello, am I on?

Jim: You're on the air.

Caller: I'm afraid that I'm not going to have a chance to get this question in, because it's moving, you know it's a closing door. And I think I'm rushing the program a bit, but the hour of 2 O'clock is getting here. Doris, you're a very interesting woman. I know of you and I've heard of you, and I admire you very much. I'd like to know—your husband is also very interesting—how you met him, when you met him, when you were dating, was it here in Fairbanks? What it was like then, and maybe even how he proposed. Would you mind telling us that?

Jim: My, that's quite an order. Doris, are you ready for that one?

Doris: I s'pose so. Yes, the lady wanted to know when I met Joe.

Jim: She wants to know about your love life.

Doris: Well, it was about 40 years ago, back in the late '40s that I met Joe Vogler. And I had a labrador retriever I named Lucky, and also a station wagon, and I was coming back one weekend from Anchorage, and my labrador retriever—I'd been rather cruel to him; he hadn't had an opportunity to do any hunting or anything. So I saw across from Donnelly Dome there was a big pool down there, and there were some ducks swimming around just in the middle, and they just swum around in the middle, and I didn't know that anybody else was down there. So, I pulled up in front of this big old truck sitting there—it wasn't a pickup, it was a big old truck, and god, it had bear, it had moose, it had everything, you name it. And there was a big old gruff voice came up and said, "You come one step closer and I'll shoot you." And I kind of backed off. And Ralph Peyton happened to be down there with Joe Vogler. He says, "Oh," since he knew who I was, he says, "Oh, she's got a labrador." He says, "She'll get our ducks for us." So, sure enough, my dog went down and got the ducks. Well, they had a dog named Topsy, and Topsy would just go out and swim around those ducks and come back. And I believe it was a water spaniel dog, Topsy was. Anyway, my dog went out and retrieved their ducks and what have you. And you know, he never gave me one duck or anything else for getting his ducks for him. So that's the way that I met Joe Vogler, down in a pothole, across from Donnelley Dome, on the other side of Delta.

Jim: What a romantic story, Doris. Tell us what happened after that. How did you get acquainted with Joe, following that period of time.

Doris: Well, I loaned him a book one time, on dogs. He was interested in retrievers. He brought it home and hung it on the door.

Jim: You mean when he returned it, he hung it on your door?

Doris: Oh yeah. If I'd go over to Peyton's he'd be over there. They still live here, by the way, Ralph and Linda Peyton, and I'd go over to the Peyton's and he'd come in and sit on a chair for maybe five minutes and leave. He never did stay at one place, at anybody's house, more than about five or ten minutes, that I know of, at that time. And he used to eat down at the Model Cafe and also down at Jimmie Lee's, there in the basement of the Mecca Bar. And of course, we all went to the Model Cafe and we all went to the Mecca Bar, we all went to Jimmie Lee's. So, you know, this was back in territorial days, and we were all just one big happy family, everybody in the whole town of Fairbanks. So, anyway, then I left. You might say I had one date with Joe Vogler. I was living in Anchorage, where I had my own business at that time. I was up here staying with a good friend of mine, Juanita Davis, and ran into Joe Vogler on the street. So he asked if he could take me to dinner and also have the Davises come along. So we went over to Jimmie Lee's, who then had the old cafe on seventh and Lacey, can't think of the name of it offhand, but anyway, so we went to Jimmie Lee's again for dinner. Well, he asked me if I would marry him, and that scared the dickens out of me. So I went back to Anchorage. So I ran off from him. I didn't come back.

Jim: That scared you, did it, Doris?

Doris: Yeah it did. Yes, it did.

Jim: One minute he's chasing you away from his truck and he's got all this food in it; the next minute he's trying to share it with you for the rest of your life. Strange things happen in the land of the midnight sun.

Doris: Well. Anyway, I was in the Lower 48, and I was thinking, "Well, I'd come back to Fairbanks," because Fairbanks was always my favorite over and above Anchorage. So, I had written him a letter up here, and sure enough he wasn't up here. I was in Oklahoma when I wrote the letter, and he was in Canada, and I didn't know that. His mother was ill, so he was down there with her, just for a short visit. Somebody up here, Howard Sparks, was picking up his mail, so he sent him the letter. Oh I corresponded with him a little bit, but then he'd write and then I never would answer and I'd move around, and that was about the end of that. So what he did was come to Oklahoma City, because the address I gave him was my cousin's address in Oklahoma City. So he called my cousins, and they said, well, that I wasn't there and they wasn't going to tell him where I was, because they weren't telling anybody. So anyway, they called me then—I was in Dallas, Texas—and they called me and said, "There's some guy here in Oklahoma City by the name of Joe Vogler, and he's looking for you." I said, "Oh, my gosh." They said, "Yes, he's staying at the Black Hotel." So they gave me the telephone number. I called him. Well, he said, he's at least going to come down to Dallas. And I said, "Well, I'll go meet you at the airport, then." So I went out to the airport. He was supposed to come in on Pan American, I believe, and I'm sitting in Pan American office—not Pan American, American Airlines—and he came in on Braniff, and somebody tapped me on the shoulder and I turned around and looked at him and he's come in an hour early. Well, I happened to have just got there. Anyway, so I married him.

Jim: In the airport, Doris?

Doris: No, no. I married him in Dallas, Texas.

Jim: What did you do, you went and got the license?

Doris: Well, yeah, I mean, went and got a license, had to have a blood test and all those kinds of things.

Jim: Well, I'll say this for you, kid, when you make up your mind, you just go right ahead and do the job.

Doris: Oh, it took a long time for me to make up my mind. He carried that wedding ring around for a long time. I was kind of shy.

Jim: Doris, I've never known you to be shy.

Doris: Well, I was then.

Jim: You know, it's been fun knowing you all these years, Doris. I've enjoyed you. I have one little comment that I wanted to bring out to the listening audience, that a couple of years ago the Alaska Women in Mining voted you and Joe Vogler the Man and Woman in Mining of the Year. And that was a nice festive occasion. Fact is, at that period of time my wife Leah was the President of AWIM.

Doris: Yes, she was.

Jim: We had a wonderful time. And I made a videotape of that. Did I ever give you a copy of that?

Doris: No, you didn't.

Jim: Did I ever promise you one?

Doris: Yes, you did.

Jim: Well, that goes to show you what kind of guy I am.

Doris: Well, you said you were a perfectionist, and it had to be perfect, and you were working on it to perfect it. I don't know how.

Jim: Oh, it is so close to perfection, Doris, I might as well just give you a copy.

Doris: Well everything you do, Jim Madonna, is perfect.

Jim: Oh yes, kid. We know that to be true. Look, there's one other question. We had the ice carnival, which used to be a real big event in Fairbanks. Do you remember the annual ice carnivals back in the late '40s and early '50s?

Doris: You better believe it.

Jim: Oh they were fun, weren't they.

Doris: Oh yes. That was back, yes, I was living in the Rose Building.

Jim: Oh. Tell us about the Rose Building.

Doris: Well, not many people would probably know where the Rose Building was. But the Rose Building is a building right across from the News-Miner, and downstairs there used to be, I think, Wagner's finally moved there. And then the Gatzer that had the agricultural department, he was downstairs. But anyway, I lived upstairs in the Rose Building. I was working for the Road Commission then. This was back in territorial days too, I believe it was in '49 or somewhere back in there. And this was before Joe and I were married, or anything like that. So, anyway, I lived there in the Rose Building, and the ice hockey team from Canada lived there also with their wives and what have you. So, they played hockey down there. And I used to go down and watch the hockey games all the time. And by the way, I used to run into Joe Vogler down there, when I was down watching hockey games.

Jim: You did?

Doris: Yes, I did. But anyway, I used to go down there, but the winter carnivals were absolutely fabulous. And I had an old 8mm camera and I took a bunch of carnival pictures down there, which I still have. And Gareth Wright, I think, one year won the dog race and they were handing him a crown and I believe he was married to Vera Stragg, and she was the queen of the carnival. It was real fun back in those days. But living in the Rose Building is something else. It's upstairs, it's kind of crickety, and the bathroom is just unbelievable, or it was at that time.

Jim: Come on, take it easy, now, kid. It's a great place.

Doris: You want to live there, Jim?

Jim: No, but my affiliation with it at the moment is nice.

Doris: Well, yes. But I'm surprised the building's still standing.

Jim: What kind of guy do you think I am?

Doris: Well, we used to have the railroad station right next to it. And the train used to... boy, it'd wake you up, too, and you'd think it was coming right through the middle of your bed. That choo-choo train, no kidding.

Jim: Yeah. I have got to tell the listening audience that I'm currently the owner of the Rose Building, and it's where George's Saw Shop is located, right at this time. As Doris pointed out, when the train came by, it made a lot of noise. There have been a lot of businesses in there over the years.

Doris: Yes, there was.

Jim: One donut shop, I believe, back in the late '40s early '50s.

Doris: Oh yes. The Spud-Nut Shop.

Jim: Yeah, the Spud-Nut Shop.

Doris: Hey, you go back a long way, too, Jim Madonna.

Jim: Well, you know, when I was going to school here, now we've only got a minute left, but it was always nice because I lived over in that area, and I passed the Spud-Nut Shop every morning on the way to school, so I'd stop in there and I'd get a hot glazed donut. Boy, they were great. They were just made, and off to school I'd go with this hot glazed donut. I'll never forget that.

Doris: Now, that was right across from the hospital there. They did make good donuts.

Jim: Well, Doris, you know, I've had a nice talk with you. Is there anything you'd like to say before we close out here?

Doris: No, except one thing. I think you have very nice sponsors. Thank you for having me on, and I hope I answered everyones questions alright.

Jim: Thanks for joining us, Doris.

Doris: You bet.

Joe Vogler
with
Jim Madonna
April 1, 1988

Jim: Hello, Joe Vogler, welcome to Alaska Gold Trails. It's a pleasure to have you on the show.

Joe: It's a pleasure to be here, Jim.

Jim: Let's just get this started right. Where did you come from and what year did you arrive on the planet?

Joe: Well, that was about April 24, 1913. I don't know where I come from. I'm not sure where I'm going, but that's the statistics that show up on my birth certificate.

Jim: And where do they have your birth certificate?

Joe: That was in Barnes, Kansas. It's a little town in eastern Washington County. It's in the northeast part of the state, due south of Beatrice, Nebraska, about 30-35 miles. Little wind-blown plain, little limestone, few trees in the bottoms.

Jim: And tell us, Joe, is there a lot of mining around that part of Kansas? Is that where you got interested in mining?

Joe: No, Blue Rapids, in the next county east, mined an awful lot of gypsum. There's terrific acres and acres and acres of underground caverns there where they took out gypsum at Blue Rapids and made wallboard. That's an old old industry in that country. But that isn't where I got my interest in gold mining. I think that probably came from my grandfather, because when I was about nine years old, I'd just moved to the country and I'd started in a little country school—had one room and I think about fifteen kids, and a potbellied stove in the middle for heat. One teacher, and you heard everybody recite. So you got an education from the first grade through the eighth, no matter whether you wanted it or not. And the teacher asked us what we wanted out of life. And I told her I wanted ten acres of ground, paid for, I wanted a rock house that couldn't burn, I wanted an orchard and a garden, and I wanted enough gold buried to pay taxes as long as I lived. This was in 1921 or 22, and the panic of '21 had pretty well cleaned out the farming area in Kansas; every other farm was either owned by a bank or an insurance company, and times were tough. The "poor farms" were filled with people—the county poor farms. And so something impressed upon my mind that it was necessary to pay taxes.

I figured that was the best hedge. And I probably can blame my grand-father for it, because he used to sell cattle and the rumor was that he brought it home in gold coins and buried it somewhere. As far as we know, it's still there.

Jim: Tell us, Joe, did you go all the way through school in Barnes, Kansas?

Joe: Well, I got four grades there in two years, then I moved to a farm.

Jim: What did you do, get in a hurry?

Joe: I don't know. Maybe I was obnoxious or something, but I took the first and second grade in one year and then I took the same the third and fourth, you see, so I got a couple years out of step with my classmates, which didn't help any. We moved to the farm in January first of 1921. They had a little country school there where I picked up and went on.

Jim: Beginning in 1921, how far did you go in that little country school?

Joe: Well, let's see, I went there through '24. I went there three, three and a half years and graduated from the eighth grade, I think in '24, then I spent four years in Waterville, Kansas—that's a little town in Marshall County. I lived on the farm and went there for high school and got out of high school in May of 1929, 16 years old and things weren't too good. The farming area was still in a depression although the October crash hadn't hit yet. But it was not good, I'll tell you that much

Jim: From that time, you went on to college, right?

Joe: Yeah. I took a scholarship examination in summer of 1929. Summerfield Scholarship—it's in Kansas—and I was one of the ten selected, and I got four years of college out of that. $500 a year, and that put me through school, and I borrowed $600 for my final year. I graduated in 1934 with a law degree and was admitted to the bar the following month or so, about June of '34.

Jim: So, you didn't get your degree in mining, you got it in law?

Joe: Yeah. You see, I'd planned on having to work my way through school, and I'd dreamed about going to the School of Mines. But that didn't work out. My father wanted me to be a lawyer, and when I wound up with a scholarship, why that's all I heard. You didn't argue much with Papa at that time.

Jim: From what I've heard, you don't argue much with Joe Vogler at this time. Joe, tell me something about education. You came up here to Alaska, and I don't want to jump too far ahead, but did you take some of these mining classes here at the University?

Joe: Oh, I think I took that short mining course three times, I guess. They figured I was dumb and I was afraid they'd look at me. Larry Dohemie taught one of them, and I don't know who the other teachers were, but I was fascinated by it and I got in the bush every time I got a chance, but I took it three times. I think Earl Beistline got tired of seeing me around too, if you'll ask him.

Jim: They're fun classes aren't they.

Joe: It was real good. It was real pleasant. It started in the fall, you know, in late September and they ran on through into probably the first of December—fascinating to get up there and do the tests and to listen and to talk to other people who were interested in mining. It was really a wonderful experience.

Jim: We've got those. We've still got the program going on, and a new course they offer there, and I might bring it out at this time, many times placer miners don't quite know how to go about evaluation of property, and one of the things that we just developed here is the placer evaluation workshop, which is scheduled for the 14th, 15th and 16th of April, and that particular program is going to be taught by the heavyweights—that's Ernie Wolff, Doug Colp, and Don Cook, and a young chap, Kevin Adler will be presenting geophysical prospecting information. Jumping back on track, Joe, after you graduated from law school, things were kind of tough around there.

Joe: Yeah, June of '34 was no picnic, I guarantee you that much.

Jim: Tell us what was going on at that time.

Joe: Of course the WPA was in full swing and the federal transient service was taking care of the people that wandered across America. That was my first job. You couldn't get in a law office for love nor money, and I worked for them, for I think 65 bucks a month, in Kansas City and Poplar Bluff and Springfield. When they found out I was from Kansas, why that was it. They didn't want me, and so I got fired for that. I went back home and worked on the farm, and did a lot of things. CIT, Dunn and Bradstreet, I picked up whatever work was available. You weren't particular then; if there was a job you took it and did the best you could with it. It's sort of amusing now to watch people turn up their noses at jobs, because if the time ever comes again when it's as tough as it was then, why we'll see just how well these people stand up to the test. I'm a little bit pessimistic.

Jim: It was interesting, as a follow-up to that statement, I recently gave a paper at the Alaska Placer Mining Conference that suggested that small scale mining was used during the depression periods to extract enough to put bread on the table. And a lot of people aren't familiar with that, but that occurred a number of times, probably during your lifetime, that people resorted to small scale mining.

Joe: Oh, I'll tell you. I didn't happen to see it in our part of the country, but since coming up here, I've become acquainted with a lot of people from the west coast, and I guess the people just went to the hills there and made do with what they had. I heard of one man that took an old Model-T rear end and took the ring gear off of the rear end and welded spring leaves on it, made impellers and used it as a pump. Well they got by, they made enough to live on. The government moved gold up to $35 an ounce in 1933, from $19, and that gave the people a lot of encouragement. No, there was lots of people... See the drought came in the early '30s and we had three years with absolutely no rain at all. We planted 180 acres of corn one summer and didn't raise one single cob. And the government bought up the cattle and shot them, dug big trenches and run 'em into it, and shot them, covered 'em up, made another trench, covered 'em up, and did that. They were starving to death. Lots of cattle starved to death, and the heat killed them. It was 108° in the shade in 1920 in Kansas. I seen cracks in the ground that if you didn't step across them you could drop a heel in them. It was not good times. I can understand why people went west, and I heard about them in the northern part of California, in Oregon. I talked to many people who said, "Yes, we survived there." A lot of people who've moved to Alaska are the children of those people.

Jim: What year did you come to Alaska, Joe?

Joe: I arrived in Kodiak on March 28, 1942.

Jim: Joe, tell us about what happened when you came up to Kodiak. What did you do there?

Joe: I had a job in the office, and I didn't like that, so it wasn't too long before I went to work in the grease rack.

Jim: And what was the company, Joe.

Joe: Oh, the Sims Great Puget Sound Bridge and Dredging Company. It was a consortium of companies that were building the Naval facility in Old Woman's Bay outside of Kodiak, and they were putting in submarine pens and airplane hangars and abutments and improving the runway. It was a defense project.

Jim: How long did you work for them?

Joe: Oh, I worked, let's see, March 28th the CBs came in, the following spring we worked at Danger Bay putting in an installation for the Army Engineers. I fished a stretch in June and July of '43. Then I came across to Anchorage and hired out to Morrison-Knutsen, then came to Fairbanks on a job for them in September. We tore a dragline down at North Camp, put it up on pipe dollies and hauled it to Northway, then reassembled it for use in lengthening the runway down there. Mechanic, grease, we did anything and everything. We cut logs to lengthen the runway. The little planes that were being delivered to the Soviet Union were running off the end of the runways. They came through here just like a bunch of mosquitoes every day.

Jim: And so you had to be a Jack-of-all-trades.

Joe: Do whatever was called for. You didn't ask any questions. If it had to be done, why you did it. People didn't worry about crossing over union lines or duties or anything else. That's the nice part about Alaska—if you can't do this, why you can do something else and get by.

Jim: How long did you work for Morrison Knutsen?

Joe: We worked there 'til Christmas time, then I came into town and went to work for Metcalf, Hamilton, Kansas City Bridge, at Six-mile (I believe I was there a year), and then went to work for the Army Engineers at Ladd Field out here, worked there 'til '51, when I quit to go placer mining.

Jim: What did you do out there at Ladd Field?

Joe: Oh, mechanic.

Jim: Same type of construction and maintenance.

Joe: Construction equipment. It was in the heavy duty shop. Draglines and Cats. I learned what I knew about them there under Carl Johnson, Don Miller. They almost gave up on me a couple of times, but I guess they were pretty patient.

Jim: That was the background you needed to go placer mining, wasn't it?

Joe: You can do a little bit of your own work, and you learn what a machine is and what it takes to keep it going. I worked in the grease rack too. I've done a lot of things.

Jim: Something must have stimulated you to drop a paying job to go placer mining. Was there somebody or something that dangled some plum in front of you that caused you to abandon the security of a job?

Joe: Oh no. I'd always been interested in mining. I spent quite a bit of time on Banner Creek with Fred Campbell down there, and had the promise of a lease and he went back on it, but I'd had my nose in the creeks here ever since I got here. And so I went rambling' in the hills every chance I got.

Jim: And all the time you were looking at the rocks.

Joe: Looking at the rocks. They fascinated me and I don't know where a nine-year-old boy gets the idea that gold's a valuable medium. Why, it's pretty difficult to trace it back, except to my grandfather, and if you get it that early you'll never lose it.

Jim: Did you ever have an interesting experience with a bear?

Joe: Oh yes. Oh yes.

Jim: Tell us about that, Joe.

Joe: First time we went bear hunting, I didn't realize that they were as big as they are. I wear about a number 11 boot pac, and we were on the beach there, I think, in either Terror or Barracuda Bay, and there'd been a bear down there on the beach, and I could put the heel of my boot in the back end of the bear's hind foot and put the other foot right in front of it, and you just barely filled up the track lengthwise, which means it's twenty-two or three inches. It's not quite as wide as your boot pack is, but it's a big animal. And we tied into one fellow up there on the hill, knocked him down. There were three of them. He wandered around there in the brush, but a guy setting up there on the hill said he wasn't sure if we were stalking the bear or the bear was stalking us. But anyway we got the job done, and I peeled his hide off and got it back to the states, finally, to be tanned. It was an interesting time. I've had a lot of encounters since then too. So far they've all been successful for me and unsuccessful for the bear, but you never know.

Jim: Thank goodness for that. Let's take a look at that placer mining activity that you went into. Joe, tell us, where did you first go mining and how did that all materialize?

Joe: Well, the first place we tried was on Homestake—that's a left limit tributary of Charity Creek, which is one of the creeks that makes up Faith Creek. Faith, Hope and Charity, become the Chatanika there. McManus comes down along the highway and Faith Creek runs into it, and from there on it's Chatanika. We went there in I think '51. We bought an old D-8 with a broken transmission case from M-K that was using it on the airport job down here. We hauled a transmission case up from the states and we took the frame arms off and everything out of the old case and stuffed it in the new case, built the Cat from the ground up, hauled it in to Homestake Creek, that's about mile 71 or 72 on the Steese Highway—it's in there where MacIntosh is operating. We went back in there about six or seven miles, and tried it that summer. It wasn't good enough to make too much money at $35 an ounce, so we eventually pulled out of that. But it's quite an experience living in a white-wall tent. Freddie Wilt and Dick Townley (he drowned off the west coast there in the undertow one time), but Freddie Wilt and his wife and my brothers and I went up there and worked that, summer of '51. Very interesting place, and very well mineralized.

Jim: Well, tell us how your processing plant was structured?

Joe: We built a sluice box out of wood—I remember putting that together right there on the ground—two-by-fours and I think one-by-ten planks. We found a couple of old truck beds, and made a slick plate to doze onto, and the slick plate channeled the gravels to the wooden sluice. They were using that method up on Mastodon Creek, and I got to take a look at it, constructed ours and then began dozing away with the Cat.

Jim: And the water just ran from the stream, right through?

Joe: No, no. There was an old ditch up on the hill, used to channel water for hydraulicking on the lower end of the creek, in the early days. Frank Miller at Miller House had mined there, see, and a number of other people. And we took water out of the ditch and brought it into the sluice box. I'll never forget. They talk about grayling not being amenable to mining. We shut the water off and I heard something flopping on the slick plate, and there was still a pile of rocks, and here was about a 14-inch grayling, that had swam up the creek, right through the discharge, and was on his way up to that ditch, if he could just get there, so I helped him on his way. We didn't bother him any.

Jim: We've got a call, Joe. Hello, welcome to Alaska Gold Trails. You'er on the air with Joe Vogler. Do you have a question?

Caller: Hi. Yes, I do. The story that you're relating, Joe, what year was that?

Joe: This was '51.

Caller: Was the Davidson Ditch still being used very much, or was this after that?

Joe: The Davidson Ditch, they were still maintaining it. There were ditch walkers there. Those cabins were maintained, and if I remember right I think they were still doing a little mining out here at Fox. I'm not certain on that because my interest was up the road a ways. But the ditch was maintained at that time. Now, shortly thereafter, why there was a group bought the ditch and put in a power generation system there, where the ditch comes down off the left limit of the Chatanika, upstream from Chatanika on the Steese Highway, about four miles. But that was a little bit later, I think, that they put in that power generation. I know the ditch was washed out up there one spring, and it made quite a mess, there at about mile, oh I'd say 56, 57, and they cribbed it up and filled it in, I know that.

Caller: OK, you just used a term that a lot of people probably aren't familiar with. You said "ditch walkers." Can you explain that a little more.

Joe: Oh yes. The F.E. Co. maintained the ditch. They had a cabin at 66-mile and there was another one down about 44-mile, is it Camp Creek? Is that right? Where that two-story building...that was an F.E. Co building there. They had people there, and the ditch required constant maintenance you know, and they were on that all the time. They called them ditch walkers, and they walked back and forth.

Caller: It was subject to problems at the time, then?

Joe: Oh yeah, you've got to maintain those. You keep the brush out of them, and I heard a time or two that the muskrats digging holes in them gave them some trouble. I can't be sure of that, but I've heard things to that effect.

Caller: Well, thank you for the information, Joe.

Joe: You bet.

Jim: Joe, Hope, Faith and Charity are all relatively well-known placer mining creeks, and some of us in the industry have recognized that some relatively large nuggets have come out of that area. How many seasons did you mine in that vicinity?

Joe: Let's see, we worked that one season. I held the ground, went back and prospected it, and it was pretty skinny, at $35 an ounce. I know we picked up one beautiful nugget right off the slick plate on Homestake Creek. Yes, there were nuggets come off of that. Frank Miller had a little sack of them at Miller House that he and Graziella had taken off of Home Stake Creek, and I don't know whatever happened to them, but he showed them to me a number of times. There's some coarse gold in there. There's a couple of big porphyry humps in there. There's also a little cobalt and some other minerals in there. It'll be a big producer some day, but I'm not encouraged at the present time.

Jim: Well, where did you travel to after your experience there?

Joe: Well, the next trip I made, Earl Hurst and I took a look at Morlock Creek. Dick MacIntyre flew an outfit down there for us in the wintertime. We went down there and it was 40 below when we got there. Got a tent set up, and then that spring I bought an eight by ten pump from Freddie Johnson, and I took a D-2 down, put it on the river barge, in high water—why, they just run it right off on the bank, and we worked there that summer. We were going down the next creek hard rock prospecting, and I had the misfortune of being skewered by a stick in my groin and had quite a time—very lucky to get just skewered. So I didn't go back down there. In the meantime I'd gotten interested in Ketchum Creek. But before I got to Ketchum, why we made a trip prospecting into the headwaters of the Robertson River, looking for some hard rock down there, and then the next trip was Ketchum. I bought that in '59 from Mrs. Zimmerman, worked there and then wound up buying Woodchopper Creek from Dr. Patty—leasing it first, then buying it in the early '70s. Bought Ketchum Creek in '59. At $35 an ounce it was pretty tough to make a living, and what I really did was to accumulate ground that I figured would eventually pay off, and sooner or later why the price went up, as you've seen. Now you've got the government saying you can't do it. We've got three injunctions against us on Woodchopper.

Jim: Are you still holding Ketchum Creek?

Joe: Oh yes. We're holding Ketchum Creek.

Jim: Is there any mining going on there at present?

Joe: Oh yes. Fred Wilkenson's on the lower end of that did reasonably well this last year.

Jim: I wanted to ask you about Fred. Do you think he'd be a good guest on the show here?

Joe: Well, Fred Wilkenson was born in this country and he knows more about mining. His Daddy wouldn't even hardly let him go to Circle Hot Springs just a few miles away. It was all work. He could tell you. Fred'd be a good guest, you bet.

Jim: And he probably knows a lot about the history of the Circle area.

Joe: Oh yeah, he could tell you things that I've never even heard of.

Jim: Well, we might try to see if we can't get Fred on the show here. It might take some arm twisting.

Joe: Well, you do a pretty good job of it.

Jim: Well thanks, Joe. Everybody'll see me coming and run for the other side of the street. Joe, you went to Ketchum, it was lean pickings, then you finally got Woodchopper. There's a gold dredge on Woodchopper, isn't there.

Joe: Yeah, there's a gold dredge on Woodchopper. Well, you know, believe in three things: real estate, gold, and Caterpillar equipment. That is wealth. It isn't money that we pass around; that's a medium of exchange. It's a form of confetti that everybody accepts and that's about all. And so I felt that eventually gold would assume its true station in our economy, and so I figured that it was about the best investment a man could make, and I proceeded to do so at every opportunity. It's easy enough to buy it, but it was awful tough to pay for at that time, but I haven't regretted a bit of it.

Jim: Joe, tell us a little bit about the Woodchopper Creek property.

Joe: Well, the Woodchopper Creek property has been known since before the turn of the century. Coal Creek is known as a place where you can rock out a grubstake. Woodchopper, of course, was where the first major discovery was made on the creek. And the Mineral Creek Mining District was set up in November of 1902. And it was mined sporadically. There was drift mining on Mineral Creek. In fact there was a lady there that was running a windlass for a while. There was eight crews there, and then from there they expanded into the main creek. There's a story about that: There was a group of English and Germans working there below Green's Gulch, and the story goes that the propaganda that came out in 1912, you know, that preceded the conflict in Europe—World War I—was taken to heart by these people and they broke up their combine, burned their cabins, burned their boiler house, burned their wood. And so help me there's a winch, a two-drum winch setting over a shaft, and the babbits melted out of the bearings, as a result of the fire. The cabins are gone. So, I've wondered if that wasn't really what happened. But then Patty arrived in the '30s. He came to Coal Creek first, then he came over and drilled Woodchopper. I think Bruce Thomas was still living in the city. He was one of the gentlemen who had the misfortune of being beaten up this winter. He was over there. So was Stampy and Smitty and, I think, Woody Johansen—they all worked there for Patty. They were his boys on Woodchopper. You could talk to some of them; they could really go into the history. I just know that it happened. But I wasn't there at that time.

Jim: How many times have you run for governor, Joe.

Joe: Three.

Jim: Three times. Are you going to do it again?

Joe: No, no, no. I'm 75 here in a few days. There's some young blood coming up and we have the party established now, and I think it's time somebody else gets in the fray.

Jim: Thanks, Joe Vogler, for joining us on Alaska Gold Trails today. It's been a pleasure.

Joe: Thank you, Jim.

Ernie Wolff
With
Jim Madonna
October 16, 1987 and November 6, 1987

Jim: Our guest this afternoon, ladies and gentlemen, is Dr. Ernie Wolff. I met Ernie when I first came to the University of Alaska, in pursuit of a Master of Science degree, and it was Dr. Ernie Wolff who helped me and a score of other students in getting settled in here at the University. Ernie was a professor at the University of Alaska at that time and director of the Mineral Industry Research Laboratory. Welcome to Alaska Gold Trails, Ernie, How are you today?

Ernie: Oh, just fine, Jim.

Jim: Well, Ernie, our show deals with Alaska, past, present and future, and what we'd like to do here is perhaps find out just how you happened to come to Alaska and the sequence of events that attracted you here.

Ernie: Well, let's see. Like a lot of other fellows at that time, which was 1938, we were trying to put up with something called a depression, that seemed like it had gone on for all of my life. It hadn't really, but it had gone on long enough so that it was making life unpleasant, and we thought that perhaps somewhere far away might have a better opportunity. So, Alaska was about as far as we could go, and I scrounged up all the money I could get and took a train from northern Minnesota across to Prince Rupert, and then got one of the Canadian national ships into Juneau. It didn't take but a week to tell me that Juneau was no place for a fellow from the midwest; it rained continually for that week. I don't think it let up for one minute. So I caught the *S.S. Aleutian* for Valdez, and I think I was on the gulf on the longest day of the year, which would put me into Valdez towards the end of June, and the Valdez Trail (the Richardson Highway) was not kept open all winter, so the trucks of that era were just going back and forth all the time hauling supplies in the spring. While I was on the steamship, I'd talked to a lot of fellows from Alaska and they said, "Just go along the dock, there, and find somebody that's loading up for Fairbanks, and tell them you want to go to Fairbanks. The going rate is $5 in steerage, that was with the load, or $10 in the cab." So I did that.

Jim: You got a ride in the cab.

Ernie: I got to ride in the cab. I got a special rate. I rode the cab for $5, and I ran into a fellow going north, and it turned out to be Pete Smith, whom many of you remember as a wood dealer at that time and miner. So we went on up and I asked him if he knew where there was a place called Fox Farm, and he did. It was 50 miles south of Fairbanks on the road, and there were two fellows I knew there from northern Minnesota. They were trappers. We got in there about six o'clock in the morning, and Pete let me off and I ran up to the door of the shack and they were there all right. So I went the rest of the way in with them and they showed me a little bit of the town, and then I was on my own.

Jim: What was Fairbanks like in those days? Was it a rough frontier town like we think of the old west, or exactly what was the atmosphere in the Fairbanks area at that time?

Ernie: It was a frontier town but it certainly wasn't a rough town. It was a town of about 3,000 or 3,500 people, completely dependent upon placer mining, gold mining. The town had hit rock bottom in about 1922, when the population had shrunk to about 1,200 people. The richest of the ground was worked out, that is the ground that could be worked profitably by hand methods. The United States Smelting, Refining and Mining Company had decided that since they were in the placer gold business, that this would be a great place to install dredges. A fellow named Norman Steins had come in here and consolidated the district. This is usually what has to be done before you can interest big capital and big companies to come in and become more efficient and revive the camp like this. They took the ground. They called it the United States Smelting, Refining and Mining, Fairbanks Exploration Department, and the Fairbanks Exploration Department of course was exploring for gold, and they started a drilling program, a very extensive drilling program, and continued it for several years, starting in about 1924. Within a few years they had large areas of ground outlined that would support dredges and they started building the dredges. I've forgotten when the first one started, but it was in the late twenties. And they continued to develop the district and add more dredges, I believe there finally were eight dredges operating before it was over. The town itself, with approximately 3,000, residents, was laid out. It had gravel streets, or no streets at all, or no gravel at all anyway. Dirt streets, pretty muddy at times, pretty dusty at times. There were a great many boardwalks in evidence, but it wasn't a wild west town by any means. In fact it's probably one of the most peaceable places that I'd seen. Naturally, a lot of young fellows a long way from home, you would expect a lot of fights. Well there weren't that many fights, compared to other places I've been. I think people were working too hard to make a living to cause much trouble. The commercial and financial center of the camp, of Fairbanks, was a concrete block building on Illinois Street, which is still there, and that was the office of the Fairbanks Exploration Company. They had a number of engineers. It was divided into departments and there was an engineer heading each department. There was Exploration and Dredging and Stripping and Thawing. It was very well organized and very efficient and the people that worked for it were hard working people. The dredging operations were booming. Living conditions were pretty much, oh halfway between the real early days and what we have now, although all the buildings were of wood, except I think there was one concrete building in town at the time, and that was the Empress Theater, right in the middle of the main block of Second Avenue. But there were just wooden structures scattered around, and then, of course, the main F.E. Co. office was a concrete block structure on Illinois Street. That structure is still there and it still looks like a pretty good building, but it hasn't been occupied for a very long time. I think it belongs to the Golden Valley Electric people. I've been told it would take a lot of money to bring it up to modern standards.

Jim: What was the year that you arrived, again, Ernie?

Ernie: 1938.

Jim: 1938. How many dredges were operating in the Fairbanks area at that time.

Ernie: Oh, I think there were seven. I'd have to figure them up again, but the next one, the last one that they put in service was Dredge Ten at Cripple Creek.

Jim: Were the dredges different sizes, Ernie, or were they all the same size?

Ernie: They were different sizes. The dredges are rated by cubic foot bucket capacity, which of course can be converted into yards pretty easily. The smallest dredge was the Pedro Dredge up on Pedro Creek, and that's the road leading over Cleary Summit. The biggest one was ten-cubic-foot, and that was at Chatanika, and then when they got the Cripple Dredge on line, that was also a ten-cubic-foot dredge.

Jim: How deep were these dredges capable of digging? Do you have an idea on that?

Ernie: Well they varied. I think somebody may want to correct me on this afterwards, but I think about a hundred feet for the Chatanika Dredge and about the same for the Cripple Dredge when that finally got going. They had to strip a hundred feet of muck off of that area, and then they had to strip quite a bit of barren gravel, and that was done with a big dragline. It was one of the biggest in the country at that time. You can still see it out there at Ester.

Jim: Well, what are the basic components of those dredges and how do they work, Ernie? Can you give us an idea?

Ernie: Yeah. The dredge floats on a barge, and it has what they call a ladder

going down off the front of the bow. They use somewhat nautical terminology on a dredge—port and starboard, bow and stern, and that sort of
thing. There's a continuous bucket line turning on the front of the dredge
that carries material continuously up and dumps it into a hopper, and
from there it goes to a circular screen called a trommel and it's thoroughly washed there. The oversized material goes on out and drops onto
another endless conveyor belt that's called a stacker, and that piles the
tailings behind the dredge. The undersize drops through holes in the
trommel and into a series of sluice boxes called the tables. Of course,
gold has about a ten to one ratio with sand for settling, and it drops out
very rapidly and then the light stuff goes on out the tail sluices and drops
out behind the dredge. Some of that sand is the bane of the winchman—
it keeps crowding against the stern and they have all kinds of trouble—
but a dredge is still about the most efficient gold digging machine there is.

Jim: When you arrived in Alaska and there were seven dredges operating in
the area of Fairbanks, did you go to work on the dredges, or what did you
do when you arrived in Fairbanks.

Ernie: No, I didn't go to work on the dredges. I guess I would've liked to,
but a fellow had to take whatever was available so I went to work on a
section gang for the railroad, just to try to get a grubstake. We had to do
something, and the railroad was hiring, so I went out and worked for a
couple months, I guess. And it was starting to get dark and cold, and it
was going to be over pretty quick, and actually the mining season was
going to be over, so there wasn't much point in trying to get another job
in the mines. So we were coming in on the railroad one Saturday night,
and an old timer pointed up on the hill, he said, "There's the School of
Mines." So that's what I did; I left that little job on the railroad and
enrolled in the School of Mines that fall. In those days you could get an
education pretty cheap. There were lots of rabbits in those days, and
there were plenty of woods around the college. Some of the fellows
built what they called "yurches." They were simply poles and moss
piled up, and in the wintertime they were pretty comfortable. They're
kind of damp and mosquitoey in the summer, but in the wintertime they
were all right. We were lucky. Dr. Bunnell, who was the president of the
University at the time, handed a guy that had got there a day or two
before me a hammer and said, "Go down and pull the hasp off an old
cabin down here and move in." Well I was looking around for something like that and I saw this fellow coming out of that cabin and he said,
"Well, might as well move in here," which I did. So we had a place to
stay. We rustled up a few utensils and there was an old stove in the cabin
that we replaced a little bit later, and there was wood in the woods around
there, so we had the heat and way to cook, and about all we had to buy
that fall was a Coleman lantern and a few things like that, and then the

books and the tuition, of course, at the University. I can still remember that. It was $56 for books, fees and tuition, which was quite a fortune in those days, but I had it from working on the railroad.

Jim: Tell us about Bunnell, Ernie. What was Bunnell like?

Ernie: I think Bunnell was a remarkable man. He had been a federal judge. He had learned law, as they all did in those days, by reading law and working as a law clerk in various places in Alaska. He had graduated from Bucknell, with an education in the classics—Greek and Latin, and that sort of thing. But of course, by the time I met him, he was an ex-judge and a lawyer and an educator, and he believed that it was possible to start a college in the wilderness, that far north. He pushed it with all the legislators he knew, in the territorial legislature, and they finally got the appropriations and they built a building, and he held it together for his whole lifetime. He was the moving force there. Because he was the first president of the University. The University really was his creation, his baby. There is a building up there named for Charles Bunnell and there's been a subscription among alumni and others to have a statue of Bunnell created and set up.

Jim: Is there any single person who is responsible for the idea of erecting a statue in recognition of his work in developing the University?

Ernie: Yes. Glen Franklin, an early graduate of this school and a lifelong placer miner spearheaded that, and it's moving right along. I don't know how long it'll be, probably a year or two, before it's done and up. You'd asked about what kind of a man Dr. Bunnell was. As I pointed out earlier, he'd worked very hard to establish or have the school established. The state was not a state yet, it was a territory. It was called the Alaska Agriculture College and School of Mines. He worked night and day to get the school established, and when it was established he worked to keep it going. It was pretty tough. There wasn't any money. He used to deliver the mail. He used to pack the mail out from Fairbanks. He'd walk along the railroad tracks because it was closer that way. He seemed to know just how much help a potential student had to have to enroll. In my case he provided an old cabin I could stay in. Another person might need a little more help and he'd give them a job waiting tables so he could live in the dormitory. They say he'd do anything to get a student. Well, it wasn't quite that; he liked to help young people too, and as we got into the thing, the University had a little loan fund and we could borrow some money from these loan funds, but we had to have a signer, a co-signer, and Dr. Bunnell—well, they called him Judge Bunnell, too— he was the co-signer for many of these fellows. He was a benefactor to all of us. He had a terrible temper, and a lot of people didn't like him. I didn't like him at times when I was on the receiving end of the temper, but then generally he was quite a good man. He was a benefactor to many many students there, and managed to keep the school operating and to help many people get a college education, which they wouldn't have gotten otherwise. For people that might want to know more about Dr. Bunnell's character and his achievements, a few years ago, Bill Cashen wrote a book called *The Farthest North College President*, and I'm sure people could get it in the library, or maybe it's still available to buy. This pretty much gives his career. Speaking of being a benefactor, I recently ran into a former student who's now ended his career and he's retired. I saw him for the first time in 40 years, and he said that he had corresponded with Bunnell up until Bunnell died, and he was very faithful in keeping up correspondence with former students that he remembered and that he had liked. I think people that are interested in this man's character should get hold of that book by Bill Cashen and they can learn a lot more than I could tell, because my experience with him covered a shorter range of time.

Jim: How long did you attend the University of Alaska, Ernie?

Ernie: Well, I went to school that year, and by that spring I was pretty well broke, and I had borrowed some money. Bunnell, of course, supplied us with jobs cutting wood. He owned all the surrounding country there. That would be the flats down below the college now, and I stayed there that year, and then the next summer I got a job with the newly organized Territorial Department of Mines, and it was a pretty good job for a young fellow because we traveled around the different mining districts of the Interior. The territorial mining engineer was supposed to keep track of what was going on in the mines, and he also had an experimental geophysical prospecting program going. So I was able to see quite a bit of the Interior. At Livengood for example, at that time they were just getting ready to build a dam. Most of you know that there's a big reservoir there, and they started that dam that summer. Then I saw the Circle District, the Fairbanks District, and I actually worked for him pretty well into the winter, when we completed the office work. So I laid out, I didn't go to school that year, but rather, tried to get enough money ahead to go the next year, which I did. I graduated in 1941, just as the war was heating up.

Jim: Reverting back to your early days in Fairbanks, Ernie, In addition to Cashen's book there were a number of other books written in the past decade or so, regarding Fairbanks in the early days, somewhere around the late thirties and early forties. Tell us more about your early days and attending classes, Ernie.

Ernie: Well, It was the University by then. I think it was the third year it had been a University after having been started as the Alaska Agricultural

College and School of Mines. Well we were living in that old cabin, and living pretty much as probably the early prospectors lived, but it worked right in with the life of a student. We were able to get by without spending a great deal of money. We walked to school. We used to set rabbit snares going to school and we'd pick up the rabbits on the way home. And we got along fine. There were other students who were doing that. There was a good article reprinted from the *Farthest North Collegian*, which was the school paper by the Loftus brothers, and they had built a big nice cabin on the banks of the Noyes Slough, or the Jenny M. Slough, and the title of the article was "A Homestead Frat House," a frat house being a fraternity house—very interesting and good pictures. By the way, for a description of Fairbanks, in the thirties Carl Mach, who recently is deceased, was written up in the Heartland, little Sunday section in the *Fairbanks Daily News-Miner,* about two months ago, and if anybody could get ahold of that and see the pictures and see his description of the town, it would be a very good description of Fairbanks and the work in the middle and late thirties. Well, I went to school, and they were all wooden buildings. There was one concrete building finished, and that was the girls' dormitory, and there was what I think they call Founders' Hall (now Signers' Hall), which has been refurbished, also there. The downstairs was being used for the gymnasium and the upstairs was the library, with about 20,000 volumes at the time, which is nothing now—I think some of the branch libraries for the University have more books than that, but it was an accomplishment. The teachers were excellent. I think we got just as good an engineering training as you could get anywhere, even though the teachers would have to make some of the equipment and demonstrations themselves. But there wasn't much money anywhere, so they were just doing what everybody had to do. I went to school that year, and then I, along with a lot of other folks, had to lay out the next year and try to get a little money ahead and to pay some of the debts that I picked up from the first year. So it took three years to finish the two that I had to do.

Jim: What did you do to generate those funds, Ernie?

Ernie: Well, the first work was cutting wood down at the foot of the hill. There is, I don't know if you'd call it a "little" settlement down there now—I guess there's some businesses, a number of businesses—but we cut the wood there. President Bunnell was the only fellow in the country that seemed to have any money, 'cause he had a steady job, and it was a period of recession, or depressed times, although the gold mining was booming. The people that had taken homesteads were disappointed and had to drop them, and as they would drop, he would buy the homesteads. He told about a lady named Widener. Her husband had died. They'd taken a homestead down close to the University, and he had gone to see her to see how she was doing, and he knocked on the door of the homestead cabin and she told him to come in, and he found her skinning a rabbit in the middle of the floor. She was destitute and hungry almost all the time, so she came to him a few days later and said, "You're the only one I know who's got any money. I want $1,000 for that homestead so I can get outside." He gave it to her. It might seem like a great bargain and that he might have taken advantage of her, but actually he had done her a great benefit because she couldn't have gotten outside any other way.

Jim: What an interesting story. Tell us more about your work.

Ernie: Well, in the year that I didn't go to school, I spent most of the year working for the newly created Territorial Department of Mines, as I said before. But interestingly, one of the fellows who had been a professor at the school was doing experimental geophysical exploration, and I worked as his field assistant for two summers and then part of the winter working up the data.

Jim: Was that Joesting?

Ernie: Yeah, Henry Joesting, his name was. He had quite a career with the United States Geological Survey and Geophysics. He died about fifteen years ago.

Jim: Then you went back to school, following that year of, what do you call that, leave, Ernie?

Ernie: It was just a necessary vacation to re-coup finances, I guess you'd call it.

Jim: I see. Tell us a little more about your education.

Ernie: I had at that time completed two years of college work when I got here, so I had two years to put in. I did those two years in three years, trying to make a little money on the side. We've had fellows from that School of Mines that took, I think the record was twelve years, to get through, but they got through and they had professional careers during and after the time they were going to school. I just thought of another source, for people who might be interested in that era. The first dean of the School of Mines was Dr. Ernest M. Patty, and he wrote a book I think in the sixties, called *North Country Challenge*. It gives a very good description of the early years of that college, and he had a very successful career in placer mining and dredging after he left the college as dean, and then he came back as president and his years as president were very successful too. He did a lot for that school. Let's see now, we were talking about going to school. I graduated in 1941, and there was a war going on and it was beginning to look like we would be in that war. And it was also becoming obvious that the gold mining effort in the district was slacking off. I had an offer when I graduated from the Carnegie

Institution of Washington, which was doing geophysics of the Earth. Mostly, it was terrestrial magnetism, and I did go to work for them. We got into war that winter and from then on that job became part of the war effort, and I put in the war years in the Interior. There was fighting in the Aleutians, but even the fellows at Ladd Field (and most of the people of my age that were at Ladd Field—it's Fort Wainwright now), we didn't hear much about that Aleutian campaign. So that's what I did with my education for the first couple of years.

Jim: We have a call. Hello, you're on the air with Ernie Wolff.

Caller: Yes. Say, I hear a lot about gold mining in Alaska, and particularly in the Interior, and especially right now when we have what some call a downed economy. What kind of future, if all the EPA rules were modified so that mining could develop as it might in the state, what kind of an employment base are we looking at in the Interior? Is there an extensive reality for employment in gold mining, in numbers?

Ernie: Well, Jim, you'll have to help me out here.

Jim: This is one of those futuristic questions.

Caller: Yeah, well we keep hearing that this is the answer for our economy up here. My impression has always been that the gold claims have been family businesses, you know, family owned, and I haven't really known anybody who's employed in mining, as such, so I'd just like to extrapolate that information. What kind of employment base is there, if all these rules are removed?

Ernie: Well, I'll take that one. You'd have to know a little bit about the history of mining in Alaska. The people you've known have been small miners, but things started out in 1902 here, and it was hand mining, and then it dropped off and things were pretty depressed even in those days, and in 1924 the Fairbanks Exploration Department of the United States Smelting, Mining and Refining, consolidated all the claims here. Up until the fifties and early sixties big mining on the dredges were the going mode of operation. So it hasn't always been small miners. The small miners really came into their own when the price of gold went up, but that's really all we have now, that's right, as far as placer mining goes. But the industry is looking toward big things in new types of what they call lode gold mining. Ester Dome now has two operations. They're not big, but they employ a number of people. We have high hopes for the other end of the district, the west end, which is the Cleary Summit area. We're looking for disseminated gold there that could make a large base. Now, as far as numbers go, we might just try to compare it. The oil boom is over. It looks to me like hard rock minerals for Alaska are what we have to look forward to, and I don't know that they would supply all the employment that we have now, but I think we're looking at several thousand people working throughout the district, and throughout Alaska, not just this district.

Caller: OK, well that was mainly my question. I was just looking in terms of what kinds of outlet do we have. I'd like to see mining open up, but I wasn't sure that it was really going to make a significant impact on the unemployment situation.

Ernie: Well, you hit the nail on the head about all these regulations, but right now we have 2,000 to 2,500 seasonally employed people throughout Alaska.

Caller: Now that's seasonally. That's the other point, it's not really full-time employment, when you talk about mining, is it?

Ernie: No, but it will be when we get some of the hard rock deposits operating. It'll make quite a difference.

Caller: What kind of a time frame do you anticipate at the present rate.

Ernie: Well, I would say, if all the things went well, maybe five years.

Caller: OK. Thank you.

Jim: What did you do after the war, Ernie?

Ernie: After the war I became interested in the Chandalar District and spent several (I think altogether parts of ten) years, either in that district or the eastern Koyukuk District, prospecting.

Jim: Is that where you met this fellow O'Keefe?

Ernie: Oh yes. Danny O'Keefe was one of the younger old-timers in the camp, and he had come there in the late '20s, come to Wiseman and worked in the drift mines with the old timers.

Jim: What's a drift mine, Ernie?

Ernie: Oh. It's an underground placer mine and it (placer drift mining) was practiced in California in the semi-consolidated gravels, tertiary gravels, there. But it was ready-made for Alaska, where the gravels are frozen. You could just sink a shaft, just as in hard-rock mining, on the center of the paystreak, which was some elongated strip down the middle of the creek that had the gold in paying quantities. You sink a hole there and you run a drift upstream, and then run two lateral drifts out to the edge of the paystreak, and then start working back towards the shaft. They would thaw the gravel with steam. Well, they sink the hole with steam. You'd have a boiler on the surface and they run a pipe down and introduce the steam through the special pipe called a steam point. You'd drive that steam point in while the steam was going into the frozen gravels, and you'd have to turn it and twist it and pound it through. When you got the point down, maybe six feet or eight feet, then you let it steam about an hour to the foot. But after the main drift and the lateral drifts were in, they would start working back towards the shaft. They would drive longer points horizontally, back into the gravel, and they might have a room in there, finally, six or eight feet high. After the gravel was thawed, of course, they'd have to pick it down and shovel it into wheelbarrows and wheel it back to the shaft, and then it was raised, hoisted in a special carrier, and I think there are probably some in the museums around yet. This thing would pull the bucket up, and then when the bucket got to the surface it would run up a high line and dump on what they call the winter dump. By spring, of course, that pile was frozen and you'd have to thaw it with steam before you could sluice it. But that was drift mining.

Jim: And then you'd just recover the gold in a standard sluice box, Ernie?

Ernie: Yeah, in the spring you'd just process the gravels through a standard sluice box.

Jim: We've got less than a minute. Give me a few moments on the book that you wrote. What was the name of the book you wrote, Ernie?

Ernie: Oh, that's the *Handbook for the Alaskan Prospector*. I spent several summers in the Chandalar District drilling, and after that brief interval I worked for the School of Mines and I did a little teaching there, although I had to go back to school to get an advanced degree, and while I was doing the teaching I wrote that book.

Jim: Well that book gained a lot of recognition throughout the mining community of Alaska, and it's currently in its third edition. Ernie, time has just simply slipped away on us, and I want to thank you for coming in and sharing your time with us today. I also want to thank the listening audience for taking part in the program. It's been fun, folks. Until next week, Happy Prospecting.

Dr. William Wood
with
Jim Madonna
October 13, 1988

Jim: I would like to introduce our guest, Dr. William Ransom Wood. Everybody in Fairbanks is probably familiar with Dr. Wood and many of the things that he has done for our community. I want to welcome you, Dr. Wood, to Alaska Gold Trails. Thank you for joining us today.

Dr. Wood: Thank you, Jim. It's a pleasure and really an honor to be on your program. I think that the mining history of Interior Alaska is something very very special. And it isn't ended yet.

Jim: No, it certainly hasn't, Dr. Wood. Why don't you give us a brief history about where you were born and raised and what kind of environment you were raised in.

Dr. Wood: Well, Jim, I'm a farm boy from the prairie state of Illinois, but we did have on our farm in Morgan County, an outcropping of coal. One of the creeks ran through the pasture lands, and we'd go down, and it's about a four-foot vein, but we could get coal for the winter, and the neighbors would come in and load up wagons with it. It wasn't really mining, it was kind of scavenging, I suppose, of what was available.

Jim: An interesting comparison here in Alaska occurs along the coastal communities near coal seams where the coal washes up on the beaches and people would collect it and scavenge it in that sense as well.

Dr. Wood: This was a bituminous coal, and there's a lot of it back in Illinois. There's a whole sheet of coal. This happened to be a thin seam of about four feet.

Jim: You were raised in Illinois and then went to school there?

Dr. Wood: Oh yes. I was raised there, and attended Murrayville Community High School—little town of about 525 residents, and I don't think it's grown very much over the years, but it was very fine farm country for corn and later soybeans. We grew oats and wheat and clover and raised some stock. And then of course there was all the orchards and the berries and the vegetables and potatoes and what not that we had. So it was a real farm experience.

Jim: You also attended college there in Illinois, didn't you?

Dr. Wood: Yes, at Jacksonville, I attended Illinois College, which is the oldest private liberal arts college in the Midwest. It was founded in 1829 by a group of seven from Yale. They were Presbyterian Congregational, a ministerial group I guess, and they came into the Midwest to help set up small colleges, and this happened to be their first venture. It's still running, at about 1,000 students now, and it has been for nearly 160 years, it has always run in the black, financially.

Jim: After finishing your education at that college, did you go on to a University?

Dr. Wood: Yes. I went on for graduate study, for one year, at the University of Illinois at Urbana, studying English Literature. But then after one year I became a teacher up in the copper country of northern Michigan, the Keewenaw Peninsula, at Lake Linden—a teacher and a coach—and that was a very interesting experience. Then the next year after that— and this is, remember, the time of the depression—I went to Wakefield, on the Gogebick Iron Range, and spent about six years there. Then, when it looked as if I never would make any headway—because I would have to borrow money in the summer to make it to the next fall, and then by the time I would pay that off during the next school year, I would have to go borrow some more money to live through the summer—I tried to break that by going to the University of Iowa for a master's degree, and stayed on to take a doctorate degree in 1939, from the University of Iowa—in Keats's poetry, by the way, pretty far removed from mining.

Jim: Following your education experience, Dr. Wood, what was your first activity? I understand, by the way, that you played a little basketball.

Dr. Wood: Well, I did. While I was coaching in the upper peninsula of Michigan, I played what was in those days called professional basketball. It really wasn't, but we played all of the teams in the country at that time—the Cleveland Rosenblums, and the New York Celtics (it was New York then, not Boston), the Green Bay Packers had a team, and there was one that traveled, called the Olson's Swedes, and we played the Harlem Globetrotters nine games, as I remember—managed to win four of them, over a period of a half a dozen years. The team was made up of coaches. One time we were known as the Michigan Mentors. Another time we were the Kelly Springfields, out of Detroit. It really wasn't professional ball, but it was called that in those days. Let's see, that was in the late '20s, early '30s. It was a different ball game than what you have today. Very different.

Jim: Were you playing basketball at the same time you were coaching?

Dr. Wood: Yes. Coaching and teaching. Both at Lake Linden High School. That's up in the copper country, and then over in the Gogibick Iron Range at Wakefield. I'd like to reflect a minute on that experience, because it was a memorable one. I had the good fortune of having some very good players. In the mining towns you had first generation born Americans from almost all of the central and northern and southern European countries. We had many Poles and Fins and Irish and Norwegians and Germans and Italians and the like, and they were wonderful young people, and they took to sports avidly and did a great job. But the thing that I remember is that I had one young man by the name of Cavender, at Wakefield, and he was a fine player and a brilliant student. Later he became a medical doctor and is still practicing and is still very well known in the midwest. His grandfather's name was Bonino, and he had spent 10 years in gold mining in Juneau, Alaska, and was always telling us about the good days of the A. J. Mine there, in Juneau. I haven't thought of that in a long while. I was back just a couple of years ago, to the upper peninsula. The occasion was the celebration of the centennial of the discovery of iron on the Gogibick Range. I had been there just 50 years before, teaching, and was asked to come back and speak there at Wakefield. It was something that bothers me even yet. I've been there in the time of depression, but when everything was working, at least at the beginning. The mines were operating, the big stamp mills were operating, the smelter was operating, the ships were coming in on the Great Lakes, to take out the ore, and the Northwestern Railroad was taking out the shipment—the ingots of copper, on the rail. The timber was being harvested, and there were great sawmills and planing mills and plyboard mills and whatnot. And everybody was employed, and it was a sort of happy and thriving time. Fifty years later, in the same place, everything was closed down, with the exception of government employment and tourism. They had built some ski resorts, which we didn't have in the old days. And that provided some employment and they operated in the summer also, as recreation camps. But there was absolutely no employment, except for government and recreation. Result—all of the young people of the community were gone. Now by young people I mean those in their 20s and 30s and early 40s. They were gone. They'd gone to places like Detroit and Milwaukee and Chicago and St. Paul-Minneapolis, Duluth, and there was an emptiness in the town as a result. There were many old people there, and it was still a very pleasant place to live. It was much like Interior Alaska. In fact, the winters are considerably more severe in the upper peninsula of Michigan than they are here, because it's a snow belt and you will get up to 20-30 feet of snow in the wintertime, and you drive on the highways always on six or eight feet of snow that's packed down, in the wintertime. I recall, my first winter there, all these snow fences, and I wondered what in the world they were, I'd never seen a snow fence. But I also noted that the houses all had doors on the street side at the second story level. I asked an acquaintance, "Why in the world would you have a door up there? Window's are all you need." He said, "Well, wait 'til winter comes." And in winter the exterior entrance was at the second level; you walked out on that snow. But you get storms there, from Lake Superior, and heavy winds. And of course you do not get winds of that sort in the Interior of Alaska. And the cold—I remember it dropping as low as 50 degrees below zero. But with a howling wind, the cold penetrability was extreme.

Jim: Regarding the deterioration of the economy within the area that you were speaking about, I would like to share a similar experience with you. This past year I visited a town in Nevada that at one time was a thriving gold mining community, and then after the gold mining waned, in the early or mid-part of the century, it had an empty, ghost-like atmosphere for a while. Then with the renewed interest in gold, several large mines opened up in the area, and this time when I visited it—this was about the third time—the people were happy and they were all smiling, and the economy was up and the community was thriving. And along those same lines, I'd like to point out a characteristic of the Fairbanks area. Back in the 1970s, when Gerald Ford, released ownership of gold, to the public, which took place in 1974, our gold mining industry started to blossom once again. And in that period of time, of course, a lot of people came into the Alaska area and they began gold mining the various creeks around, and some of the people took a glimpse into the future and saw an opening to start manufacturing certain items. And one of these people was Hector, out at Hector's Welding. He began building sluice boxes. Well, it was recognized that the old style single-channel sluice boxes weren't very effective at collecting fine gold, and so Hector, along with a lot of advice from many of the miners in the Interior of Alaska, began building multiple-channel sluice boxes, which captured a larger concentration of the fine gold. And so, with that, we began a manufacturing plant here in the Fairbanks area, which lent to our economy and helped us and helped our mining industry. And at the same time, when you think about it, he had to order his steel from outside for the manufacture of the sluice boxes, but by the same token, we also had an increase in employment, in that he had several people working for him, and Hector then slowly but surely began manufacturing some of the most well-respected gold recovery units, not just in the state, but in the world. So with that, the miners began collecting more and more of the fine gold, and of course, property that at one time was uneconomic to mine became economic to mine.

Dr. Wood: He's a member of the Interior Alaska Manufacturers. There are about 80 or more of them now, and it's an extraordinary range of talent that we have in this area. And I have a notion that manufacturing, which is either fabricating or assembly or any form that would go under the general term, is a very important aspect of the future. You know, I just reflect again, when I look at all of the land that we have, the words that come to me are "stewardship" and "husbandry" and it seems that we have a purpose, as human beings, not to destroy, not to desecrate, and not to just take off the cream, but to discover somehow what the total utilization could be that would have lasting value. That is, that we could use this land intelligently, so that there would always be a resource available for the generations that follow. And the timber is a fine prospect for us. And think in terms of what are all of the uses that could be made of 1,000 acres of boreal forest.

Jim: Well, there is something interesting about not just harvesting timber but other types of businesses that spring up from that type of work? Using the local gold mining industry and Hector's work as a parallel example, we acquired more gold, and as a result other types of businesses spring out of that. For example, Oxford Assaying and Refining was established in Fairbanks, Alaska, in the late 1970s. They began buying the miners' gold. Up until that time, there were some buyers in the area, but Oxford developed a strong, stable base here and has become one of the most well known gold buyers within the state. Let's change gears here, Dr. Wood. You had some teaching and educational experiences in Nevada, if I'm not mistaken.

Dr. Wood: Yes, after the Michigan experience—there I was in both the copper mining area and then in the Gogibick Iron Range mining area— I went to the University of Iowa for a couple of degrees and subsequently to Evanston, Illinois, to teach and be an administrator at the Evanston Township High School, and later we set up a community college there, and I taught at Northwestern part time; I was a lecturer for about 10 years. Then I went to the U.S. Office of Education as a specialist in higher education and worked extensively with the new community college concept as a form of continuing education beyond the high school level. Afterwards, I had an opportunity to go to Nevada. I was an academic vice president at University of Nevada, and Jim, I just recall, I had the opportunity to set up what we called Nevada Southern—it's now the University of Nevada Las Vegas—and I drove from Reno to Las Vegas and back every week—that's 455 miles, and if you started early enough in the morning, you'd get down to Las Vegas by noon and work all afternoon and then you could drive home that evening. It made quite a day of it but we did get the University started. But driving through that desert, you know, there's mile after mile just straight, and you can open it up and average about 90 to 100 miles an hour.

Jim: If I recall there was no speed limit then.

Dr. Wood: No, no speed limits at all, and nobody else to bother you, so you just drove along. But that was an interesting experience because I had to deal heavily with mining people—not only the gold mining, but also the copper there at Harrington, the gold up at the Golconda-Hyacin, Winnamucca area and beyond, and then of course the old silver mines in Virginia City area. But tungsten was much in demand at that time. I remember one interesting experience. We were building a new facility—whether it was a student union or a new college of business or a new library or what it was on the campus in Reno—and we needed iron. And we bought it and found out that the ore had been mined at Lovelock, about 100 miles north of Reno, and then it had been shipped to Japan, and then it had been brought back, and we bought it then from American dealers in California, but the price was considerably less—to buy the Japanese-processed iron ore from Nevada—than it was to buy from the Kaiser Fontana plant, which was what, a couple of hundred miles, at most, from Reno. And I'm still puzzled about that. If you could mine it in Nevada and ship it to Japan for smelting and processing (whatever you did to it) and then get it back cheaper than what you could process the same ore in a plant 200 miles from you in California...It was an interesting experience, believe me. I come back to that notion that we should examine in some depth the notion of stewardship. I believe it is Biblically-based, that man has a responsibility that is different from that of other living things, whether a plant or animal or insects or whatever. And I'm not certain that we are exercising our responsibilities, or carrying out our responsibilities, in connection with our stewardship of Alaska and its resources. Now the word "husbandry" comes in there too, that needs to be examined. As you well know, all of the new wealth that we know in the world comes from two sources: It comes from mining and it comes from agriculture. Both very broadly conceived. Mining would include the use of the gravels or whatever. But agriculture is the fisheries and the furs and the timber and the berries and the fruits and the vegetables, and everything that grows. I'm not at all certain that we are using our best intelligence in carrying out our responsibilities of stewardship. We've been more or less in the high grade activity—come in and take out the top of something, the cream—and when that's gone, then we scratch around to find something else we can high-grade. And I doubt that that's a very intelligent approach. But as Alaskans, we ought to examine this whole concept of stewardship. What is the total usage that you could make, on a continuing basis—that is, without destroying or desecrating or degrading, but continuing it. And we need to spend a lot of thinking on this before we get too deep into the doing. It's more than multiple use, in my book; it is total use. What's the ultimate utilization that you can make. I also think in terms that idle resources are an expense that man cannot afford indefinitely. You may be wealthy enough at one point, by high-grading some one type of thing, to let everything else lie idle, but it is both a social and an economic expense to have un-utilized resources, and especially the land resource. That doesn't mean that some of it isn't at its best use when it's simply there in its pristine state—it does something for the soul. But where do you draw the line? That whole notion of stewardship and husbandry needs to be critically examined in depth by all of us.

Jim: Dr. Wood, tell the listening audience a little bit about what drew you to Alaska. And I understand you came in about 1960, is that correct?

Dr. Wood: That's correct. Jim, the short answer is, I was offered a job.

Jim: Is that right?

Dr. Wood: But it was so attractive, in terms of the things that interested me a great deal, that I would have jumped at taking up the offer, even if I'd had to pay money for it, which of course I didn't have. Here you had an entire state, and you had a constitutionally based state University, which was the entire system of public higher education in the state of Alaska...in the whole state. There was everything to do. Now, I was familiar with the situation, because at the Office of Education, for nearly five years, it was my assignment to visit all the states in the union, and I think I was on the campus of 2/3 or maybe 3/4 of all the institutions of higher learning in the United States, in every state. And the one place that had everything to do was Alaska. And since my interests are always to explore and to try to find new ways to do something—to create, to build—this was simply an ideal chance. And I never was much interested in tinkering with the operation of something that is already structured, already built. Much more interested in the building than in the operation. That's everything—not only facilities, but the faculty, the student body, the staff, the whole bit. And this was ideal. I came, not only because I was asked, but because it was a job that was, to me, the finest job in all higher education in North America.

Jim: How long were you president of the University of Alaska?

Dr. Wood: Thirteen years.

Jim: Thirteen years. You retired in 1973, then.

Dr. Wood: That's right. Overaged and grey, as we say in the Navy. And then we just stayed in Fairbanks, and that was 15 years ago, so I've lived here, now, this is the beginning of my 29th year.

Jim: Twenty-nine years and a lot of service to Alaska. We don't have a lot of time, but I would like for you to briefly describe the activities surrounding being city mayor, and what you accomplished as city mayor, in terms of upgrading the appearance of Fairbanks, Alaska.

Dr. Wood: Well, I was asked to declare for mayor. I was fortunate enough to win the election. I served for the two years, from '78 to '80, during which time I had a heart attack, and spent some time in the hospital. It probably would have happened anyway, but being mayor isn't the calmest assignment that you can pick up. Well, during that two years, in October of 1980, a resolution was put forth, the city was asking that we prepare to celebrate the silver anniversary of Alaska's statehood, which was coming along in 1984. And from that came the project of the Gary Statue, the sculpture in Golden Heart Park, and all the plaques with the names on it. And then also came the book about Interior Alaska, called *Interior Alaska - Journey Through Time*, which was, by the way, manuscripts lent to Jim Michener, and he uses it as the basis for the first three chapters of the recently published, *Alaska*. And we did many other things. It was a year-long celebration, even had a stamp issued, for the 25th.

Jim: We have a caller. Hello, you're on the air. Do you have a question for Dr. Wood?

Caller: Yes. Speaking of the park and the Alaskan Family, I would like to ask Dr. Wood, our family has been in the area for seven years, and most of us are on the plaques. But my new daughter-in-law and grand-daughter are not. Is there a possibility to add names to the plaques?

Dr. Wood: Not on the existing ones. The series of 49 is complete. However, there is a likelihood—the board has been discussing this—that we will have one or two additional plaques just for the things you mention. I have a new granddaughter that came along after the fact, and then there's another one in the wings, apparently, about to come along, and there is considerable interest in that. There are people that never heard about it, although for four or five years we did a lot of advertising; the people that didn't hear about it feel neglected. So we probably will open up one or two more plaques in the park, possibly a total of three. But a decision hasn't been firm, as yet, but it looks as if we might.

Caller: Now, Dr. Wood, a follow-up on that previous question that I gave you, how would one become listed?

Dr. Wood: Well, we're taking now the names and addresses and the telephone numbers, but not accepting any money. So you just send in your name and your address and say you're interested, , and as soon as the decision is made we'll notify you and send you the form.

Jim: Where do we send the information?

Dr. Wood: The address is 514 Second Ave., Suite 102, Fairbanks, Alaska 99701. That's the Lathrop Building; it's owned by the University of Alaska Foundation.

Jim: We are just about to the end of the trail on this particular version of Alaska Gold Trails. I want to thank you, Dr. Wood for joining us on the show today.

Dr. Wood: Thank you for inviting me, Jim.

Shorty Zucchini
with
Jim Madonna
May 18, 1989

Jim: Today we are here with Shorty Zucchini, an oldtimer here in the Fairbanks area and my very special guest. Shorty, welcome to Alaska Gold Trails .

Shorty: I'm very happy to be with you here, Jim Madonna. It's a real pleasure to have the opportunity to share some of my experiences after 40 continuous years up here in the north, which is just like mining paradise, in my way thinking. Very happy years they were, and I wish I could share every minute that I've had, the good parts and the bad parts. That made it sort of a variety, you could say. So, Jim, what would be more interesting in, say, my career in Alaska. I want to say this. Until I come to Alaska, I was pretty free, I was really a bum. I traveled all over. But after I got here, I kind of settled down and had many wonderful years with the fine people in the north. I traveled over a good part of the world and met so many people, but none of them compare with Alaskans. I don't know, maybe it's that 50 below that makes people so kind and so considerate of their neighbor. It's just great. Since I've been up here, over these many years, I've traveled all over the state, generally speaking, in all directions from Fairbanks. Fairbanks has always been my headquarters.

Jim: Shorty, some of the oldtimers around here call you Junior. Why is that?

Shorty: Well, I'm only 78 you know.

Jim: Where were you born, Shorty?

Shorty: I was born in a rough and ready situation in St. Louis, Missouri. And you know, to have this experience to go from the blacktop to the wilderness up here in Alaska has been fantastic. But I've moved into good company, with the old prospectors, you know. I'm not old yet.

Jim: What made you leave the blacktop?

Shorty: Well, I'll tell you. For some unknown reason I can't explain, there was a dissatisfaction living within the big community there. Well, I guess that's one way of expressing that. Really, getting out here and knowing nature, this is the answer, Jim. This is what really gave me everything, the lifestyle provides me with what I need. So I can say that I feel, in my own mind and heart, that I've been most happy and I appreciate what the Alaska people have provided for me.

Jim: You think you're fortunate that you arrived in Alaska.

Shorty: Oh yeah. I really didn't know what living was until I come to Alaska, and I've been over a good part of the world, as I've said.

Jim: Well, where did you go?

Shorty: Well, I was pretty free. I was out of control.

Jim: Nobody had any control over you?

Shorty: Nobody did.

Jim: Has anybody ever had any control over you?

Shorty: Well, I tell you, generally speaking, no. I never really had any. That's my downfall, but it had some good results too. I feel like I've benefited by that—what's that—philosophical type of thing, you know. This is what comes to you when you travel out there with only the bears and the bees and a bug or two around you. You sort of start thinking your life over a little bit. But that's good. So, I would say, in the long haul, it's given me a freedom of mind, and I enjoy and appreciate every day, every minute. What more can I have than that? So, anyway, today, I believe in spiritual life, that's true. But I also am very strong in the fellowship and the love that we're giving—accept that any way you want to. But it's the care that you have for your brother Alaskans. That's what's made me love everybody in Alaska, is they share this affection for each other.

Jim: Let me ask you this question. When you first came to Alaska, was there a camaraderie among all the pioneers that were up here? What year did you arrive?

Shorty: That was '47, 1947.

Jim: You got here a year before me, didn't you.

Shorty: Yeah, well you're really a cheechako in my eyes, Jim.

Jim: Yeah, Shorty. You were saying that you traveled all over the country and you've had a pretty good life. But there was a time that you weren't quite so free, and that was the time that you went into the service. Tell us about that.

Shorty: Well, I'll tell you. Like all people who want to assume some responsibility and obligation to our country, every day I'm more thankful that I'm American, when the rest of the world has such a terrible time getting together or even realizing what humanity is. Well, anyway, in World War II, I felt like all Americans do—if I can do a little bit for my country, that's it. So I had some Navy training I wound up in the Merchant Marines. I sailed on tankers, mostly with Standard Oil, which was very good, seeing a good part of the Pacific and met many people. That was very interesting. However, when the hostilities terminated, I was ready to quit; I'm not a natural sailor—I'm, as they say, a land lover.

Jim: Following the service, then, is that when you came to Alaska?

Shorty: No, I took a vacation then, in southern California, and then I started thinking about all the treasures that might be up here in Alaska (which I didn't find, I'm happy to say). But the amusing part of it is, I was carrying these treasures around with me and didn't realize it, believe me or not.

Jim: How did you get here, Shorty?

Shorty: At that time, in 1947, there was a small outfit that had prop planes (we didn't have no jets, you know) and of course I signed up. But I got a roundtrip fare just in case things wouldn't work out. But I knew that I hit my high peak in life just after I landed here and met these wonderful Alaskans. I don't know why the people are different unless it's putting snowshoes on and knowing what 60 below is and dark nights or freezing my feet or having these doggone mosquitoes bite the hell out of me, you know, when you put all this together, it changes your life, Jim.

Jim: It creates that wonderful atmosphere that you're talking about?

Shorty: Oh, absolutely.

Jim: Sixty below. Mosquitoes. The tourist information bureau would love to have your ad on that one. Did you ever use the other half of that ticket to go back out?

Shorty: No. I tore it up, to tell you the truth. That's right.

Jim: Some guy said he went way out in the bush one time, and he said he got way out there and it was like 50 miles from anywhere, up a river by boat, then he had to hike in 10 miles someplace and he had packs and he had help with some friends, they were out prospecting, and they walked into this canyon, and there was Shorty Zucchini down there, staking some claims ahead of them.

Shorty: Well, that's possible.

Jim: What was Fairbanks like when you got here?

Shorty: Well, I'll tell you, it was just like a wide place in the road. Nobody even thought about Airport Road, and they were building Eielson. It was called 22-mile, at that time. Now if you went from what was then Fairbanks out to 22-mile, if you got out there without a flat tire, you had a good mark, you really had an achievement, see? It wasn't really a gravel road, it was more like a stone road. Sometimes you had to push these stones out of the way if they were in your way. Same way out to a place called Big Delta down the same road another 70 miles.

Jim: Is that right? Rika's Roadhouse, was that operating at that time?

Shorty: I'm sure it was. I don't exactly recall, but I know there was Donnelly Dome and two or three others out there. They were popular stops.

Jim: You said you've been all around Alaska, but Fairbanks was your headquarters.

Shorty: That's true. For one reason or another, it's been my favorite headquarters, so to speak.

Jim: In Fairbanks, Alaska, when you first got here, were the roads paved? Or were they gravel?

Shorty: Oh no. I don't think there was even a trail out to where we are here, out on Airport Road, out by University Center, or whatever you want to call it.

Jim: There was nothing, not even a trail here?

Shorty: I don't recall even a good trail. Probably a dog team. I don't know why we don't go back to the dog teams. What do we need all this oil for, and all this stuff, and all these fancy cars. Just think of the fun of the dog teams and a swede saw and an axe and cut all the wood you want free, how can you beat that?

Jim: Can't beat it, Shorty. When you came here, were there a lot of dog teams around? Was dog racing a major outdoor activity?

Shorty: Oh yeah, there was a lot of them. You couldn't really make it without a team if you lived out of town any distance.

Jim: Did they compete? Did they race?

Shorty: Oh sure, that was one of the fun things to do in the winter.

Jim: Lets change direction here, Shorty. Did you ever work in a drift mine?

Shorty: Yes, I did. I know what it is. I was a little shaky when I first got broke into that, but you know, you wonder if the ceiling's going to be on you, but after you've spent some time there, that doesn't seem to matter at all.

Jim: I've had some experiences working at one of the drift mines that was developed more recently based on the old time drift mining method, and it was like stepping back into history. Keep in mind that the gold was distributed at the interface of the gravels and bedrock down there. These chaps dropped the shaft some 35 feet to bedrock and then drifted out laterally and found the paystreak and were hauling the gold-bearing gravels to the surface where they stacked it in a large pile and then waited for the spring, which would bring the thaw, and ultimately the water that was used for sluicing the gravels, and they had their pay day. That's basically the same as what went on in the early days, isn't it Shorty?

Shorty: Oh yeah. Very definitely so. Well, it appeared to me, I always had the thought that the simple life that we knew back then was so we didn't miss anything.

Jim: Shorty, tell us a little bit more about your prospecting and mining activity in the Interior of Alaska. You say Fairbanks was the core that you worked out of. Did you work up in the Chandalar area, in the Brooks Range?

Shorty: Yes, I did do a minor amount of work and activity up there. That's another beautiful, isolated and remote place in Alaska. And anyone that hasn't had the opportunity to see this natural beauty, I certainly encourage them to do that.

Jim: And did you work with some of the other young guys that were up there, like Ernie Wolff and some of those chaps?

Shorty: Oh yeah, Ernie, as a matter of fact, I was fortunate enough to meet Ernie up there during his activity at Coal Creek. He does a good job. He's a little opinionated, like I am, like all Alaskans eventually get if they stick around long enough, you know what I mean.

Jim: Is it a traditional character about the old time Alaskans, that they send gifts and things that people might need out in the bush environment.

Shorty: Yeah. You've got to keep that in mind, Jim, if you want to be a regular, you know.

Jim: I heard that it was traditional when you go for a visit into the bush that you take a bottle with you, have one drink with the miner then leave the bottle. It's worked well for me. I've had some experiences where things arrived unexpectedly and I certainly did enjoy receiving some of the gifts that were sent to me when I was out in the bush.

Shorty: Jim, that's a surprise to me. I always figured you were a blacktop prospector. I didn't know you ever left Fairbanks. This is amazing. Well, I'm glad to know it, anyway, Jim.

Jim: Well, tell me, what is a blacktop prospector?

Shorty: A blacktop prospector has to have a vehicle to drive right up to the sluice box. That's a blacktop miner, see what I mean. He's got to have a paved road to get right where he's mining.

Jim: And you thought I was a blacktop prospector?

Shorty: Yeah. I couldn't associate you any other way, Jim.

Jim: That's because of my frail build and because I'm short.

Shorty: Well, that's true, that's partly it.

Jim: Shorty, tell us about some of your experiences in Alaska. Have you had any encounters with bears or ice problems or airplane crashes or narrow escapes or something of that nature?

Shorty: Well, you know, in my lifestyle up here, I've been real close to grizzly bears, and I often wonder why they were so friendly, but they were, you know. Maybe it was because they didn't think I was big enough to be interesting. But anyway, I generally had a good relationship with the bears. I've had a few close ones. I was thankful that I didn't fall through the ice, a couple of times, but came real close. And being lost, you know, if you've never been lost, I tell you, it's a wonderful experience, I'm telling you, it really shakes you up real bad.

Jim: It's a wonderful experience to be lost? Tell us how it's a wonderful experience.

Shorty: Well, I tell you. I was up north there a couple hundred miles, on the south fork of the Koyukuk River, and I thought I would make a sharp cross-country deal there, and I got lost. Now, in places a creek or a river might just zig-zag. You'd think you were going upstream, you'd go a little ways through the bush, and here it is going in the other direction. So you really easily get lost, you know, because you don't know. You think the river's taking you up or taking you down, but that isn't the way it is in flat country. But anyway, I got lost and got pretty hungry too, and well, I tell you, it's kind of a weird feeling to be lost, I'll tell you for sure. And then you fall back on your spiritual life at a time like this, and you say, how about the supreme power? If you give me another chance to have another day, I'll be a good guy from now on. And that's the way it was. So, that's part of it.

Jim: You're still lost, Shorty. Did you get out of this mess? Obviously you did, but how did you get out of it?

Shorty: Well, I tell you, I was pretty shook up, and I almost gave up hope. You know this builds your confidence and builds your spirit. I finally come to the realization that if I got up into the highest peak in the general area—which I did—by getting up high, I could read the terrain, you know what I mean? So I got oriented. I got a brief idea of where I was, and believe me, Jim, I can't tell you what a wonderful relief and spirit of thankfulness it is to be lost and be alone, and then find your way. Wonderful.

Jim: This brings us to another question. Do you think, Shorty, if you were to give somebody some advice regarding entering the wilderness of Alaska, would you suggest that they go alone, or would you suggest that they have a companion?

Shorty: Well, I'll tell you, as it developed, I've been with a lot of bears. So you really don't know, but I've had a relationship through the years with the bears, and if you give them plenty of room and don't surprise them, why I figure you're reasonably safe. If they've got a family, why that's something else. You better respect that.

Jim: Would you prefer to enter the bush area with a companion?

Shorty: Well, it's always better. I would recommend this, but a lot of these cheechako or blacktop prospectors don't want to take that opportunity, you know what I mean? But it's all right. Being alone, it is lonesome, and you overcome that. There's a beauty of the woods; where else but Alaska can you enjoy this? So there you are. Alaska will provide everything to sustain your energy. The salmon and various other edible animals or whatever, even the berries. You can sustain...I've made it on berries. It's kind of thin. You kind of keep your weight down, you know.

Jim: You want to travel light, anyway, don't you?

Shorty: That's right. You might as well get used to that, 'cause if you get lost again, it eases your problem.

Jim: Shorty, tell us a little bit more about some of the prospecting adventures you've had. Have you staked a lot of claims in Alaska?

Shorty: Yes I did. There's been several instances where I would stake some claims and then I would move away from that area and discover something that was more promising or better. And so it's just been, until not too long ago I discovered the greatest of treasures. Can you believe that? The greatest of treasures. I feel like I have more than anybody else that I can even think about or know.

Jim: Shorty, let me ask this question. Do you have a message that you'd like to give the public?

Shorty: Well, I'll tell you. To every one of my dear Alaska friends, remember, number one, it's not what you put in your wallet that is going to make your life full. It's what you have built inside of you.

Jim: So you think it's what's in your heart that counts the most, is that right?

Shorty: The heart and mind is the greatest treasure you'll ever own. Even if the world was paved with gold, it would not equal that, believe me. One of the things you do, the first thing to get started on my trail, is go over—you might even go over to Alaska Prospectors and see Leah—and start with a gold pan. And if you don't know how to pan, come out to Ester and we'll help you. We want to share our wonderful life in Alaska. That's the beginning.

Jim: I remember one time, Shorty, that I saw you in one of the businesses here in town, and some people were asking how to gold pan and where they could gold pan, and you happened to walk through the door, and you took these people who were visitors to our state and you took them out to Ester and apparently showed them how to pan gold. And they panned gold, and they were very happy with what you gave them and you became good friends with them. You made a comment about them living down in what, Los Angeles, and that you have now become good friends with them and you go visit them every time you get down in that area, is that right?

Shorty: This is what I call a treasure, Jim. When you do something nice that's not monetary, then you're on the right track, you know what I mean?

Jim: You know, Shorty, you're a treasure in itself, to have you here in Fairbanks, Alaska, we're very fortunate. We're running a little close to the end of the show here, but I want to thank you for coming on Alaska Gold Trails with me this afternoon, and I'm certain that all the people out there that have listened to this show today appreciate you and the kind of person that you are, and I certainly respect your integrity and regard for Alaska and its people.

Shorty: Only way to go, Jim. Thank you.

Paul McCarthy
with
Jim Madonna
November 30, 1989

Jim: Today our guest on Alaska Gold Trails is Paul McCarthy. Welcome to Alaska Gold Trails, Paul.

Paul: Thank you very much for the invitation, Jim.

Jim: Paul, we know that you're affiliated with the University of Alaska, at the library, and before we talk about what you do there could you give us a little background of where you came from—who you are, where you are, and what you have done through your life, in capsule form?

Paul: Sure, Jim. I'm currently the director of libraries at the University. I came here in 1964, from Syracuse, New York. My wife, Lucy and I had two small children at the time, and I was working full time at Syracuse University and going to school full time. I had a friend who moved up here, Ted Reiberg, who was a director of libraries, and he asked me if I'd ever be interested in coming to Alaska, and I said, "Sure," not thinking too much, but having read about Alaska as a teenager and growing up and just really entranced by it. So, he made an offer about a year later, in '64, and Lucy and I grabbed our two kids and ourselves and about 300 pounds of gear total, and came to Alaska. And you know we flew in Pan Am's 707, at the time, and we looked at all the mountains and the snow, and we got to Fairbanks and there was a small airport and a dirt parking lot, and we thought, "We have come to the end of the world."

Jim: Paul. What time of year was that again?

Paul: It was in the summer. But there was still a lot of ice and snow in the mountains on the way up. And we got here and had a place to stay, and we picked our gear up off a wooden table on the outside of the airport and drove into town, and you know it was summer, and it was just a stunning difference from upstate New York, Many people were still doing tasks and chores at 11 to 12 O'clock at night.

Jim: You had quite a cultural and social shock, in terms of climate, people and activities.

Paul: Really, we did, and I think, when I reflect back over the changes, we didn't call home very often because it was nine dollars for the first three minutes, and we were pretty poor at the time and relatively cut off from our outside families. One of the things I've really reflected on, Jim, as you and I've talked about, is the great people we've met here over the years, and the good experiences we've had. We've raised two kids and brought two more up here in the state, and have really enjoyed that experience, and enjoy the experience of working at the University, too.

Jim: Now, when you came up in 1964, Paul, did you go directly to work for the University?

Paul: Right. I was the six-area services librarian, and Ted Reiberg and I had talked about developing a special collections emphasis to the library. I had worked at Syracuse University, in the archives there, and they had a very aggressive program on developing resources on railroads and different economic areas—art, writing—so that the students and faculty of the University could use those to do research. That was kind of Ted's dream, and Dr. Howard Cutler at the same time, shared that dream, and so they created a position the next year, and I took that position and began developing the archives and manuscript collections.

Jim: What a lot of people are interested in, Paul, is the archives, and some of the facilities and materials that you have available there at the University of Alaska library, and how they might be able to use it. Tell us a little bit about some of the services you have there at the library and things that you've developed and worked on, specifically.

Paul: Part of what we attempted to do when we started the program in '65 was to look at Alaska and try to develop resources—whether they were diaries or photograph collections, corporate records—the things that would document Alaska's history and development. You know, one of the first people I ran into was Ivar Skarland, who kind of set a tone with his enthusiasm and interest in Alaska, and it's been almost non-stop really enthusiastic and supportive people, all the way along. What we try to do is contact a variety of people, including native individuals, like William Paul, some political figures like Gruening and Bartlett. and miners. I know one of the collections we got earlier was the Tanana Valley Gold Dredging Company, in terms of looking at gold dredging opportunities and operations in the Tanana Valley. Ted Reiberg and I went down to Juneau at one time (it was about 50 to 60 below zero) to rescue some mining records that were stored down at the Alaska Juneau Mining Company, and were going to be disposed of. We were using an old University vehicle (you might have had some experience with them) to go to Juneau and collect the documents. It was about 60 below zero and we blew an engine in one of the passes. Besides, it didn't have any internal heater, so we had to stop every 40 miles or so to thaw ourselves out. But we finally got down to Juneau, after a few days, and were able to retrieve the records and bring them back.

Jim: So these are available today, in the archives?

Paul: That particular set we transferred back to Juneau when they became interested, but we did work with the people at Kennicott and retrieved a number of records there before they were lost.

Jim: We've got a call, Paul. Welcome to Alaska Gold Trails. You're on the air with Paul McCarthy.

Caller: Work it in wherever you can, but don't forget to tell us about your canoe trip with Reiberg down the Yukon. OK.

Jim: Paul, I think you also made a trip over to Porcupine Creek, is that right? Or was it one of the streams off the Yukon?

Paul: We went down the Yukon, down to the Charlie, but we stopped at all the rivers and all the places between Eagle and Circle. We just recently, three years ago, returned to Coal Creek to retrieve some records, but the trip that the caller just referred to was a trip that was suggested to us in 1966 or '67, of going down and trying to survey the historical sites along the Yukon, and to retrieve any records that were abandoned, and to document that part of Alaska's history. So Ted and I took off, and we had to drive through the Chicken forest fire, at that time—I think it was about 500,000 acres—and were delayed.

Jim: What year was that?

Paul: Either '66 or '67. And then we spent a week on the Yukon. Ted and I had envisioned that we would get from Eagle down to Tanana in about a week and a half to two weeks, and we recognized early on that we were going to get nowhere near that distance, because we'd stop and we'd really look at the sites—which would now be historical sites or cabin sites or mining sites—and just get an idea of what was going on along the river.

Jim: The caller had something to say about your trip down the Yukon. Was there any adventure that was particularly dangerous that occurred along that trip, or was it just the timing.

Paul: Not on that trip. We've had plenty of others where there's been a little bit of adventure, unplanned adventure, but not on that one.

Jim: I think the word I was looking for was adrenaline flow.

Paul: Well, there were a couple of ones where we had a little adrenaline flow. We were flying into Kodiak, or flying out of Kodiak, and we had gone in there on the state ferry, and this was I think the late '60s, early '70s. And there was a storm with winds up to about 100-120 miles an hour which had taken off cannery roofs, as well as done other damage. We flew out to a small village and then flew back, and the fog was so bad and the wind was still so bad that the plane was actually fairly close to the water—we could see the wake of the engines in the water. A couple things like that, when I look back on what we did in collecting archives, probably have not occurred in very many places in the United States.

Jim: Let's see, there were a couple of other places that you traveled to, Paul, in terms of collecting archival materials.

Paul: We went into Kennicott. There was a project funded, and the project leader was Mike Sullivan. He was in Anchorage; now he's in Washington state. He was really trying to preserve the mine there. And so he had gotten some funding—I think it was from Kennicott, and we went in and surveyed the mining operation records that were left in the store. There were several hundred cubic feet, as I remember, and we decided we couldn't retrieve them all, but we did retrieve about 40 or 50 cubic feet of records, and sampled the records that were there, and then grabbed some of the early health records of miners, and then had a really thorough tour of the mine. It's a really magnificent structure and magnificent mining operation. So we brought those back in what I guess would be a flying boxcar. We had our picture taken; we looked like the last three veterans leaving Vietnam—We looked haggard. And we took off. It was one of those things where the plane was leased to fly back to Fairbanks, so we actually landed in Gakona, where we'd left the University van, and just loaded the van and all records right into the plane and flew home. That's traveling in style, which we never got accustomed to.

Jim: Only in Alaska.

Paul: Really.

Jim: We have a call, Paul. Hi, you're on the air with Paul McCarthy.

Caller: Yes. What kind of records is your guest trying to salvage?

Paul: We're really interested in a variety of business records. We have different kinds, but we certainly would like to get some quality mining records, that would show operations. We have worked with Earl Beistline out at some of the creeks collecting records. Anything that provides an overview of what it meant to be a miner—the difficulties, operations, costs, those kinds of things.

Caller: I was in the Kennicott years ago. I took what records I could read out of the hospital, that's why I was asking.

Paul: Oh, that would be interesting.

Caller: Deaths, people that had died there and what not.

Paul: Those would be very interesting to us, really.

Caller: Do you have a phone number?

Paul: Surely. 474-7224 is my number, or you can call David Hales or Gretchen Lake at 474-7261 that's the archives.

Caller: Thank you much.

Paul: You're entirely welcome.

Jim: Thanks for the call, sir. Paul, we were talking a little bit about your trips around Alaska. You got a couple more you'd like to tell, and some adventures that you might have had, other than loading your car in the airplane and bringing it back?

Paul: Well, I'm trying to think. A really humorous one is a continuation of this one that we went to Juneau on. Ted and I spent three days in the top of Three Guardsmen's Pass. That was when the Alaskans were maintaining that part of it. And then we towed the truck 75 miles, to Haines, and then had to put it on board ship, and then take it to the DOT facilities in Juneau to have it repaired, because there was not a good internal engine heater in it. As I said, it took us five hours to start it at Beaver Creek, and I think the engine never survived that well. That and a few others around the state. We once had to charter an aircraft out of Juneau, because I had an appointment I could not miss, and we could take a small aircraft out and just go above the water and go over to Sitka and catch your regular commercial craft out. So, just different things that archivists and librarians are usually involved with up here.

Jim: You know, you never think, Paul, that a librarian could have as many adventures as you've had. I once got stuck in a snowstorm on top of 75-mile on the Haines-Haines Junction Pass. You know that's not fun.

Paul: That's not fun at all, and it was one of my early trips, and I didn't have anything to read, and the quality of reading materials left there at the camp was real marginal. So I always carry enough in Alaska to read for a day or two.

Jim: I don't know if maybe a lot of people out there recognize the full magnitude of what Paul is talking about, when on some of the travels you get caught a little bit short, in terms of quality of not only the reading material that's available but the transportation vehicles as well. You have to be very careful they are prepared for the journey—both aircraft, boats and of course cars. Paul, tell us a little bit about what you do with the archival materials, in general, that you have here at the University of Alaska archives. What is the procedure for carrying it through. For example, the gentleman that just called suggested that he might be willing to donate some archival materials to the University of Alaska. What would you do with that material?

Paul: OK, what we would do—and Jim I'd like to emphasize that we are really open to anybody who thinks that they have material that might be of interest to us, that's significant—what we do is take a look at the material and see how it might document Alaska's history and development, and then if we can negotiate an agreement to have the material given to the University, we do an inventory of it, and then we try to arrange it so that a student or a scholar or a lay person can come in and use the material. We usually make some kind of a subject arrangement, or reconstruct how the donor might have put that collection together. We then put together what we would call a finding aid—it's like a list of the subjects folders, or just an outline of the design of the collection so that if you come in, there is some guide to find your way in the collection. It's like a map of the collection, so that you can find your way around. It still involves a lot of work for the user, but it gets them pretty close to the subject areas or the sequences of the people they want to look at. So, we create that finding aid, then it's put in the archives. The archives is open five days a week, from 9 to 5, and we make the finding aids available outside of those hours, if you need that additional help. I would like to emphasize that I am not in charge of the archives. The archives operate under my general supervision, but I did spend 23 years trying to develop that collection. What I would like to emphasize with that collection, and with the Alaska collection, is that over 50% of our users come from off campus. So the materials are available to residents of the state of Alaska as well as visitors from the lower states or foreign countries.

Jim: Well then, this is truly an international public service, as well as a local public service.

Paul: It really is. Right now we have a Swiss couple, Hubert and Beatrice Fonget, who spend two or three weeks with us at least once or twice a year, doing research on early exploration of the Arctic and Inuit people. So, they're not by any means the first. We do have a small stream of international visitors, but a very steady stream of Alaskans and people from Canada and the lower states.

Jim: Paul, tell us a little about how somebody in town can come up to the University of Alaska library and look at the archives, and how they might be helped from a personal standpoint. For example, if I was a local person, interested in coming up to the archives to look up some information for perhaps a paper that I was writing or a story that I was writing, how would I go about that?

Paul: Well, Jim, if I could step back just a little bit, I'd like to look at the entire library, since that is open to the citizens of the state. You can get a very good idea of what we have in the printed collection, the book collection, by just dialing in. We have our catalog on-line, so if people have a modem then they can dial in. They can come up to the University and get a really quick good overview of what we have in almost any subject area.

Jim: If a person has a computer and a modem at home, they dial in and this information will flash up on their computer screen?

Paul: It's a pretty easy routine to use, if you type S, slash (/), and the subject. You use standard subjects, but we can teach people how to do that. We've got log-in procedures for people to do that. We also have a bibliography of Alaska, which I think is really valuable, and we would love to have more people use it. That's dial-in also, so if you or somebody else is interested in what is currently being published on mining, in any periodical we have, you can dial in, get into the bibliography and we index material on about a ten-day turn-around. So if something's in the archives or in the Alaska Polar Regions today, it'll be indexed and available on-line within say five to ten business days.

Jim: Is that right. Well, tell us, what is the number?

Paul: You have to come in—you have to dial in to 474-6910, which is what they call the INX—and then you need to log on, and it would be easier just to describe to somebody over the phone, or we could give them a sheet and we could show them how to use it on site, and then they can get into it.

Jim: So they would just call the reference people, and they would explain the procedure?

Paul: Right. Or they can come up and we will give them a demonstration. Much of the Alaska material is not yet on line, although we're describing it and then putting it up on line this year. We've over 100 descriptions of the archival collections, and I would like to emphasize that there's a tremendous amount of material in there relating to mining or commercial operations. Almost anything you can think of. They might be buried in collections, you know like if you were looking at mining, you'd certainly want to look at some of the political collections, because the senators and representatives had an interest, and they would develop the subject areas and expertise about that. We have some geological scientists who have donated their field notes. We have some fabulous photographic collections of gold mining—both in this area and along the Yukon—all over the state. So, you can come in, there's a list of collections in the Alaskan Polar Regions department. The staff there would help you identify the collections that are appropriate. They can show you photographic collections. We have 47,000 photographs on microfiche that are available anyplace in the state. We have a lot of oral histories that deal with mining operations, with early pioneers, that kind of thing. I think we have about 1,500 oral interviews. And these, again, there's an index there, and very shortly we're anticipating that all these will be searchable on-line—not the full text, but at least a citation to it. So if you're interested in an area or person, within say a one to three-year window, we'll have an enormous amount of this on-line, like we do with the entire book collection and the periodical index right now.

Jim: If somebody needed that information, they could, if they had computer capabilities, dial in, or if not they could simply come up to the University and some of the staff would help them through the necessary avenues to reach their goal, is that correct?

Paul: Right. And we have some, I think, despite the hard times, we have some really really very exciting things coming on line. One of those, for people interested in business operations, whether they relate to mining or hospitals, is a thing we call ABIN form. It's a CD round, the size of a small record. It has 200,000 citations and abstracts relating to anything to do with business, whether it's hospital management or mining management. It's searchable—you can search any term or combination of terms; it identifies 100 citations and abstracts a second. And we have this both for business and education. We intend to broaden this to some science areas and perhaps engineering this year. Ultimately, we're going to create what we call a local area network, where you'll be able to get into any of these from about six or eight stations on campus, and then pretty soon we hope to link it up with the University's computer to link it to off-campus status.

Jim: We've got a caller, Paul. Hi, you're on the air with Paul McCarthy.

Caller: Hi. I was listening a little while ago and I thought I heard him say that he had reference material on-line, and I would say that I'm familiar to some extent with this Gnosis. Is that the same thing?

Paul: Right. There's a second part that you may not be aware of, in terms of that index to Alaska-related articles. That's not as widely known as the other part.

Caller: I guess what I was wondering is, all I ever knew about was that you could get indexes of materials that were available in the library, on Gnosis. Can you actually read the material through there?

Paul: No, you can't read the material through that. It's just a citation to the books or to the periodical articles. We're experimenting with the other, but we don't have anything that we could demonstrate yet.

Caller: OK, thank you very much.

Jim: Paul, we've got a few minutes left here. Tell us a little bit more about the library. One question that I have, and many of my students have had, at the University of Alaska Mining Extension, is do you have a set of U.S.G.S. bulletins and works.

Paul: Yes. Yes, we do. As far as I know we have a very comprehensive set of the bulletins. We endeavor to collect extra copies of any that relate to Alaska, and we're always scouting for additional ones, additional duplicates, because they're a real high-use item. So, they're available both in government documents, and most of them if not all of them should be indexed in the Alaska collection, available on-line.

Jim: You know, one of the pioneers in Alaska for the U.S.G.S. was Alfred Hulse Brooks, and of course our Brooks Building is named after him, and he had done a lot of work out on the Seward Peninsula and first identified the fact that there were not only submarine beaches, but also beach lines that existed on the upland areas, away from the present beach strand. And I was wondering, does your literature on U.S.G.S. publications go back as far as Brooks, or farther than Brooks, back into the 1890s?

Paul: It would go back I think to the 1890s, and we were fortunate enough to acquire a good deal of the Brooks library from Alfred Brooks, and lots of it is still autographed with his name and we've incorporated much of that into the collection. We also have a fellow named Katz who did a lot of work, and we have his manuscript collection and much of what he published. So, I think the geology would be one of the really strong collections, and we're continuing to work with people like Brent Washburn and Troy Péwé, to increase the richness of those collections.

Jim: I had one more thought here, and we've got a couple of minutes. Just quickly, could you comment on the Skinner Collection—how it came about.

Paul: Sure. The Skinner Collection—well, there are really two different strands that weave together in what is called the Skinner Collection. When Bunnell first became president, he immediately began developing a library and writing to people. In the early '50s, it was brought to the University's attention that there was a very very good book collection in the custody of a Mr. Erskine in Kodiak. And Mr. Skinner, of Alaska Steam, funded the purchase of the book collection, which I think at that time was about 3,000 or 3,500 books relating to Alaska. And that was brought from Kodiak to Fairbanks, courtesy of Alaska Steam and Mr. Skinner. But much of it was generated by Mr. Erskine, who also had collected some of the early Alaska Commercial Company records that we also acquired at about the same time. So, that forms the basis of what we would call the Alaska and Polar Regions collection, and it has grown to at least 40-50,000 discrete titles, probably 60-70,000 volumes of material.

Jim: You attempt to keep that updated at all times.

Paul: That is kept updated, and we've broadened the focus to include kind of a pan-Arctic interest, so we collect northern Canada, Greenland and northern Scandinavia, and we have a very strong collection of Russian literature relating to Soviet geology.

Jim: Paul, I want to thank you for joining us here on Alaska Gold Trails today.

Paul: Well, thank you very much, Jim. I really enjoyed it.

Jim: It's been a pleasure. Folks, I want to make a little comment regarding Alaska Gold Trails. We have had 97 shows on Alaska Gold Trails to date. These shows have all been taped on cassette tapes. A copy of the tapes have been prepared and will be donated to the University of Alaska library, so if you or any of your friends have been on Alaska Gold Trails and you care to hear the show once again, or make a copy of that tape, you merely have to call the University of Alaska library and let them know your desires. This is Jim Madonna, I have enjoyed presenting Alaska Gold Trails each week. I have a rather large research project which will take up most of my time for the next couple of years. I want to thank Bill Walley, Michael Dresser and Frank DeLong of KFAR Radio for allowing me to visit with you over these past three years. Most of all, I want to thank my guests who made this show such a success. And of course I want to thank you, the listening audience for your interest and participation. It has been wonderful, simply wonderful.

Part IV

Where
The Trail Winds

Where the Trail Winds

Following the Alaska Gold Trails Radio interviews in 1989 the guests and I, where possible, have stayed in touch. The following summaries provide the reader with a brief history of these pioneers over the past decade.

Jim and Mary Binkley

Between 1989, when they appeared on the Alaska Gold Trails program, and 1993, Jim and Mary Binkley continued to operate their riverboat tours. In 1992 they moved from their home on University Avenue to a new house on the shores of the Chena River near the riverboat dock. In 1993 they began to restore *Discovery I* for the purpose of training interested young people in the art of riverboating. Since that time they have willingly shared their memories and experiences with the passengers on the riverboat tours, but for the most part they are now enjoying the comfort of watching their children take over the family tradition of riverboating in Alaska.

Robert Charlie

Robert and his wife Cathy live just off Badger Road near Fairbanks, Alaska.

During the past twelve years Robert has organized and directed the Cultural Heritage Education Institute, which is dedicated to preserving Interior Athabascan native cultural heritage.

One of Robert's special interests is his native band, which plays at various functions including dances, fund raisers and state fairs, all of which are alcohol-free gatherings.

Both Robert and Cathy are in good health. Robert says: "My life is dedicated to serving and improving cross-cultural communications in Alaska and reducing the tragedies of drug and alcohol abuse among Alaska's native people."

Doug Colp

Doug Colp continues to live in Fairbanks, Alaska, with his wife Marcel.

Doug continued mining at Candle until 1992 then he and his mining group moved to Tofty, near Manley Hot Springs, where they began placer mining gold on Cache Creek. Cassiterite in this deposit encumbered profitable gold extraction even though they shipped a number of 1800-pound drums containing 65% tin to Vancouver then to Singapore for processing.

In 1996 Doug and his group moved from Cache Creek and began a drift mine operation on Little Eldorado Creek near Fairbanks. In 1998 the company sold out and Doug began development of a new property on Ketchum Creek in the Circle mining area. Simultaneously he began an ongoing evaluation of a gold property on a ranch in Northern California near Hayfork.

Doug says that at 84 he is "too old to quit and too young to retire."

Tony Gularte
1908-1995

Anthony "Tony" Gularte, 86, died April 2, 1995, at the Anchorage Pioneers Home. Mr. Gularte was born June 15, 1908, in New Bedford, Massachusetts. He came to Alaska with his family at the age of seven. They settled in Flat. He married Liza Demientieff in 1935 in Seattle, and in 1945, moved to Fairbanks.

The family moved to Anchorage in 1957. Mr. Gularte worked on the Alaska Highway, Distant Early Warning (DEW) Line near Point Barrow, and the Alyeska Pipeline. He was a working member of Operating Engineers Local 302.

Mr. Gularte participated in the Prospectors, Fairbanks Chapter of Pioneers of Alaska, Anchorage Senior Center, and the Friday polka nights at St. Patrick's Parish. His family said "He cultivated relationships and friendships throughout his life."

From Anchorage Daily News, April 5, 1995.

Juanita Helms

Juanita Helms still lives in Fairbanks, Alaska, with her husband, Sam. She completed her second term as Fairbanks North Star Borough mayor in 1991.

From 1992 through 1995 she worked on several projects in Russia including marketing workshops, business conferences and methods of updating Russian election processes. From 1995 through 1997 Juanita was content to work as a housewife and share landlord duties with her husband on several Fairbanks properties. However, in 1998 she once again got itchy to become heavily involved in community government and ran for Fairbanks city mayor. Although she received a good public response Juanita did not receive the majority required for election.

While Juanita's children are all grown, she and Sam still enjoy frequent visits with them and have close family ties. She and Sam are both happy and healthy and have begun making plans for extensive traveling in the future. At this time she is heavily involved with several public service community activities. Juanita says, "Although I am semi-retired I will always be involved with community organizations that benefit the Alaskan residents."

Cliff and Orea Haydon

Cliff and Orea Haydon still live in Fairbanks, Alaska. In 1993 they were selected as the King and Queen Regents of the Pioneers. As regents they traveled to many of the Alaskan communities then ended their trip at the Pioneers Convention in Valdez.

In 1996 Cliff fell ill and spent almost two months in the hospital. About that same period of time a friend started a nursing home where Cliff went to stay. He has adjusted nicely and all his needs are met, including the snacks that he has always enjoyed so much.

Orea still lives in their home of 50 years located on Badger Road. She makes several trips a week taking pies and other baked goods to Cliff at the nursing home. She also busies herself by writing historical stories for the Heartland section of the Daily News Miner, and is currently preparing a historical book on her family.

Duke Kilbury

Duke Kilbury has retired and since 1992 has lived in the Ketchikan Pioneers Home. Prior to retiring he completed the home he had contracted to construct.

He and Ken Eichner flew one last time into the headwaters of the Unik River, to their cabin on Sulpherette Creek. They prospected and for the most part reminisced about old times.

Duke and his wife were both living in the Pioneers Home in 1995 when his wife passed away. At 87 years old Duke is in relatively good health, although he does have problems breathing. His son George suggested that he could quit smoking. Duke's response was: "I am not a quitter". This is a characteristic that Duke has carried with him throughout his life. He always finishes the tasks he is committed to.

Don May

Don still lives in Fairbanks, Alaska, with his wife Ruth. While all six children—three girls and three boys—are grown and have left home, they all live in Fairbanks and get together often.

Don continued to run Polar Mining, one of the largest placer mining operations in Alaska until 1993 when he suffered a serious illness. At that time he turned the operation over to his sons. Although he has made continuous recovery from his illness he is now semi-retired from the business. He has begun to travel a fair bit and has visited Hawaii, Florida, and Arizona, and has made three trips to Israel.

His more recent activities include teaching Bible classes at the Fairbanks Rescue Mission, which he indicates is a very rewarding experience.

At this time Don says that both he and his wife are healthy and happy and are thankful for this and for their fine children.

Don Nelson
1924-1997

Missionary Donald L. Nelson of North Pole passed away at the age of 73, on May 8, 1997.

Dick Olson, a close friend of his, said Nelson had planned to be on the Alaska Highway by Thursday (May 8), headed north for a final visit to his North Pole home.

Instead, Olson and other members of Nelson's radio family had to face the fact that Nelson wasn't coming back.

"His goal was to get up here before he passed away," Olson said. "It wasn't meant to be."

Nelson died early Thursday (May 8) from complications of pneumonia and heart disease. Gov. Tony Knowles ordered state flags in the Fairbanks area lowered to half-staff in honor of Nelson.

His death has silenced a religious voice that permeated Alaska's Interior for three decades.

"He touched a lot of lives," Olson said. "If it wasn't for his drive and incentive in getting things done, we probably wouldn't be here today."

Olson was sitting in a small studio at the KJNP AM-FM radio and television station cabin in North Pole. He recalled building that cabin and others with Nelson in 1967 on a 46-acre parcel of land. It all started with a 10,000 watt AM radio station.

"We hauled all our own equipment up over the highway," Olson said.

Olson said he and Nelson hauled a trailer and radio tower with a pickup. They were followed by an 18-wheeler that carried the transmitter.

"He was a man with a vision," Olson said.

Nelson's vision came to him after some trying times. The World War II veteran was a ball turret gunner on a B-17 bomber when the plane was shot down during a mission over Berlin. Nelson breathed toxic fumes as he jumped from the burning aircraft. He spent the next several months in a prisoner of war camp. He returned home to Minneapolis in the post-war years and led a hard life.

But Nelson saw the error of his ways and was saved at Soul's Harbor Church in Minneapolis. He headed north to Alaska and ended up in Fairbanks, then he left for Stevens Village when he learned the community needed a pastor.

Nelson learned to fly airplanes and spent the next 7 1/2 years visiting Interior villages. "His first love was the Bush of Alaska," said U.S. Rep. Don Young. "he was a young man full of ambition."
From Fairbanks Daily News-Miner, June 1997.

Hector and Jeannette Therriault
Hector and Jeannette Therriault still live in North Pole, Alaska. While Jeannette continues to be active in the welding and fabrication business, acting as both secretary and treasurer of the corporation, Hector has retired and turned the business operation over to his son Ken.

Jeannette has enjoyed some traveling to Taiwan and Hong Kong. Her impression of some parts of Taiwan was that it closely resembled the area around Valdez, Alaska.

These days Hector spends several months each winter in Arizona and the summers fishing in Valdez and Chitina. His newest hobby is creating gold nugget jewelry which he sells at an outlet in Valdez.

They are both well and happy. Jeannette says she is old enough in some ways and too young in others.

Rudy Vetter

Rudy Vetter still lives in Fairbanks, Alaska, and indicates that after so many years in this state, living anywhere else is unthinkable. Following our radio interview Rudy continued to support and promote the Alaskan mineral industry and conduct his private mineral exploration and mining activities.

In the fall of 1995 Rudy became seriously ill and was paralyzed. He began a long slow recovery and, to the amazement of many of his friends, was released from the hospital with his mobility recovered to the point where he could once again begin his prospecting activities on a limited scale. Since that time he has continued to recover, as evidenced by his discovery and development of several rich gold deposits in Interior Alaska.

At 82 years old Rudy is still in good health and spirits. He says, "I am to mean too die and intend to live and prospect in Alaska until I am 105 years old."

Rudy's current interest is in making a video about his life as a prospector in Alaska.

Doris Vogler
1919-1992

Doris Vogler died in her sleep early Saturday morning, January 8, 1992.

Doris had fought lung cancer since being diagnosed in January 1990. Doctors told her then that she probably wouldn't live to see the summer According to her husband, she had quit smoking six or seven years ago, but it was apparently too late.

Mrs. Vogler was born in Oklahoma City, Feb. 5, 1919. She came to Alaska in 1946 with her first husband, who is deceased. She married Joe Vogler in 1964 and worked with him in politics and mining.

As treasurer of the Alaska Independence Party, she remained active even though she could no longer leave her home.

Doris Vogler is buried next to her husband in Dawson City, Yukon Territory, Canada.

From Fairbanks Daily News Miner January 12, 1992

Joe Vogler
1913-1993

Joe Vogler, the 80-year-old founder of the Alaskan Independence Party, disappeared from his home in May of 1993. After an extensive search his body was found in a shallow grave off Chena Hot Springs Road on Oct. 12, 1994.

Vogler, during his life in Alaska, made three unsuccessful bids for governor and was well-known for his fierce and tenacious battles against the federal government and for Alaska independence.

Rev. Jim Kolb pastor of the University of Alaska Fairbanks Catholic Parish conducted the service at his funeral. Vogler was characterized as a man whose wisdom showed through his often forceful and colorful tirades. "Joe was wise and eloquent and learned and well read. His mind was truly a gift from God and one that we'll miss. Whether we liked it or not, he forced us to think," said Rev Jim Kolb.

Tom Snapp, longtime editor of the now-defunct All-Alaska Weekly, attended in remembrance of a man he often wrote about. "He had strong language and he was blustery. When you got beneath the exterior he was very considerate," Snapp said. "How he had that much energy at that old age, I don't know," said Snapp.

Following Vogler's vow never to be buried on American soil, his body was buried in Dawson City, Yukon Territory Canada, next to that of his wife Doris.

From Fairbanks Daily News-Miner—October, 1994 .

Ernie Wolff

Ernie Wolff still lives in Fairbanks, Alaska, which has been his home for over fifty years.

In 1996 Ernie completed a book titled **"Frank Yasuda and the Chandalar,"** which centers on the life of a man who lived in the Chandalar area in north-central Alaska.

Ernie has had some medical problems, mainly pinched nerves in his back which have affected his mobility. Although his health is not the best he is in good spirits. These days he enjoys visits and reminiscing over past experiences with his life-long friends.

William R. Wood

Bill Wood continues to live in Fairbanks, Alaska, with his wife Dorothy-Jane. They both feel that after the Fairbanks experience anyplace else would be dull.

Dr. Wood is still active in community activities, including the Chamber of Commerce, Rotary and Farthest North Press Club. He is also involved in Festival Fairbanks, a non-profit service organization that devotes its efforts to beautification and promotional projects for Fairbanks, such as the maintenance of Golden Heart Park, airport exhibits about Fairbanks businesses, and organization of the 1997 International Symposium on Mining, which attracted speakers from around the world.

Dr. Wood says: "My health is good for my age and Dorothy-Jane and I have enjoyed the thirty-eight years we have lived here and feel that Fairbanks, Alaska, is and always will be our home."

Shorty Zucchini
1911-1998

Albert A. "Shorty" Zucchini, 87, passed away at Denali Center on September 8, 1998.

Al was born in St. Louis Missouri on August, 3, 1911. He mined in Colorado and Nevada during the 1930s, served in the Merchant Marines during World War II, and came to Alaska in the mid-1940s. He mined in the Fortymile and Circle areas, dealt in surplus equipment, and enjoyed attending all surplus sales. Al had many friends throughout many communities in Alaska.

For several years before his death, Al spent the winter months in the desert outside Yuma, Arizona, always returning to Ester fully invigorated for spring and summer work. He loved Alaska and Alaskans.

Al was a most generous person and will be greatly missed.

From the Fairbanks Daily News-Miner, September, 1998

Paul McCarthy

Paul McCarthy retired from the University of Alaska Fairbanks in 1993. For the following two years he worked on grant projects while simultaneously serving on the board of directors of WLN, a telecommunication and library database organization. In 1995 the CEO of WLN retired and Paul was asked to take the position. Since that time he has found a great deal of satisfaction with his new employment duties. The downside is that he was required to leave Alaska and create a new home in Washington state.

Although his children have all grown and left home he still has the joy of frequent visits with them. Paul's wife, Lucy, is actively engaged in art quilting, producing both picturesque quilts and coats for exhibition and sale. Paul continues to enjoy outdoor activities, including a form of mountain climbing called scrambling.

Paul and Lucy are both well and happy and visit Alaska on occasion. If the opportunity arises they hope to return and make their home here in the future.

Appendices
and
Suggested Reading

Appendix I: Alaska Facts

Appendix II: Alaska Gold Discoveries

Appendix III: Alaska Pioneers Featured in Volumes II and III

Suggested Reading

Appendix I

Alaska Facts

Alaska Highway: Begins at Dawson Creek, British Columbia (mile 0) and runs 1,520 miles to Fairbanks, Alaska. Prior to its construction in 1942, travel to Alaska was primarily by water.

Arctic Circle: Approximately 66°30' north from the equator. Also is the latitude at which the sun does not set during the summer solstice (June 20 or 21) or rise during the winter solstice (December 21 or 22).

Aurora Borealis: Commonly known as Northern Lights are light displays in the northern hemisphere that occur in response to charged particles entering the Earth's atmosphere. The result of these charged particles striking gas particles is the creation of light displays which as often observed as variably colored movement of serpent type arcs and draperies in the Alaskan skies.

Alaska Bush: areas of wilderness outside the major population areas; includes numerous small towns and villages.

Cabin Fever: A state of discontent produced when a person is snowbound in a small cabin or room.

Cheechako: A newcomer or greenhorn that has recently just arrived in Alaska.

State Capital: Juneau.

Population (1998): 607,800

Size: The largest state; approximately one fifth the size of the conterminous 48 states, with an area of 570,374 square miles (365,000,000 acres).

Coastline: 6,640 miles.

State Bird: Willow Ptarmigan.

State Fish: King Salmon.

State Flower: Forget-Me-Not.

State Fossil: Woolly Mammoth.

State Gem: Jade.

State Insect: Four-Spot Skimmer Dragonfly.

State Marine Mammal: Bowhead Whale.

State Mineral: Gold.

State Motto: North to the Future.

State Sport: Dog Mushing.

State Tree: Sitka Spruce.

Appendix II

Alaska Gold Discoveries

1862-Placer gold discovered on the Stikine River.

1870-Placer gold found at Sumdum Bay, Southeastern Alaska.

1871-Placer gold found near Wrangell, Southeastern Alaska

1872-Gold in quartz found near Sitka (Stewart Mine).

1875-Placer gold found on Shuck River, Windham Bay, Southeastern Alaska.

1880-Joseph Juneau and Richard T. Harris, discover placer and lode gold at Juneau.

1884-Lode gold found at Unga Island in Southwestern Alaska.

1886-Lode gold discovered at Berners Bay, Southeastern Alaska.

1886-Howard Franklin discovers placer gold on Fortymile River and on Franklin Creek.

1887-Placer gold found on beaches of Yakutat and Lituya Bays.

1888-Placer gold found on Resurrection Creek, Kenai Peninsula.

1893 Pitka and Sorresco discover placer gold on Birch Creek (Circle District).

1896-Placer gold found in the Klondike District, Yukon Territory, independently by Robert Henderson and George W. Carmack.

1897-Placer gold found on Ophir Creek, Seward Peninsula.

1898-Klondike Stampede.

1898-Placer gold found in Porcupine District near Haines.

1898-Placer gold found at Nome by Jafet Lindenberg, Jon Bryantson and Eric O. Lindblom.

1899-Placer gold discovered on Upper Koyukuk River.

1899-Nome beach gold discovered.

1902-Placer gold found in the Tanana District (Fairbanks) by Felix Pedro.

1903-Placer gold found in the Bonnifield District.

1903-Placer gold found at Denali (Valdez Creek) on upper Susitna River.

1905-Placer gold found in the Kantishna District.

1906-Placer gold found in Tenderfoot District.

1906-Placer and quartz gold found in Chandalar District by Frank Yasuda and Thomas G. Carter, partners.

1906-Gold in quartz found in Willow District.

1906-Placer gold found on Games Creek, Innoko District.

1907-Placer gold found in Talkeetna (Yentna) District.

1907-Placer gold found in Ruby District.

1907-Gold discovered on Nolan Creek, Upper Koyukuk District.

1909-Placer gold discovered in Iditarod District by John Benton and W.A. Dikeman.

1909-Placer gold discovered on Klery Creek, Kiana, Kobuk District.

1910-Placer gold discovered near Hughes, middle Koyukuk.

1900-1914-Lower Kuskokwim, Arolik River and Wattamus Creek stampeds.

1910-Gold bearing quartz found at Valdez.

1911-Placer gold found on Hammond River, Upper Koyukuk. First copper shipped from Kennicott.

1912-Placer gold discovered at Chisana (Shushana).

1913-Placer gold discovered at Nelchina.

1913-Placer gold discovered at Marshall, lower Yukon.

1914-Placer gold found at Tolavana District (Livengood).

1924-Large scale dredging program at Fairbanks planned.

1926-Placer platinum discovered at Goodnews Bay: small scale mining until 1934 when mining with mechanical equipment began.

1942-Gold mining prohibited by law because of war.

1945-Gold mining again allowed by law.

1970-I.L. Tailleur recognizes potential Red Dog deposit.

1972-Record low gold production of only 8,639 ounces statewide.

1973-O'Dea vein at Grant Mine property discovered by Roger Burggraf and Gilbert Dobbs.

1974-Private ownership of gold permitted.

1974-1983-Rise in gold prices to $850 per ounce stimulates gold rush to Alaska.

1977-Greens Creek silver, lead-zinc prospect near Juneau discovered.

1981-Gold production jumps to 134,200 ounces nearly doubling previous year's total.

1983-Joe Taylor Jr. discovers hardrock gold in the Cleary Summit area near Fairbanks which leads to development of the Fort Knox project.

1985-Underground hardrock ore production begun at the Grant Mine near Fairbanks in October.

1987-"Bima" dredge begins offshore placer mining near Nome June 16.

1987-Surface hardrock ore production begun at the Grant Mine near Fairbanks in October.

1987-Citigold Alaska heap leaches first gold from Ryan lode near Fairbanks.

1989-Greens Creek hard rock silver, lead-zinc mine near Juneau goes into operation.

1990-Red Dog lead-zinc mine near Kotzebue opens.

1991-Cambior Alaska reopens Valdez Creek placer gold mine near Cantwell.

1993-Greens Creek Mine near Juneau closes in April because of low metal prices.

1995-Valdez Creek placer mine near Cantwell closes.

1995-Sumitomo announces gold discovery at Pogo prospect near Delta Junction.

1995-Nixon Fork hard rock gold-copper mine near McGrath goes into production in October.

1996-Greens Creek Mine near Juneau reopens.

1996-Fort Knox hard rock gold mine near Fairbanks goes into production in November.

Appendix III

Pioneers Featured in Volumes II and III

VOLUME II	VOLUME III
Del Ackels	Ed Ashby
Gail Ackels	Bob Cowgill
Steve Agbaba	Janet Cowgill
Paul Barelka	Bob Hamilton
Bill Boucher	Jerry Hassel
Freida Chamberlain	Bob Jacobs
Emory Chappell	Neville Jacobs
Don Cook	Leah Madonna
Bettye Fahrenkamp	John Miscovich
Mack Fenton	Tom Snapp
Harold Gillam	Sandra Stillion
Mary Hanson	Oden Strandberg
Roy Larson	Mary Lou Teal
Enid Magill	Jack Williams
Fred Magill	Leah Madonna with Joe and Doris Vogler
Irene Mead	
Cy Randall	Most Memorable Pioneer Christmases
Hazel Randall	
Stu Rothman	
Bill Suess on Leon Tromley	

Suggested Reading

Alaska Northwest Publishing Company, 1998, The Alaska Almanac. Alaska Northwest Publishing Co., Anchorage, Alaska.

Cashen, William R., 1972, Farthest North College President. University of Alaska Press, Fairbanks, Alaska.

Cohen, Stan, 1979, the Trail of 42 - A Pictorial History of the Alaska Highway. Canada Friesen Printers, Altona, Manitoba.

Heller, Herbert L., 1967, Sourdough Sagas. The New World Publishing Company, Cleveland, Ohio.

Wharton, David, 1972, The Alaska Gold Rush. Indiana University Press, Bloomington, Indiana.

Wolff, Ernest, 1969, Handbook for the Alaska Prospector. Mineral Industry Research Laboratory, College, Alaska.